P9-DNV-412

YAS

▼ *exclamation*

An affirmative exclamation. The number of *A*s and *S*s can vary depending on the tone and use. The gesture of quickly waving the index finger with approval is sometimes done to emphasize the expression. Often used in the phrases "yas, queen," "yas, girl," and "yas, gawd."

The LGBTQIA+ Dictionary

The Queens'
ENGLISH

Clarkson Potter/Publishers
New York

The Queens' ENGLISH

CHLOE O. DAVIS

THE LGBTQIA+ DICTIONARY

OF LINGO AND COLLOQUIAL PHRASES

ST. JOHN THE BAPTIST PARISH LIBRARY
2920 NEW HIGHWAY 51
LAPLACE, LOUISIANA 70068

Copyright © 2021 by Chloe O. Davis

All rights reserved.
Published in the United States by Clarkson Potter/
Publishers, an imprint of Random House,
a division of Penguin Random House LLC, New York.
clarksonpotter.com

CLARKSON POTTER is a trademark and POTTER with
colophon is a registered trademark of Penguin Random
House LLC.

Library of Congress Control Number: 2020945849

ISBN 978-0-593-13500-6
Ebook ISBN 978-0-593-13501-3

Printed in China

Photography by Chloe O. Davis
Illustrations by Troy Lambert with contributions from
Cassandra Fountaine, Mark Uhre, and Shanée Benjamin
Editor: Sara Neville
Designer: Danielle Deschenes
Production editor: Mark McCauslin
Production manager: Kim Tyner
Composition: Merri Ann Morrell, Zoe Tokushige
Pre-press manager: Neil Spitkovsky

10 9 8 7 6 5 4 3 2 1

First Edition

This dictionary is dedicated to all of you who take the courageous path each day to completely be yourselves.

You encourage us all to love our inner beauty and ideas, even when faced with the challenges of not being embraced by others. I write to affirm and remind you that you are exceptional and more than enough. Thank you for opening your life and world to me unselfishly and allowing me to share the essence of your words.

INTRODUCTION

The idea to write *The Queens' English* was spawned when I landed my first job as a professional performing artist at a Philadelphia-based dance company in 2006. We traveled often for shows, and bus conversation—our ultimate entertainment pastime—was typically led by a few charismatic MVPs at the back of our tour bus. Jokes and witty remarks were always being tossed around, and the better the joke, the louder the laughs, the more fun everyone had. The back-of-the-bus group had the 411 on all the good gossip, and the rest of us were always glued to their conversations. But sometimes their jokes sounded like a code to me, filled with terms I could not decipher.

One day I called to the back of the tour bus and asked, "What does 'snatched' mean? You are always calling people 'snatched' like it's a compliment. What is it?"

With a bit of shade, a company member said, "Something you need to be when you are in this company, snatched for the gawds!" Laughter erupted, but I was still confused.

Another company member, who was willing to break it down, said, "Let me give you the T. We are gay, honey, and we have our own language that only *we* get. Other people in the company eventually get it, too, because it's fierce backboots. That's why you are here looking through the window trying to come inside our world. So, here's a little breakdown . . . five, six, seven, eight! 'Snatched' means that the body is together! You are lovely, small, lean, shapely, sexy, you are SNATCHED! And to be in this company, our boss wants us to be snatched for the gawds! So, that means you have to be extra lean, extra sexy, and extra lovely! You are eating air and drinking hope with a wheatgrass shot for dessert." The whole bus exploded with laughter. And so it began.

I wanted to kiki all the time! I was fascinated with the language I was learning from gay culture. As an eager newbie (cough, cough, I mean eager *gaybie*), I started a running list of terms and expressions my friends taught me, and bus conversations soon revolved around the entertainment of me trying to pair "academic" definitions with words like "beat," "fierce," "living, "ovah," and "werk." Jokingly, I told a friend that this was a fully developed language and there should be a dictionary for these words.

"When you write it," he said, "call it _The Queens' English_. It's a language for all the queens."

Over the years, I added more terms as I performed all over the country. Colleagues—actors, artists, dancers, and performers—who identified as LGBTQIA+ shared their favorite lingo with me and introduced me to friends so we could collect more. I even learned terms from friendly strangers in gayborhoods, at LGBT centers, and during Pride events. The list of terms eventually became a glossary that represented a diverse group of gay and queer people, lifestyles, and communities.

My research eventually led me to explore the complexities of my own sexual identity. Learning new words like "demi," "bi," and "flexible" gave me labels that identified the fluidity of my attraction to others. Throughout my life, I've identified as heteroflexible, bi-curious, and at a time, struggled with being a semi-closeted bisexual; I've explored polyamory, and now I'm a proud and openly biromantic, demisexual bisexual. These words helped articulate my developing sexual expression as I grew to understand myself. It was the support of my community—family, friends, dating partners, the theater, dance—and the writing of _The Queens' English_ that gave me the courage to express my truth and become an advocate for understanding the spectrum of identity and sexuality.

WHAT IS _THE QUEENS' ENGLISH_?

The Queens' English is a dictionary that celebrates the etymological diversity of over eight hundred terms used to describe our collective gay and queer experience. It is an epic journey of understanding identity, sexuality, gender, equality, humor, community, and pride.

A vibrant and rich history has been captured by the unique language created by and for the lesbian, gay, bisexual, transgender, two-spirit, queer, questioning, intersex, asexual, gender nonconforming, nonbinary, and nonheteronormative community—commonly abbreviated as LGBTQIA+. This dictionary is a resource with modern definitions, real-life examples, synonyms, important usage notes, and supporting background information to further enhance the understanding of each term. Interstitial how-tos and history lessons about trailblazing people, places, and events that have impacted the language within the LGBTQIA+ community are included throughout.

Much of my research came from the cultural heartbeat of our queer community, consisting of personal interviews and group discussions with people who identify as LGBTQIA+. I filled in the gaps using digital and print references and content from queer and mainstream media outlets, taking sensitive measures to define every term appropriately and inclusively, while respecting (and encouraging!) the flexibility of other interpretations. I also committed to

ON THE WORD "QUEER"

"Queer" was once a derogatory slur for homosexuals. By the 1980s, HIV/AIDS activists were determined to reclaim the term as a badge of honor for the LGBTQIA+ community. Since the eighties, the younger LGBTQIA+ generations have adopted "queer" as an umbrella term for anyone who identifies as lesbian, gay, bisexual, trans, two-spirit, queer, questioning, intersex, asexual, nonbinary, gender nonconforming, or nonheteronormative.

There are many identities within the LGBTQIA+ community and each person's label preference and interpretation of that identity should be respected. Only use the term(s) with which a person identifies. If you don't know, just ask!

PLEASE NOTE

The term "queer" is used throughout this dictionary as a catchall for people who identify as anything other than heterosexual and/or cisgender. *But!* Please be aware that not *all* members of the LGBTQIA+ community feel comfortable using the word "queer" in this way. While it has largely been reclaimed as an inclusive term for those of us who have been marginalized due to sexuality, gender identity, and/or gender expression, the term still holds negative connotations for some.

highlighting the diversity of language that lives within our community—from the New York City ballroom scene to the San Francisco leather community and everything else in between.

However, my research only captures a sliver of the subcommunities that make up LGBTQIA+ culture. *The Queens' English* is merely a starting point for the important conversations around inclusivity, sexuality, gender expression and identity, gay slang that's been co-opted by mainstream culture, and queer American terminology that's been around for decades.

WHY DO WE NEED LABELS?

Years ago, a close friend asked how I wanted to be perceived. He knew I had been with both men and women, and he was testing me. I told him I was open to identifying however I saw fit and asked him, "Why do I need a label?" He replied, "You don't need a label, I just recommend you live in your truth." His words prompted me to challenge myself. Over time, I gained the courage and confidence to love myself and the many layers that shape me.

Research for *The Queens' English* has provided me with a new understanding of human identity, and as a result, I feel empowered by who I am. I believe that outward **expression** and feelings of **attraction** are two inherent components of every human—gay, straight, cis, trans, and beyond. These two ideas of expression and attraction show the layered depth of each person's existence.

While our unique expression and attraction—our labels—are used by society to categorize or even divide people, how we express our identity to the world and the spectrum of attraction we feel for others actually unite us. Our similarities *and* our differences unite us, and as a result, labels do, too. Let's celebrate that!

We are *all* fluid in some ways—a little bit feminine, masculine, androgynous, vanilla, kink, and drawn to cisgender and/or transgender men and/or women and/or gender nonconforming people. We all have a relationship with race, religion, music, books, sex, self-expression, feminism, patriotism, money, power, and culture. *The Queens' English* is a way for all of us to explore our common humanity, whether or not we identify as queer in some way.

BUT IS IT APPROPRIATION?

Queer lingo carries with it a vast history. It is important to understand that much of the language in this book has been adopted from subcommunities of LGBTQIA+ culture. Some terms originated in Harlem's Black gay scene in the 1920s or white working-class lesbian bars in the 1940s, while others came from New York's drag scene and have since been appropriated by the gay community at large, or, in some cases, by mainstream culture, too.

Many of the terms in this book come from a community of Black and Latinx gay and trans people who faced systematic attacks for being queer and people of color. This language was created to supplement a marginalized community's self-worth and ideas.

Mainstream culture views queer language as cool, hip, fresh. Today, words like "shade," "fierce," "slay," and "yaaaas!" are all used freely by the masses without acknowledging the Black and Latinx queers who created this language as a form of survival. Buzzwords are printed on clothing, are used candidly and by nonqueer celebrities and predominately white social groups. This appropriation is emphasized by social scientist Dan Zarrella: "Subcultures often create terms to describe things that mainstream society does not have words for. . . . Sometimes a slang term pops into the culture sphere that is so useful it crawls under the brainskin, no matter the historical stigma implied."

Appropriation is a major concern within the LGBTQIA+ community. When our language is subjugated by mainstream culture, its value is minimized—especially if terms are not used correctly and respectfully. I created *The Queens' English* to give proper documentation to queer vernacular and to appropriately credit the LGBTQIA+ subcommunities for their contribution, while acknowledging that the creation and re-creation of jargon is an ongoing process.

You hold something very valuable in your hands. Even if you are not part of the LGBTQIA+ community, this is an opportunity to gain insight into our culture. With access to our language comes a responsibility to be sensitive and respectful to a community that persisted in the face of hate. Before RuPaul graced us with "Shantay, you stay" and Wendy Williams co-opted "tens across the board" from

New York's underground ballroom scene, living as a lesbian, gay, bi, trans, or queer person in America often meant living in fear and secrecy. This book is not permission to use this language flippantly; it is meant to be an educational tool, a conversation starter, and a celebration of the history of gay coded language, queer spaces, and the LGBTQIA+ experience.

ON USAGE NOTES

- ▶ Language is always evolving. There may be definitions that are not present in the dictionary that are still valid.
- ▶ Not all of this language is used by everyone in the LGBTQIA+ community.
- ▶ Many of the terms are not appropriate for people *not* in the LGBTQIA+ community to use, either.

While *The Queens' English* encourages all readers to engage with this vibrant language, usage notes have been attached to terms that need extra context. Several terms, while considered derogatory or slurs, have been a part of gay language for decades. The intent of the dictionary is to document queer language in its entirety, not to censor it.

The saying "speak, so you can speak again" (often credited to she-ro Zora Neale Hurston), holds great relevance today. In speaking now, *The Queens' English* will use the nuances of queer language to celebrate the people who define LGBTQIA+ culture. It shows the brilliance, strength, and power in queer voices telling our unique stories and is a testament to the value of marginalized people's voices.

So, come indulge in *The Queens' English*. This dictionary welcomes all readers. All of us have a gender identity, a way of expressing our gender, a sexual orientation, and a romantic orientation, as well as a need to understand those who are different from us. Be PROUD of the lingo within our diverse LGBTQIABCDEFGHIJKLMNOPQRSTUVWXYZ+ community because, yes, ladies and gentlemen and gender nonconforming queens alike, this lingo does slay!

AGENDER

ALLGENDER

ANDROGYNOUS

BIGENDER

BUTCH

DEMIGENDER

FEMALE

GENDERFLUID DEMIGIRL

MALE

NEUTRAL

THIRDGENDER

TRANSGENDER

The Queens' English

Lowercase words and phrases in quotes provide alternative ways you might hear a term used in everyday encounters.

TERM

▼ *1ˢᵗ part of speech*
First definition. Often used in the phrase "abc xyz."

Second definition.

SEE ALSO

TERM A, TERM B

Capitalized words and phrases are cross-references that can be found elsewhere in the dictionary by looking them up alphabetically.

▼ *2ⁿᵈ part of speech*
Definition. The terms XYZ and ABC can also be used.

RELATED

TERM C, *part of speech*

"Highlighting real-life examples of how to use the term in a sentence!"

Related terms provide alternate parts of speech to familiarize yourself with.

WANT MORE INFO? *THINK:* **HERE'S A QUICK SYNONYM FOR THE TERM.**

USAGE NOTE For understanding the origin and appropriate usage of the term.

DID YOU KNOW Historical references and/or information that contribute to the understanding of the term or phrase.

Aa

AAPI

▼ *noun*

An acronym for Asian American and Pacific Islander(s). "API" (Asian–Pacific Islander) can also be used.

"Queer AAPI organizations are working on cultivating support, visibility, and coming-out resources for our Asian community."

 WANT MORE INFO? *THINK:* **A PERSON OF ASIAN DESCENT.**

DID YOU KNOW Many queer Asian icons have made substantial contributions to both the AAPI and queer communities. Activists like Cecilia Chung, *Star Trek* icon George Takei, actors Maulik Pancholy and BD Wong, comedian Margaret Cho, and the first openly gay congressman of color, Mark Takano, have all received recognition for their dedication to queer AAPI pride.

ABIGAIL

▼ *noun*

A gay, bi, or queer man who is discreet about his sexuality.

"When I think of my dear Abigail, Francis Underwood—in the show House of Cards—*comes to mind."*

 WANT MORE INFO? *THINK:* **A GAY MAN WHO KEEPS HIS SEXUALITY UNDER THE RADAR.**

USAGE NOTE This term is commonly used in the gay male community.

ABLEISM

▼ *noun*

Discrimination in favor of able-bodied people.

"Let's begin to address ableism by having qualified sign language interpreters at our events."

 WANT MORE INFO? *THINK:* **LACK OF CONSIDERATION FOR DISABLED PEOPLE.**

ABOUT THIS LIFE

▼ *idiom*
To be completely interested and involved.

"Yaasssss, honey! We are in Miami, boo! I am about this life!"

 WANT MORE INFO? *THINK:* **TO BE TOTALLY, WHOLLY ENTHRALLED.**

 This term originated in Black American culture and is used in the Black gay and queer community. It has been appropriated by mainstream culture.

ABSOLUTE CODE

▼ *idiom*
A pledge to not disclose someone's sexuality without permission. The term GOLDEN RULE can also be used.

SEE ALSO
"Coming Out 101," *p. 26*

"Absolute code, dude! It's my choice when I want to come out, not yours!"

 WANT MORE INFO? *THINK:* **AN UNSPOKEN AGREEMENT TO KEEP SOMEONE'S SEXUAL ORIENTATION PRIVATE.**

About this life ▲

AC/DC

▼ *adjective*
Referring to a person who has a sexual and/or romantic attraction toward men and women.

"I mean, I kind of feel AC/DC. I can date a man or a woman. I like both energies."

 WANT MORE INFO? *THINK:* **BISEXUAL.**

USAGE NOTE This term may carry negative connotations as it limits bisexuality to the gender binary. It is inappropriate to use this label if a person has not self-identified as such.

DID YOU KNOW AC/DC is a commonly used electrical term that stands for Alternating Current/Direct Current, which are two different methods of delivering electricity. The queer community began to use this acronym to show how a bisexual person could receive power (or sexual energy) from people of different gender identities.

ACE

▼ *adjective*
An abbreviation of the word "asexual."

"Here is the formula: 'gay' for homosexuals, 'straight' for heterosexuals, and 'ace' for asexuals."

 WANT MORE INFO? *THINK:* **THE MIGHTY (AND GROWING!) ASEXUAL POPULATION OF SEVENTY MILLION PEOPLE WORLDWIDE.**

ACEPHOBIA

▼ *noun*
Aversion, fear, or hatred toward asexuality.

RELATED
ACEPHOBIC *adjective*
ACEPHOBE *noun*

 WANT MORE INFO? *THINK:* **DISLIKE OF OR PREJUDICE AGAINST ASEXUAL PEOPLE.**

SEE ALSO
BIPHOBIA, FEMMEPHOBIA, HOMOPHOBIA, LESBO-PHOBIA, QUEERPHOBIA, TRANSPHOBIA

"I just read an article about all the harmful things people are saying about asexuality. Acephobia is so real. There's nothing wrong with someone who doesn't want to have sex."

ACE QUEEN

Ace queen ▶

▼ *noun*
A gay, bisexual, or queer man who grooms and styles himself in a traditionally feminine way.

SEE ALSO
QUEEN

"Honey, an ace queen will spray his Chanel No. 5, pluck his eyebrows, and have major points on his Sephora BeautyInsider card."

 WANT MORE INFO? *THINK:*
A SUPER-FEMININE QUEER MAN.

ADORBS

▼ *adjective*
An abbreviation of "adorable."

"O-M-G! Leah and Nora's engagement pictures with their Goldendoodle puppies are adorbs!"

 WANT MORE INFO? *THINK:*
DELIGHTFULLY SWEET.

AESTHETIC ATTRACTION

▼ *noun*
An admiration based solely on the way someone looks.

"I don't want to be with her, I just have an aesthetic attraction because she is beautiful."

 WANT MORE INFO? *THINK:* A
**NONSEXUAL, NONROMANTIC
ATTRACTION.**

AFAB

▼ *adjective*
An acronym for "Assigned Female at Birth." This term is used by a range of people—including transgender, nonbinary, gender nonconforming, and/or intersex individuals—as a way to communicate to others the gender assigned to them at birth (based solely on their sexual anatomy).

SEE ALSO
AMAB

"Katie was AFAB but is actually bigender."

WANT MORE INFO? *THINK:* **THE BOX LABELED "FEMALE" WAS CHECKED IN THE DELIVERY ROOM.**

USAGE NOTE This term is commonly used in the transgender, nonbinary, and gender nonconforming communities. The use of this term relies on an individual's preference. Do not assume that an individual wants to be identified by this term. Please ask for and use a person's chosen name and pronouns.

AFFECTIONAL ORIENTATION

▼ *noun*
See ROMANTIC ORIENTATION

AFTERCARE

▼ *noun*
Time and compassionate attention given to a partner after sex, scenario role-play, or BDSM activities.

"After our scene, Frank broke down. He needed aftercare so I put my Dom side away, wiped his tears, and hugged him tight."

 WANT MORE INFO? *THINK:* **CHECKING IN WITH YOUR PARTNER AFTER INTENSE SEX OR SCENE PLAY.**

USAGE NOTE This term is commonly used in the BDSM, leather, and kink communities. For all BDSM-related terms, the power exchange is a part of sadomasochistic play and should be consensual between all partners involved.

AG

▼ *adjective*
An abbreviation of "aggressive." When used in the lesbian community, it usually refers to a masculine woman who has a dominant personality. The term "femme AG" can also be used to distinguish an AG woman who identifies as femme.

SEE ALSO
STUD, "The Lesbian Spectrum," *p. 194*

"I like to control shit in my relationship. I'm AG with it."

 WANT MORE INFO? *THINK:* **WANTS TO RUN IT ALL.**

USAGE NOTE This term originated in the Black lesbian community. It has been appropriated by the larger lesbian community.

DID YOU KNOW Many Black lesbian communities in northeast American cities like Baltimore, Philadelphia, and New York use the term AG to identify a woman who has a dominant personality and/or is the dominant partner in a relationship. Black lesbians and bisexual women are often overlooked in the larger queer community, but documentaries like *The Aggressives, U People,* and *The Same Difference* explore the diverse identities and relationship dynamics seen in the Black lesbian community.

AGENDER

▼ *adjective*
Not identifying with any gender.
The terms NONGENDER and
GENDERLESS can also be used.

> SEE ALSO
>
> **NEUTROIS, GENDERQUEER,
> NONBINARY**

*"Unisex bathrooms are for
everyone. Transgender, agender,
bigender people, and those who
identify within the gender binary.
We can all pee together!"*

 WANT MORE INFO? *THINK:*
**NOT BOUND TO A SPECIFIC
GENDER.**

AIDS

▼ *noun*
See A-WORD; HIV/AIDS; "History
Lesson: HIV/AIDS," p. 160

▼   A-List Gay

A-LIST GAY

▼ *noun*
A queer person who is considered
socially elite and has power, wealth,
and privilege. The term "A-Gay" can
also be used.

*"Who runs the world? Clearly
the A-Gays."*

 WANT MORE INFO? *THINK:*
**AN INFLUENTIAL LGBTQIA+
PERSON.**

ALLOROMANTIC

▼ *adjective*
Experiencing romantic attraction.
This attraction can exist with
or without sexual desires. Often
shortened to "romantic."

▼ *noun*
An alloromantic person.

> SEE ALSO
>
> **AROMANTIC**

"An alloromantic and an aromantic are like yin and yang—one has those mushy, romantic feelings; one doesn't."

 WANT MORE INFO? *THINK:* **LOVE IS THE FAVORITE EMOTION.**

 This term is commonly used in the asexual community.

ALLOSEXUAL

▼ *adjective*

Experiencing sexual attraction. This attraction can exist with or without romantic desires. Often shortened to "sexual."

▼ *noun*

An allosexual person.

SEE ALSO
ASEXUAL

Winter: *I'm super attracted to Melissa. I want to spend every waking moment with her!*
Seth: *I don't understand you alloromantics. Love letters, long walks in the park, listening to each other's heartbeats? No thank you. I am only allosexual.*

 WANT MORE INFO? *THINK:* **JUST SEX? YES!**

 This term is commonly used in the aromantic and asexual communities.

ALLY

▼ *noun*

An active supporter of the rights and causes of the LGBTQIA+ community. The term "super ally" can also be used.

RELATED
ALLYSHIP *noun*

"Campbell's Soup wins the super ally award because their gay dads commercial was the most heartfelt ad I've ever seen!"

 WANT MORE INFO? *THINK:* **A MEMBER OF THE QUEER FAN CLUB.**

DID YOU KNOW This term identifies someone who is cisgender and heterosexual; allies are not part of the inclusive identifying label of LGBTQIA+.

Ally ▲

AMAB

▼ *adjective*
An acronym for "Assigned Male at Birth." This term is used by a range of people—including transgender, nonbinary, gender nonconforming, and/or intersex individuals—to communicate to others the gender assigned to them at birth (based solely on their sexual anatomy).

SEE ALSO
AFAB

"I was assigned male at birth [AMAB], but I've spent a good portion of my life trying to get away from the expectations that have been placed on me because of that." ▸ Nick Adams

 WANT MORE INFO? *THINK:* **THE BOX LABELED "MALE" WAS CHECKED IN THE DELIVERY ROOM.**

 USAGE NOTE This term is commonly used in the transgender, nonbinary, and gender nonconforming communities. The use of this term relies on an individual's preference. Do not assume that an individual wants to be identified by this term. Please ask for and use a person's chosen name and pronouns.

ANDROGYNY

▼ *noun*
A display of both masculine and feminine qualities. The state of being androgynous. Can be abbreviated as "androj" or "andro."

A label used to define an androgynous gender identity.

RELATED
ANDROGYNOUS *adjective*   **ANDROGYNE** *noun*

"David Bowie, Grace Jones, and Prince. Totally androgynous."

 WANT MORE INFO? *THINK:* **AN AMBIGUOUS GENDER PRESENTATION.**

DID YOU KNOW Greek philosopher Plato writes about the idea of androgyny in his text *Symposium*. In this Platonic myth, Aristophanes delivers a speech explaining that "male-female" people came from the moon.

ANDROSEXUAL

▼ *adjective*
Experiencing sexual attraction toward masculinity.

RELATED
ANDROSEXUALITY *noun*

SEE ALSO
GYNESEXUAL

▼ *noun*
An androsexual person.

"I'm gonna hit that Chippendale's revue to get my androsexual juices flowing. Wanna come?"

 WANT MORE INFO? *THINK:* **ATTRACTED TO MASC PEOPLE.**

ANGEL FOOD

▼ *noun*
A gay pilot who serves in the United States Air Force.

"That angel food is hot. Maybe I can be the PYT on his AFB."

 WANT MORE INFO? *THINK:* AIRMAN WITH THE RAINBOW BADGE OF HONOR.

 This term originated in the gay male community.

APPROPRIATE

▼ *verb*
To take ownership of something without permission or endorsement of those who created it.

RELATED
APPROPRIATION *noun*

SEE ALSO
CULTURAL APPROPRIATION, MISAPPROPRIATE, REAPPROPRIATE

"Let's talk about pop culture's appropriation of Black gay lingo— child, yas, girl, fierce, shade, read! I mean, I can go on and on."

 WANT MORE INFO? *THINK:* TO BORROW WITHOUT ASKING.

AROMANTIC

▼ *adjective*
Lacking a romantic attraction toward someone. Sexual attraction may still be present. Can be abbreviated as "aro."

▼ *noun*
An aromantic person.

SEE ALSO
ALLOROMANTIC

"Look, I'm not being selfish. Aromantic people enjoy sex without romance. I honestly don't think about doing 'romantic' things."

 WANT MORE INFO? *THINK:* MAY BE ASEXUAL, ALLO-SEXUAL, OR SOMEWHERE IN BETWEEN, BUT DOES NOT EXPERIENCE ROMANCE.

 It is important to avoid the assumption that something is "wrong" with people in the aromantic community. It is common for aro people to engage in intimate connections through platonic relationships.

ASEXUAL

▼ *adjective*
Not experiencing sexual attraction or desire. Can be abbreviated as ACE.

▼ *noun*
A person who is without sexual yearnings.

RELATED
ASEXUALITY *noun*

SEE ALSO

ALLOSEXUAL

"Unlike celibacy, which is a choice, asexuality is a sexual orientation."
▸ Asexual Visibility and Education Network (AVEN)

 WANT MORE INFO? *THINK:* **MAY NOT EXPERIENCE SEXUAL ATTRACTION BUT COULD EXPERIENCE ROMANTIC ATTRACTION.**

 USAGE NOTE It is important to avoid the assumption that something is "wrong" with people in the asexual community. It is common for ace people to engage in intimate partnerships and have families.

AUNT(IE)

▾ *noun*
An endearing term used to identify a mature, often effeminate, gay man. Alternate spelling includes "Aunty."

A respected transgender woman—often, a mentor.

"You better behave at Pride or Auntie is gonna come get you. Do you hear me?"

 WANT MORE INFO? *THINK:* **AN EXPERIENCED, RESPECTED GAY MAN OR TRANS WOMAN.**

USAGE NOTE This term originated in Black culture and is commonly used in the Black gay and trans community.

 DID YOU KNOW "Auntie" is used in Black cultures as a way to identify a well-respected adult woman. During the nineteenth century, white Europeans and Americans used the term to belittle Black women, refusing to use Mrs. or Miss as a respectful honorific. The Black community reclaimed the term to dispel its negative connotation and empower Black women.

AUNTIE QUEEN

▾ *noun*
A young gay, bisexual, or queer man who enjoys the courtship of older men. The term "auntie chaser" can also be used.

SEE ALSO

QUEEN, CHASER

"Look at Josh with that silver fox! He's an auntie queen who knows how to pick 'em."

 WANT MORE INFO? *THINK:* **A YOUNG MALE WHO SEEKS OLDER MALE COMPANIONSHIP.**

USAGE NOTE The term "chaser" varies in meaning but often implies a person who has fetishes based on harmful stereotypes.

AUTOEROTIC

▾ *adjective*
See AUTO-SEXUAL

AUTO-SEXUAL

▼ *adjective*
Using self-stimulation to satiate sexual desires; an auto-sexual person may prefer solo sexual play or may be unable to be aroused by others. The term AUTOEROTIC can also be used.

Them: *So, why no sexual partners? Are you asexual?*
Her: *No, I identify as auto-sexual. I prefer solo stimulation.*

 WANT MORE INFO? *THINK:* **"I TOUCH MYSELF" BY DIVINYLS.**

A-WORD

▼ *idiom*
A euphemism for AIDS.

SEE ALSO
HIV/AIDS, "History Lesson: HIV/AIDS," *p. 160*

"The A-Word is not taboo. We want a world without AIDS! Speak out and tell your story."

 WANT MORE INFO? *THINK:* **ACQUIRED IMMUNE DEFICIENCY SYNDROME.**

 DID YOU KNOW Human documentation of AIDS was found as early as the 1970s, and AIDS cases spread rapidly across North America, South America, Europe, Africa, and Australia. Today, the HIV/AIDS crisis is still one of the world's most serious public health challenges. More than 36 million people worldwide are currently living with HIV/AIDS.

COMING OUT 101

ACCEPT the most AUTHENTIC you

In the LGBTQIA+ community, "coming out" is a phrase most commonly used in reference to a person sharing their sexual orientation or gender identity with the world. It is part of a personal journey toward self-love, self-acceptance, and living authentically.

Coming out can happen on your terms and at your own pace. It is never too early or too late to come out. For some encouragement, a few friends share their best coming out advice:

"Growing up I didn't have the liberty to be out. But now that the world is more open to people being gay and lesbian, I am living a happy life with my wife. Always know that we all support you."

Thomasene, 66, and Alison, 55, St. Louis, MO

"It's about honoring the greatest, most authentic you. Whether that awakening inspires you to share it with the world, your immediate family and friends, or solely with the most important steward of your life (yourself), be present for it."

Sir Brock, 33, Brooklyn, NY

"Research, research, research, read, read, read. Read about trans people's experiences and learn from them. Find the right way to transition for yourself and don't let others influence that decision."

Mila Jam, 30, Atlanta, GA

"The most important thing is for you to come out when you feel ready."

"The first step is that you have to be able to accept it yourself. Talk to yourself and reassure yourself. But don't overanalyze it. If you feel it is your truth, just do it!"

Odell, 16, Washington, DC

"Seek out someone who has already come out. Hang around LGBT spaces, groups, and even message boards that will give you the ability to explore who you are."

Chris, 26, Houston, TX

"Coming out is an investment to your future happiness."

C. Barth, 19, New Haven, CT

"Sexuality is not black and white, it's on a spectrum. Trust your own voice, thoughts, feelings, and the way your heart jumps. Trust the way you perceive the world."

Sara, 30, Philadelphia, PA

"Make sure you have a safe place and space to live when you come out."

RTB, 50, Boston, MA

Baby butch ▲

Bb

B

▼ *noun*
A common abbreviation for "butt." Used mostly by gay, bisexual, or queer men in a sexual context.

"This B bounces back!"

 WANT MORE INFO? *THINK:* **RUMP.**

BABY BUTCH

▼ *noun*
A young, boyish lesbian, bisexual, or queer girl.

"Look at that baby butch over there with all that swag. I see you, young one."

 WANT MORE INFO? *THINK:* **YOUNG LESBIAN TOMBOY.**

 This term originated in the lesbian community.

BABY DYKE

▼ *noun*
A female who has newly revealed her sexuality as lesbian.

A young queer girl.

"I just came out at twenty-eight—help! I'm a baby dyke going through gay puberty, and I've got no game!"

 WANT MORE INFO? *THINK:* **LESBIAN NEWCOMER OR YOUNG LESBIAN.**

 This term originated in the lesbian community. The term "dyke" originated as a derogatory slur for lesbians but has been reclaimed by some of the LGBTQIA+ community. It may still have negative connotations for some people.

BABY GIRL

▼ *noun*
See GIRL

BACKBOOTS

▼ *exclamation*
See BOOTS

BACK DOOR

▼ *noun*
The anus. The term "back porch" can also be used.

Demetri: *You lookin' sexy as hell right now. You 'bout to let me in that back door, baby?*
Lamont: *Not tonight, Daddy. She isn't ready yet.*

 WANT MORE INFO? *THINK:* **THE G-SPOT ACTIVATOR.**

BALL

▼ *noun*
An event in ballroom culture where gay, transgender, and queer members of the ballroom scene gather and compete for awards in a series of categories based on self-expression. Free agents and competitors from different houses walk for awards based on appearance, attitude, dance, attire, and realness,

> **SEE ALSO**
> **"History Lesson: The Ballroom Scene,"** *p. 232*

"I went to a ball, I got a trophy, and now everybody wants to know me."
▶ Paris Is Burning

 WANT MORE INFO? *THINK:* **COMPETITION IN THE FILM** *PARIS IS BURNING.*

BALLAD

▼ *noun*
An unwarranted or poor excuse.

"You can stop singing your out-of-tune ballad now. I have heard every excuse."

 WANT MORE INFO? *THINK:* **AN ATTEMPT TO VINDICATE ONESELF.**

BALL GOWN

▼ *noun*
A playful reference to a man's suit.

"I'm going to wear my Tom Ford ball gown for tonight's gala. Sweetheart, do you think my velvet slippers are a good shoe choice?"

 WANT MORE INFO? *THINK:* **EXQUISITE FORMAL ATTIRE.**

◀ **Ball**

DID YOU KNOW In 1920s Harlem, gay balls were born out of racial tension. People of color were not allowed to participate in the lavish gay affairs of the white community, so the gay Black community created a social space to express their sexuality freely. Balls began as extravagant underground drag performances, but by the 1970s, the events had evolved to feature an array of themes to celebrate the performers' artistic expression, gender identities, sexualities, and ethnicities.

BALLROOM SCENE OR BALLROOM CULTURE

▼ *noun*
A distinct social community comprised mostly of Black and Latinx gay and transgender members who use ballroom competitions as a safe place to express their gender, sexuality, and artistic spirit. The phrases "ball culture," "gay balls," and "drag ball" can also be used.

SEE ALSO
BALL, CATEGORY, HOUSE CULTURE, "History Lesson: The Ballroom Scene," *p. 232*

"The fairy godmother of the ballroom scene is New York City, honey! She has graced you with the houses of Ninja, Xtravaganza, Mizrahi, and LaBeija. All of the legendary children received their first real trophies in New York."

 WANT MORE INFO? *THINK:* **THE SCENE PORTRAYED ON FX'S SHOW** *POSE*—**A SOCIAL AND ARTISTIC LIFESTYLE FOR QUEER AND TRANS PEOPLE OF COLOR.**

DID YOU KNOW The ballroom scene is centered around balls—competitions that champion self-expression. Competitors at a ball walk (much like models on a runway) for titles and awards in themed categories. The best competitors are celebrated widely within the community's social house structure. Social houses are typically made up of a house mother and/or house father and their children, all of whom take the last name of their chosen family.

BANANA

▼ *noun*
A gay, bisexual, or queer man.

A penis.

"Honey, pretty much anything shaped like a penis refers to a gay male or gay sex. Banana, eggplant, corn on the cob. Just make sure it's edible, thick, and long."

 WANT MORE INFO? *THINK:* **THE FRUIT AND THE BODY PART.**

Banana ▲

BANDANA CODE

▼ *noun*
See HANKY CODE

BANJI OR BANJEE

▼ *adjective*
Ill-mannered or unsightly.

▼ *noun*
A banji person, place, or thing.

"Why did you take me to this banji club? Look at the VIP section. They used Christmas lights to section it off and only five bulbs still work."

 WANT MORE INFO? *THINK:* **RATCHET AND RAUNCHY.**

USAGE NOTE This term originated in ballroom culture. This term can be considered negative, but it has also been reclaimed by some as a positive self-identifier, similar to "bitch," "ratchet," or "slut."

BARBIE

▼ *noun*
A drag queen who is disorganized and lacking concentration.

"Please remove this Barbie from my presence and enroll her in charm school. She is a disaster."

 WANT MORE INFO? *THINK:* **A DITZ.**

USAGE NOTE This term is commonly used in the drag community.

BAREBACK

▼ *adjective*
Having sexual intercourse without a condom. Mostly used in reference to anal sex but can be used for sex in general. Can be abbreviated as "BB."

"I had to go bareback last night. The store didn't have Magnum XL."

 WANT MORE INFO? *THINK:* **UNPROTECTED, AS IT REFERS TO SEX.**

BARFAIRY

▼ *noun*
See LOUNGE LIZARD

BARFLY

▼ *noun*
See LOUNGE LIZARD

BARSEXUAL

▼ *noun*
See BEER BI

BASKET

▼ *noun*
See BULGE

BASKET SHOPPING

▼ *idiom*
The act of looking directly at a bulging crotch. The term CROTCH GAZING can also be used.

SEE ALSO
PACKAGE, PACKING

"I was basket shopping on the train and saw the biggest bulge."

 WANT MORE INFO? *THINK:* **WINDOW-SHOPPING VERSION OF CHECKING OUT A CROTCH.**

BAT

▼ *noun*
See BIG HUNK OF MEAT

BATH HOUSE

▼ *noun*
A private sauna or spa sometimes appropriated by gay, bisexual, or queer men for sex. The terms SKIN ROOM or DEN can also be used.

"Tom of Finland, bath houses, cruising—these young gays are missing out on some good times because of these dating apps."

 WANT MORE INFO? *THINK:* **A LOCATION WHERE MEN CRUISE FOR HOOKUPS.**

BATTLE

▼ *noun*
In ballroom culture, this is a performance competition between opposing walkers.

SEE ALSO
"History Lesson: The Ballroom Scene," *p. 232*

"The kids are about to gag! The battle for the grand prize is between House of Ebony and House of Balenciaga."

 WANT MORE INFO? *THINK:* **A BALLROOM CONTEST TO WIN THE TITLE, THE TROPHY, THE PRIZE MONEY, AND THE GLORY.**

BDSM

▼ *noun*

An acronym for Bondage and Discipline, Dominance and Submission, Sadism and Masochism. It refers to the exploration of power, control, and resistance through relationships, sex, and scene play. Practices are always negotiated and consensual and, more often than not, erotic. BDSM is often used as an umbrella term for a wide range of sexual fetishes. The abbreviation S&M can also be used.

SEE ALSO

CONSENT, DOM/SUB RELATIONSHIP, FETISH, KINK, NEGOTIATION

"Pick a card, any card. I have orgasm denial, fetish, fantasy, and fisting for your BDSM pleasure."

 WANT MORE INFO? *THINK:* **SEXUAL POWER PLAY.**

 USAGE NOTE For all BDSM-related terms, the power exchange is a part of sadomasochistic play and should be consensual between all partners involved.

BEAR

▼ *noun*

A gay, bisexual, or queer man who has a large or stocky body with visible body hair, resembling a bear.

"I want a big bear to cuddle with tonight and keep me warm . . . BRB, logging into GROWLr."

 WANT MORE INFO? *THINK:* **A STURDY, HAIRY GAY MAN.**

 USAGE NOTE This term originated in the white gay male community.

BEAR COMMUNITY

▼ *noun*
A gay subcommunity that supports and celebrates the brotherhood of bears. This community also embraces other types of queer people who identify as a CUB, CHUB, OTTER, PANDA, or URSULA.

SEE ALSO
"Help! What's My Gay Type?," *p. 152*

"Urban Bear is hosting a 'Cuddle Me' party at Bubble Lounge. Calling all bear community members and admirers!"

 WANT MORE INFO? *THINK:* **THOSE WHO CELEBRATE THE BEAR NECESSITIES DURING P-TOWN BEAR WEEK.**

 This term originated in the white gay male community.

BEARD

▼ *noun*
In binary terms, a partner of the opposite gender meant to cover up one's sexuality.

SEE ALSO
CLOSET, FISH WIFE, LAVENDER MARRIAGE

"Harrison is just her beard. She dates him to make people think she's straight."

 WANT MORE INFO? *THINK:* **A FAKE PARTNER FOR A CLOSETED LESBIAN, GAY, OR QUEER PERSON.**

 This term originated in the white gay male community.

BEARDED LADY

▼ *noun*
A woman dating or married to a gay man to help him pose as heterosexual.

"I was gay in the sixties. So, yes, I had my bearded lady. The world wasn't always keen on me loving men."

 WANT MORE INFO? *THINK:* **A FAUX WIFE FOR A GAY MAN.**

BEAT

▼ *noun*
Makeup or overall appearance.
Often heard in the phrase "full beat."

▼ *verb*
To apply makeup extremely well.
Often heard in the phrase "beat for the gods/gawds."

"Her face was beat for the gawds and pulled back to her temples!"

 WANT MORE INFO? *THINK:* **THE MAKEUP ARTISTS AT MAC.**

 This term originated in ballroom culture and is commonly used in the drag community. It has been appropriated by the larger LGBTQIA+ community and mainstream culture.

BECHDEL TEST, THE

▼ *noun*
A test used to examine gender bias and female representation in fictional works—particularly film, television, and books. In order to pass the Bechdel Test, a work must feature two distinct female characters who talk about something other than a man.

SEE ALSO

THE VITO RUSSO TEST, RING OF KEYS

"My wife and I only let our daughter Sparrow watch movies that pass the Bechdel Test."

 WANT MORE INFO? *THINK:* **A FEMINIST MEASURE OF ACCOUNTABILITY FOR ART.**

DID YOU KNOW Alison Bechdel, the award-winning lesbian cartoonist who wrote *Fun Home*, an autobiographical "tragicomic" about her family, also wrote a successful comic strip from 1983 to 2008, *Dykes to Watch Out For*. It documented the lives of a diverse group of fictional lesbians alongside the cultural and political landscape of their time, and it was in the comic that the Bechdel Test was introduced, forever changing the way we look at gender bias in the media.

BECKY

▼ *noun*
See WENDY

BEEFCAKE

▼ *noun*
A man with a well-defined muscular body.

"Anderson Cooper is a freakin' silver fox beefcake. CNN me, baby."

 WANT MORE INFO? *THINK:* **MUSCLE MEN PINUPS LIKE THE CAST OF** *MAGIC MIKE.*

 This term is commonly used in the gay male community.

BEEP

▼ *exclamation*
A sound used when confirming that someone is gay or queer.

SEE ALSO
GAYDAR

"BEEP! BEEP! BEEP! My gaydar is going off facing northeast."

 WANT MORE INFO? *THINK:* **ZEROING IN ON AN LGBTQIA+ PERSON.**

BEER BI

▼ *noun*
A person who is only open to same-sex or queer encounters when under the influence of alcohol. The terms BARSEXUAL, GAY AFTER THREE, and THREE-BEER QUEER can also be used.

"Everyone gets a little 'beer bi' on New Year's Eve."

 WANT MORE INFO? *THINK:* **ALCOHOL-INDUCED BISEXUALITY.**

BENT

▼ *adjective*
Not heterosexual.

"If it ain't straight then it's bent."

 WANT MORE INFO? *THINK:* **QUEER.**

BENT STICK

▼ *noun*
A penis that is not erect.

"Based solely on his bent stick, you would have never known his magnitude."

 WANT MORE INFO? *THINK:* **AN UNAROUSED DICK.**

BETTY

▼ *noun*
See MARY

B

BICON

▼ *noun*
A bisexual icon.

SEE ALSO

DYKON, GAY ICON

"Let's not forget our beautiful brown bicon, Josephine Baker!"

 WANT MORE INFO? *THINK:* **A BI TRAILBLAZER.**

BI-CURIOUS OR BICURIOUS

▼ *noun*
Someone who identifies as hetero-sexual but is interested in exploring same-sex or queer relationships. This also can apply to a homosexual who is interested in experiencing a heterosexual relationship.

 WANT MORE INFO? *THINK:* **A PERSON EXPERIMENTING WITH BISEXUALITY.**

"Did you know Jasmine is bi-curious? She kissed Nicole in the projection room above the auditorium!"

BICYCLE OR BI-CYCLE

▼ *noun*
The changing of one's sexual attraction between men and women.

SEE ALSO
AC/DC, BISEXUAL

"I can be 70 percent gay one day and 15 percent gay the next. My bi-cycle is powered by two different wheels, what can I say?"

 WANT MORE INFO? *THINK:* **A BISEXUAL PLAY ON THE WORD "BICYCLE."**

USAGE NOTE This term may have negative connotations as it limits bisexuality to the gender binary. It is inappropriate to use this label if a person has not self-identified as such.

BIG DYKE ENERGY OR BIG DICK ENERGY

▼ *idiom*
Sex appeal based on confidence and swagger. Often abbreviated as "BDE."

SEE ALSO
LP, POWER LESBIAN, STUD, ZADDY

Sherise: *I'm doing "big dyke energy" awards on my podcast this week. What do you think about Lea DeLaria, Brittney Griner, Joan Jett, Ruby Rose, and Janelle Monáe?*
Yvette: *Every single one of them could not be more perfect. And goddess Joan Jett damn near invented BDE!*

 WANT MORE INFO? *THINK:* **STUD VIBES.**

USAGE NOTE The term "dyke" originated as a derogatory slur for lesbians but has been reclaimed by some of the LGBTQIA+ community. It may still have negative connotations for some people.

BIGENDER

▼ adjective

A person who identifies as two genders (not limited to the gender binary)—a combination of male, female, and/or another gender identity.

> **SEE ALSO**
>
> **POLYGENDER, PANGENDER, GENDER-FLUID, GENDERFLUX, NONBINARY**

Reid: Brook is bigender, right?
Sav: Yeah, they use he/him and they/them pronouns.
Reid: Great! I was thinking about getting them a set of 'His' and 'Theirs' monogrammed hand towels for Christmas.

 WANT MORE INFO? *THINK:* **SOMEONE WHOSE IDENTITY ENCOMPASSES TWO GENDERS.**

 USAGE NOTE This term is commonly used in the transgender, nonbinary, and gender nonconforming communities.

BIG HUNK OF MEAT

▼ noun

A large penis.

A well-endowed man.

"You mean the gay porn star Rafael Alencar? Now, that is a big hunk of meat!"

 WANT MORE INFO? *THINK:* **XXXL DICK.**

BINARY

▼ noun

Something having two parts.

> **SEE ALSO**
>
> **GENDER BINARY**

▼ adjective

Relating to or involving two things.

"The use of binary systems is a bit simple and uninformative to me. Do we really only want to see the world in just black or white?"

 WANT MORE INFO? *THINK:* **A SYSTEM BUILT ON A PAIR OF OPPOSITES.**

BIND

▼ verb

To flatten or conceal one's breasts/chest using constricting materials, typically using a BINDER, which is the healthiest and safest way to bind.

> **SEE ALSO**
>
> **"Tucking & Binding 101,"** *p. 130*

"Hey queer masc nation, I have some tips for you on how to bind properly. Check it out on my blog. Link in profile!"

 WANT MORE INFO? *THINK:* **TO REDUCE THE APPARENT SIZE OF ONE'S BREASTS.**

 USAGE NOTE This term is commonly used in the transgender, nonbinary, gender nonconforming, and drag communities.

BINDER

▼ *noun*
An undergarment used to reduce the appearance and size of breasts.

SEE ALSO
"Tucking & Binding 101," **p. 130**

"Avoid using tape or Ace bandages to bind. Wear a binder instead."

 WANT MORE INFO? *THINK:* **A COMPRESSION GARMENT FOR BREASTS/CHEST.**

 This term is commonly used in the transgender, nonbinary, gender nonconforming, and drag communities.

Binder ▲

BIO QUEEN

▼ *noun*
See FAUX QUEEN

BIPHOBIA

▼ *noun*
Aversion, fear, or hatred toward bisexuality.

RELATED
BIPHOBIC *adjective* **BIPHOBE** *noun*

SEE ALSO
ACEPHOBIA, FEMMEPHOBIA, HOMOPHOBIA, LESBO-PHOBIA, QUEERPHOBIA, TRANSPHOBIA

"Straight and gay people can be biphobic. I've personally been verbally mistreated more than I like to admit."

 WANT MORE INFO? *THINK:* **DISLIKE OF OR PREJUDICE AGAINST BISEXUAL PEOPLE.**

BIPOC

▼ *noun*
See POC

BIRD

▼ *noun*
A large penis.

"That bird was tasty indeed! A mouthwatering seven-and-a-half inches of goodness."

 WANT MORE INFO? *THINK:* **A BIG BANANA.**

BIROMANTIC

▼ *noun*
A person who has a romantic attraction to two genders.

"Andrew and I just clicked! We cuddle all night and write each other the sweetest letters. I think this asexual's biromantic heart has been shot by Cupid's arrow!"

 WANT MORE INFO? *THINK:* **THE ROMANTIC COUNTER-PART TO BISEXUAL.**

 This term is commonly used in the asexual community.

BISCUITS

▼ *noun*
See CAKES

BISEXUAL

▼ *adjective*
Being attracted to two genders. Often, but not limited to, being attracted to the same gender and other genders. Sometimes shortened to "bi."

▼ *noun*
A bisexual person.

RELATED
BISEXUALITY *noun*

SEE ALSO
PANSEXUAL

"I am not confused. I am not experimenting. I am not half-gay and half-straight. I am bisexual."

 WANT MORE INFO? *THINK:* **ATTRACTED TO JACK AND JILL AND JAI, TOO.**

 Bisexual attraction is often misunderstood as a sexual preference that is limited to the gender binary. Bisexuality is a personal journey and not all bisexuals share the same type of attraction model.

DID YOU KNOW Bisexual Visibility Day is celebrated each year on September 23.

BITCH

▼ *noun*
A term of endearment for a friend or a derogatory term, depending on the context and tone. Alternate spellings include "binch," "betch," and "byotch."

"Bitch, you look gorgeous! Yaaasssss!"

 WANT MORE INFO? *THINK:* **A CATCHALL FRIEND/FOE IDENTIFIER.**

▼ *exclamation*
An exclamation used to emphasize a particular feeling.

"Biiiiiitch, these sixty-hour weeks are killing me. I'm getting no sleep."

WANT MORE INFO? *THINK:* **A CATCHALL FEELING IDENTIFIER.**

ATTRACTION TO SAME GENDER

 ATTRACTION TO DIFFERENT GENDER

ALL
BISEXUAL

B

BITCHY

▼ *adjective*
Nasty and unlikable.

"Stop being so bitchy! Your face gets uglier every time you open your mouth."

 WANT MORE INFO? *THINK:* **HAVING A BAD ATTITUDE.**

BITE ME

▼ *idiom*
An aggressive way to tell someone you do not want to be bothered.

Kyle: *Bite me, Xavian!*
Xavian: *Fuck off, Kyle!*

 WANT MORE INFO? *THINK:* **"SUCK IT."**

BLACK GAY PRIDE

▼ *noun*
A movement that empowers the visibility of the Black gay, same gender–loving, and queer community. The terms "Black Pride" and "Black Pride Movement" can also be used.

"Gurl, your calendar should always include at least one Black Gay Pride! It's time to get you on the scene. Block off Memorial Day weekend for DC Black Pride right now!"

 WANT MORE INFO? *THINK:* **A CELEBRATION OF BLACKNESS, GAYNESS, LOVE, AND UNITY.**

BLACK TRIANGLE

▼ *noun*
A symbol adopted by the lesbian community to show pride in women's liberation and resistance against discrimination.

SEE ALSO
PINK TRIANGLE

"My black triangle tattoo is the perfect complement to my Venus and moon sign tattoos. They symbolize a mix of strength, tenacity, and balance."

 WANT MORE INFO? *THINK:* **SYMBOL FOR QUEER FEMINISM AND LESBIAN PRIDE.**

DID YOU KNOW The black triangle was originally used in Nazi concentration camps to mark prisoners who were considered "asocial" or "work-shy." Lesbians were included in this category. The symbol was reappropriated by the lesbian community in the 1970s as a symbol of pride.

BLAPS

▼ *noun*
Irritable bowels. The term "blatts" can also be used.

"My stomach is rumbling! I got the blaps."

 WANT MORE INFO? *THINK:* **DIARRHEA.**

BLAQUEER

▼ *noun*
An empowering identifier for a Black person who identifies as queer. The term "BlaQ" can also be used.

SEE ALSO
QPOC OR QTPOC

"The separation of the words 'Black' and 'Queer' presents a false division, a convenient (forced) circumcision of self, that is not the reality for BlaQueer people across the world." ▶ *Tabias Olajuawon Wilson, BlaQueerFlow*

 WANT MORE INFO? *THINK:* **A TERM FOR QUEER BLACK EMPOWERMENT.**

USAGE NOTE This term was coined by writer and motivational speaker Tabias Olajuawon Wilson and is commonly used in the Black queer community.

 DID YOU KNOW From prolific writers James Baldwin and Lorraine Hansberry to legendary modern dance pioneer Alvin Ailey, from civil rights trailblazer Bayard Rustin and trans activist Marsha P. Johnson and her impact on the 1969 Stonewall riots to the award-winning queer activists and Black Lives Matter cofounders, Patrisse Khan-Cullors and Alicia Garza, Black LGBTQIA+ artists and activists have played crucial roles in shaping American history for decades.

BLOCKERS

▼ *noun*

Medicine taken by transgender, nonbinary, or gender nonconforming youth to prevent puberty from starting. These drugs interrupt the production of hormones and delay the development of secondary sex characteristics, such as the deepening of the voice, development of body hair, and menstruation. The term "puberty blockers" can also be used.

"The primary use of blockers is for young people to have time to understand who they are. If a child says, 'I don't think I want breasts,' blockers can put that development on hold."

 WANT MORE INFO? *THINK:* **PUBERTY STOPPER.**

USAGE NOTE	This term is commonly used in the transgender, nonbinary, and gender nonconforming communities.

DID YOU KNOW Blockers were first used to help young girls who experienced puberty at an early age. Blockers would halt menstruation in girls as early as age seven, and when the girl reached a more mature age, she would come off the blocker to resume puberty.

BLOUSE

▼ *noun*

A feminine gay, bisexual, or queer man who identifies as a top.

SEE ALSO
FEMME TOP, TOP

"Glenn may look super-femme, but that blouse had my ankles over my head in five minutes flat."

 WANT MORE INFO? *THINK:* **AN EFFEMINATE GAY TOP.**

USAGE NOTE	This term originated in the gay male community.

BLOW

▼ *verb*

To give sexual oral pleasure, often to a penis.

To ejaculate.

RELATED
BLOWJOB *noun*

SEE ALSO
EAT IT, FELLATIO, GO DOWN ON

"I want you to blow my mind when you blow me."

 WANT MORE INFO? *THINK:* **TO SUCK A DICK OR TO CUM.**

BLUE BOY

▼ *noun*
A police officer. The terms MATILDA and MEG can also be used.

"Don't trust the blue boys. They're trying to get information to shut down the club."

 WANT MORE INFO? *THINK:* **THE COPS.**

BLUE DISCHARGE

▼ *noun*
A dated term for the discharge of a gay man from the United States Army.

"My grandfather was given a blue discharge even though his personal life had nothing to do with his service for the U.S. Army."

 WANT MORE INFO? *THINK:* **AN ARMY DISMISSAL BASED ON SAME-SEX RELATIONSHIPS.**

BODY-ODY-ODY

▼ *noun*
An attractive physique. The phrase "serving body" can also be used.

"She has body-ody-ody!"

 WANT MORE INFO? *THINK:* **A FINGER-LICKIN' HOT BOD.**

 USAGE NOTE This term originated in ballroom culture and is commonly used in the larger queer and trans people of color (QTPOC) community.

BOG QUEEN

▼ *noun*
A gay, bisexual, or queer man who looks for sexual encounters in public restrooms or public parks.

SEE ALSO
CHASER, QUEEN, TEA ROOM

"Before Grindr, GROWLr, and Scruff, there were the bog queens."

 WANT MORE INFO? *THINK:* **AN OUTDOOR OR PUBLIC SPACE SEXUAL ADVENTURER.**

BOI

▼ *noun*
A person of any gender expression who presents in a youthful, masculine way.

"I'm a girl and he's a dude but we both also identify as 'boi.'"

 WANT MORE INFO? *THINK:* **A YOUNG-LOOKING, MASC-OF-CENTER PERSON.**

USAGE NOTE This term originated in the lesbian community. It has been appropriated by the larger LGBTQIA+ community.

 DID YOU KNOW A wide range of gender identities can fall under this term including young femme gay males, masculine lesbians, transmasculine, intersex, and gender nonconforming folx (to name a few).

B

BOOBS

▼ *noun*
Breasts. The terms "boobies" and JUGS can also be used.

SEE ALSO
RACK, TITTIES

"Your boobs look great in that jumpsuit, babe! Are you wearing a push-up bra?"

 WANT MORE INFO? *THINK:* **TWO HANDFULS OF HAPPINESS.**

BOOM

▼ *exclamation*
A stern, dismissive signifier to punctuate the end of a statement.

"Just admit you forgot. The meeting has been on the calendar for two months, Tiffany. Boom!"

 WANT MORE INFO? *THINK:* **MIC DROP.**

USAGE NOTE This term originated in Black American culture and is commonly used in the Black gay and queer community.

BOOP

▼ *exclamation*
A sound effect used to signify agreement.

Jules: *I want to get that new BMW coupe after I get my bonus. I have worked so hard.*
Teddy: *Boop! Queen, you deserve it. Spend those coins!*

 WANT MORE INFO? *THINK:* **YAAAASSS.**

BOOTS

▼ *exclamation*
An emphatic word used to enhance an adjective. The superlative is BACKBOOTS.

"I just want all the freakin' food! I'm hungry boots! What time is lunch?"

 WANT MORE INFO? *THINK:* **AN ADJECTIVE INTENSIFIER.**

USAGE NOTE This term originated in the Black gay community.

BOOTY

▼ *noun*
See CAKES

BOOTY HOLE

▼ *noun*
See BACK DOOR

BOSTON MARRIAGE

▼ *noun*
A dated term for a relationship in which two unmarried women live together long-term, without the company of a man.

"People think Alice B. Toklas and Gertrude Stein were roommates?! Ha! Back then, that was called a Boston marriage."

 WANT MORE INFO? *THINK:* **AN OLD-SCHOOL EUPHEMISM FOR LESBIAN ROOMMATES.**

DID YOU KNOW "Boston marriage" was originally coined by writer Henry James in his 1886 novel *The Bostonians*, where he depicted two wealthy women living together and having an intimate relationship. Same-sex relationships were illegal in most parts of the world until the twentieth century. Women would pose as housemates or companions instead of intimate partners in order to live discreetly.

BOTTOM

▼ *noun*
The person on the receiving end of a sex act; when referring to queer or same-sex male encounters, it often implies anal penetration—for these sexual encounters, the term CATCHER can also be used.

▼ *verb*
To perform a submissive sex act; to engage in sexual activity as a bottom.

> **SEE ALSO**
> **BLOUSE, CLOWN BOTTOM, POWER BOTTOM, SWITCH, TOP, VERS**

"Welp, I got a date tonight. This bottom has to eat Popsicles and ice all day!"

 WANT MORE INFO? *THINK:* **THE POSITION OR ACT OF BEING SUBMISSIVE DURING SEX.**

USAGE NOTE This term originated in the gay male community. It has been appropriated by the larger LGBTQIA+ community.

BOTTOM SURGERY

▼ *noun*
Reconstructive surgery performed on the genitals, often performed to affirm a person's gender identity.

SEE ALSO
TOP SURGERY

"Bottom surgeries can include vaginoplasty for MTF or MTN and phalloplasty or metoidioplasty for FTM or FTN."

 WANT MORE INFO? *THINK:* **MEDICAL PROCEDURE TO ALTER ONE'S GENITALS.**

 This term is commonly used in the transgender, nonbinary, and gender nonconforming communities.

BOX

▼ *noun*
Vagina.

SEE ALSO
PUSSY

"Unwrap my box with soft passionate kisses and you will surely find a blooming flower inside."

 WANT MORE INFO? *THINK:* **VAG, COOTER, PINK, SLIT, TACO, ETC.**

BOY

▼ *noun*
A submissive role in BDSM, leather, and kink play; also known as PUP.

SEE ALSO
DOM/SUB RELATIONSHIP

"A boy is taught by his Sir— leadership, discipline, honor, and balance."

 WANT MORE INFO? *THINK:* **THE ONE WHO OBEYS.**

 This term is used in the BDSM, leather, and kink communities. For all BDSM-related terms, the power exchange should be consensual between all partners. The *b* in the word "boy" should always be lowercase when referring to power dynamic relationships.

BOY PUSSY

▼ *noun*
See BUSSY

BREEZY

▼ *noun*
An attractive woman.

"Just bought two tickets to Janelle Monáe's tour. Which lucky breezy should I take with me?"

 WANT MORE INFO? *THINK:* **A FOXY LADY.**

 This term is commonly used in the Black lesbian community.

BRING OUT THE GAY

▼ *idiom*
To persuade a heterosexual person to explore homosexuality.

"Ricky Martin can bring out the gay in anybody. It's a gift."

 WANT MORE INFO? *THINK:* **TO TEMPT SOMEONE TO EXPLORE SAME-GENDER OR QUEER LOVIN'.**

BRO OR BRUH

▼ *noun*
A term of endearment used between two masculine people.

"Bruh, what's up for tonight? I'm headed out to shoot some pool with Ty and Aisha, wanna come?"

 WANT MORE INFO? *THINK:* **PAL, BUD, DUDE.**

 This term originated in Black American culture. It has been appropriated by the larger LGBTQIA+ community and mainstream culture.

BUBBLE GUM MACHINE

▼ *noun*
A machine that dispenses condoms for sale.

"The bubble gum machine was invented by this German guy named Julius Fromm. No, not the chewing gum machine, the latex one."

 **WANT MORE INFO?** *THINK:* **A DISPENSER FOR RUBBERS.**

BUG

▼ *noun*
See LUG

BULGE

▼ *noun*
Refers to a penis, either visible through clothing or seen naked. The term BASKET or PRINT can also be used.

SEE ALSO
BASKET SHOPPING

"Mine eyes have seen the glory of his bulge."

 WANT MORE INFO? *THINK:* **OUTLINE OF A MAN'S PACKAGE.**

BULL

▼ *noun*
A man with a hyper-masculine, muscular build. Other characteristics may include a deep voice, large penis, and a dominant sexual personality.

"I rode that bull like a champion."

 WANT MORE INFO? *THINK:* **A MUSCLE MAN WITH A HIGH LIBIDO.**

BULL DAGGER

▼ *noun*
See BULL DYKE

B

BULL DYKE OR BULLDYKE

▼ *noun*

A lesbian characterized by aggressiveness and/or masculine behavior and appearance. The term BULL DAGGER can also be used.

> SEE ALSO
>
> **DYKE, BUTCH, "The Lesbian Spectrum,"** *p. 194*

"Of course the bulldyke went to save the femme damsel in distress."

 WANT MORE INFO? *THINK:* **A SUPER-MASCULINE LEZZIE.**

USAGE NOTE The term "dyke" originated as a derogatory slur for lesbians but has been reclaimed by some of the LGBTQIA+ community. It may still have negative connotations for some people.

DID YOU KNOW The terms "bull dyke" and "bull dagger" can be traced back to the Black lesbian community in the 1920s, during the Harlem Renaissance. Popular lesbian blues singers like Ma Rainey and Bessie Smith were widely known as bull daggers.

BUMMING

▼ *verb*

Anal sexual intercourse.

"Jared and I will be bumming all night. Don't bother calling."

 WANT MORE INFO? *THINK:* **EUPHEMISM FOR GAY SEX.**

BUMPER-TO-BUMPER

▼ *noun*

Vagina-to-vagina sexual intercourse.

"Hey baby, can we play tonight? A little shag? A little bumper-to-bumper? Should I shave?"

 WANT MORE INFO? *THINK:* **EUPHEMISM FOR LESBIAN SEX.**

USAGE NOTE This term is commonly used in the lesbian community.

BUNGHOLE

▼ *noun*

See BACK DOOR

BUNS

▼ *noun*

See CAKES

BUSSY

▼ *noun*

A sexual nickname for the rectum. This term is a portmanteau of the words "butt" and "pussy." The terms BOY PUSSY and MAN PUSSY can also be used.

A name for a transgender or nonbinary person's genitals.

"They are sexy. Damn, my bussy just got wet."

 WANT MORE INFO? *THINK:* **A MAN'S LOVE-MAKIN' HOLE OR GNC PERSON'S SEXUAL PARTS.**

USAGE NOTE This term may be considered limiting as it relies on the gender binary. The use of this term relies on an individual's preference, as many transgender and gender nonconforming people consider it insensitive and/or pejorative.

BUTCH

▼ *adjective*
Denoting the vast and dynamic representation of masculine characteristics, regardless of gender. Both "femme" and "butch" are often paired with adjectives soft/hard or high/low as a means of distinction.

SEE ALSO
FEMME, FUTCH, "The Lesbian Spectrum," *p. 194*

▼ *noun*
In the lesbian community, a woman who possesses a masculine appearance and behaviors.

SEE ALSO
BABY BUTCH, SOFT BUTCH, STONE BUTCH

"That butch changed my tire and then she gave me the ride of my life."

 WANT MORE INFO? *THINK:* **MASCULINE.**

USAGE NOTE This term originated in the lesbian community. It has been appropriated by the larger LGBTQIA+ community.

BUTCH/FEMME RELATIONSHIP

▼ *noun*
An intimate relationship between a butch lesbian and a femme lesbian.

SEE ALSO
BUTCH, FEMME, MAMA AND PAPA RELATIONSHIP

"I love butch/femme relationships because my girlfriends never want to wear my clothes. Well, except my T-shirts to bed."

 WANT MORE INFO? *THINK:* **LESBIAN LOVERS—ONE MASCULINE, ONE FEMININE.**

USAGE NOTE This term originated in the lesbian community. It has been appropriated by the larger LGBTQIA+ community.

DID YOU KNOW In 1940s working-class bar culture, the words "butch," "femme," and "kiki" described women who were attracted to other women before "lesbian" was widely used. In butch/femme relationships, partners assumed traditionally masculine and feminine gender roles. Kiki girls did not adhere to the butch/femme binary when it came to gender expression *or* sexual preference; they were often shunned within the lesbian community.

BUTCHKINI

▼ *noun*
The bathing suit of choice for butch lesbians, and other masculine queer people with breasts, like bois, tomboys, studs, transmasc, or AFAB gender nonconforming people: a sports bra and board shorts.

"The rainbow butchkinis were out at Miami Pride."

 WANT MORE INFO? *THINK:* **A BODY-POSITIVE SWIMSUIT FOR BUTCHES.**

BUTCH-ON-BUTCH CRIME

▼ *idiom*
An expression disapproving of a lesbian couple consisting of two masculine women.

SEE ALSO
STUD FOR STUD

"Aw, man. We lost another hottie to butch-on-butch crime."

 WANT MORE INFO? *THINK:* **WHEN TWO MASCULINE LESBIANS HOOK UP.**

USAGE NOTE This term originated in the lesbian community. It may be considered a stereotype or derogatory.

BUTCH QUEEN

▼ *noun*
A category competition in the ballroom scene for cisgender men.

SEE ALSO
CATEGORY, QUEEN

A gay, bisexual, or queer man who possesses both masculine and feminine traits.

"That's right! I said it! Butch queen! Boy in the day, girl at night."
▶ *Paris Dupree,* Paris Is Burning

 WANT MORE INFO? *THINK:* **A GAY MAN PERFORMING IN A BALL.**

USAGE NOTE This term originated in ballroom culture. It has been appropriated by the larger LGBTQIA+ community.

PEOPLE KEEP SAYING GOODBYE TO THIS POOR UNFORTUNATE WOMAN

"WHO IS FELICIA?"

BYE, FELICIA

▼ *idiom*
This phrase is used as a dismissive signifier.

Chloe: *Let's go skydiving tomorrow! Don't you think that will be fun?*
Tommie: *Bye, Felicia! Absolutely not.*

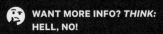 **WANT MORE INFO?** *THINK:* **HELL, NO!**

 USAGE NOTE This term originated in Black American culture and is used in the Black gay and queer community. It has been appropriated by mainstream culture.

 DID YOU KNOW The phrase "Bye, Felicia" was first coined by rapper, actor, and producer O'Shea Jackson (better known as Ice Cube) in the popular 1995 film *Friday*.

Be informed on gender identity, expression, and sexual orientation

Educator, author, and activist Sam Killermann popularized an educational tool that breaks down the complex concepts of gender and sexuality into a comprehensive, visual format for learners of all ages. The Genderbread Person serves as a basic introduction to understanding the complexities of gender identity, gender expression, and a person's sexual and romantic preferences.

Here, you will find a version of the Genderbread Person enhanced with even more terms to better account for the full spectrum of expression. Our queer community is so vast and brilliant—and the way we talk about identity is always changing—that there may be people who do not fit neatly into any of the labels provided here. Their existence is just as celebrated and just as valid as the descriptions presented here.

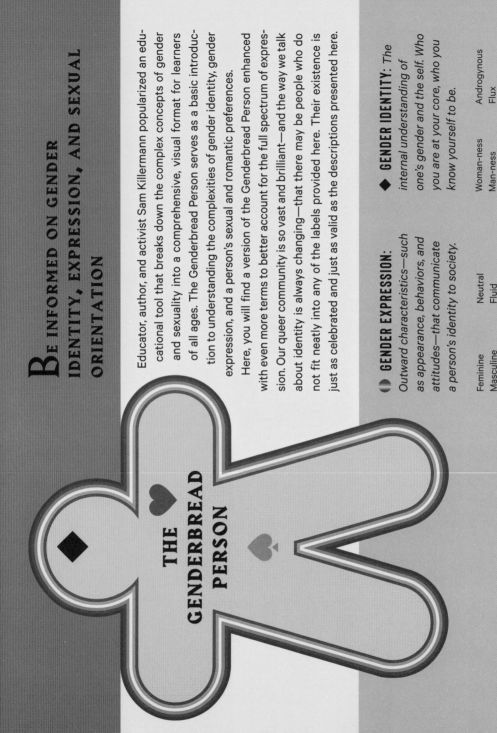

THE GENDERBREAD PERSON

● GENDER EXPRESSION: *Outward characteristics—such as appearance, behaviors, and attitudes—that communicate a person's identity to society.*

Feminine
Masculine

Neutral
Fluid

◆ GENDER IDENTITY: *The internal understanding of one's gender and the self. Who you are at your core, who you know yourself to be.*

Woman-ness
Man-ness
Trans-ness

Androgynous
Flux
Genderless

It is common to find your identity on pink, yellow, and blue!

◆ **GENDER IDENTITY**
- woman-ness
- gender nonconforming
- man-ness

● **GENDER EXPRESSION**
- femininity
- androgyny
- masculinity

ANATOMICAL SEX
- female-ness
- intersex
- male-ness

♥ **ATTRACTION**
- women and/or feminine and/or female people
- gender nonconforming and/or genderfluid people
- men and/or masculine and/or male people

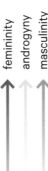

♥ **ATTRACTION:** *The sexual and romantic ways in which humans are drawn to one another. Gender and sexuality are separate entities, and someone's gender expression, identity, or anatomical sex actually have nothing to do with whom they're attracted to.*

Aesthetic attraction	Homoflexible
Alloromantic	Homoromantic
Allosexual	Homosexual
Androsexual	Lesbian
Aromantic	Lesbiflexible
Asexual	Monosexual
Auto-sexual	Non-monogamous
Bi-curious	Non-monosexual
Biromantic	Omnisexual
Bisexual	Pansexual
Demiromantic	Polyamorous
Demisexual	Polysexual
Fluid	Queer
Gay	Romantic orientation
Gynesexual	Same-gender loving
Heteroflexible	Sexual orientation
Heterosexual	Solo polyamorous

ANATOMICAL SEX: *The physical makeup of the human body, sometimes referred to as biological sex. Our understanding of anatomical sex is led by things like genitals, chromosomes, and hormones.*

- Female-ness
- Male-ness
- Sex assigned at birth: male, female, intersex

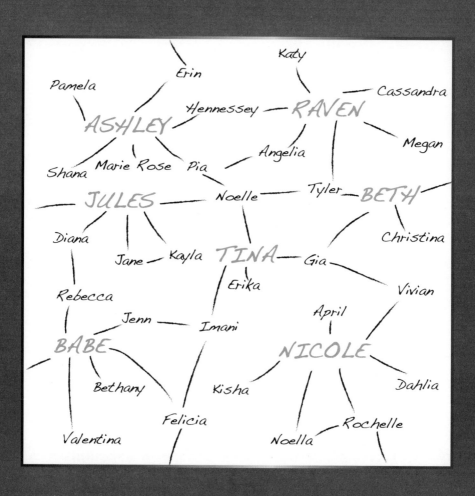

Pamela

Erin

Katy

ASHLEY

Hennessey — RAVEN — Cassandra

Angelia

Megan

Shana   Marie Rose   Pia

JULES — Noelle — Tyler — BETH

Diana

Christina

Jane — Kayla   TINA — Gia

Rebecca

Erika

Vivian

Jenn — Imani

April

BABE

NICOLE

Bethany

Kisha

Dahlia

Valentina

Felicia

Noella   Rochelle

Cc

CAKES

▼ *noun*

Enticing buttocks. The term BISCUITS, BOOTY, or BUNS can also be used.

"He got cakes! Ass for days, cakes by the pound!"

 WANT MORE INFO? *THINK:* **A NICE ASS.**

USAGE NOTE This term originated in Black American culture. It has been appropriated by the larger LGBTQIA+ community and mainstream culture.

CALL WARDROBE

▼ *idiom*

An expression of dissatisfaction with someone's style of dress.

"Why does he have on that fake fur and those knockoff Jimmy Choos? CALL WARDROBE!"

 WANT MORE INFO? *THINK:* **TO POINT OUT SOMEONE'S ABSOLUTELY UNACCEPTABLE ATTIRE.**

A complaint.

"These people and their 'call wardrobe' cries about everything. The drinks are free, the food is free, and the WiFi is free. What's the problem?"

 WANT MORE INFO? *THINK:* **AN SOS SIGNAL.**

C

CAMP

▼ *noun*
The spirit of extravagance, irony, and exaggerated bad taste.

RELATED
CAMPY *adjective*   **CAMP IT UP** *idiom*

"Mommie Dearest and Showgirls are the crown jewels of camp, with Joan Crawford and Nomi Malone as queens!"

 WANT MORE INFO? *THINK:* **JOHN WATERS'S** *HAIRSPRAY.*

DID YOU KNOW The word *camp* derives from the French *se camper* meaning "to flaunt." Camp is often associated with aesthetics, homosexuality, beauty, art, and stylization that dates back to the beau ideal seen in Renaissance sculptures. King Louis XIV is cited as an embodiment of sophisticated high camp style, which was a sign of wealth and power in 17th-century France—fast-forward to 20th-century drag culture and underground films like *Flaming Creatures*, and camp has been theatricalized, now associated with queer culture.

CARPET MUNCHER

▼ *noun*
A lesbian; a woman who performs cunnilingus on another woman. The terms RUG MUNCHER or MUFF DIVER can also be used.

"Ashley and Marissa just came out. They are newly certified carpet munchers."

 WANT MORE INFO? *THINK:* **SOMEONE WITH A BIG LESBIAN CRUSH.**

 USAGE NOTE This term is used in the lesbian community. It originated as a derogatory slur for lesbians but has been reclaimed by some of the community.

CARRY

▼ *noun*
One who overembellishes or overdoes it, referred to as "a carry."

"Did Ronnie and Adam really just make a ten-page birthday itinerary for Sasha? Yes, she is cute, but she is a poodle and they are a carry!"

 WANT MORE INFO? *THINK:* **A BIT MUCH.**

▼ *verb*
To be insulted or outdone.

"Dang, you just got carried! Why did you let him talk to you like that?"

 WANT MORE INFO? *THINK:* **DISSED.**

 USAGE NOTE This term originated in ballroom culture.

CARTA

▼ *idiom*
See FACE

CATCHER

▼ *noun*
See BOTTOM

CATEGORY

▼ *noun*
A division of ballroom competition with strict rules surrounding a particular theme.

SEE ALSO

"History Lesson: The Ballroom Scene," *p. 232*

Jamie: *Girl, what category are they on? I'll be there in twenty minutes.*
Dante: *Just finished Schoolboy Realness. But you betta hurry up 'cause Jack Mizrahi is here reading the girls!*

 WANT MORE INFO? *THINK:* **A ROUND OF WALKERS SERVING THEIR BEST LOOKS ON THE RUNWAY TO CLAIM AWARDS AND THE TITLE.**

CD

▼ *noun*
See CROSS-DRESSER

CELESBIAN

▼ *noun*
A female celebrity known or reputed to be a lesbian.

"There are just so many to name them all, but Rosie O'Donnell, Ellen DeGeneres, Melissa Etheridge, Robin Roberts, Suze Orman, and Samira Wiley are my favorite celesbians."

 WANT MORE INFO? *THINK:* **A QUEER WOMAN IN POP CULTURE AND MEDIA.**

CH

▼ *exclamation*
A sound made emphasizing a hard "ch" sound to dismiss an action or a thought, often accompanied by a smirk and/or an eye roll. Alternate spellings include "chu" or "chi," as the term is derived from CHILD. The term TUH can also be used.

Christopher: *I am so excited about my new diet! Only veggies and fruit my first week. Want to join me?*
Quinton: *Ch! I am not about to live on rabbit food. You know I need my meat! Ooh, I think that's him calling right now.*

 WANT MORE INFO? *THINK:* **A HARD NO.**

 This term originated in the Black gay community. It has been appropriated by the larger LGBTQIA+ community and mainstream culture.

C

CHAPSTICK LESBIAN

▼ *noun*

A gay woman who has a muted feminine sensibility. The term was coined as an alternative to "lipstick lesbian," for women who present in a feminine way but prefer casual clothes and ChapStick over feminine clothes and makeup.

SEE ALSO

ANDROGYNY, SOFT BUTCH, "The Lesbian Spectrum," *p. 194*

"I dig a ChapStick lesbian. There's nothing sexier than watching her code and create a website."

 WANT MORE INFO? *THINK:* **THAT FIELD HOCKEY PLAYER YOU HAD A CRUSH ON IN HIGH SCHOOL.**

USAGE NOTE This term originated in the lesbian community.

THE FUTURE IS FEMALE

CHART, THE

▼ *noun*

An extensive diagram representing the relationships and sexual connections between lesbian, bisexual, and queer women within a community. This term is a reference to the popular early-2000s television show *The L Word*.

"I created my version of the chart, using every lesbian in Omaha!"

 WANT MORE INFO? *THINK:* **THE LITTLE BLACK BOOK OF LESBIAN LOVE AND SEX.**

CHASER

▼ *noun*

Someone who pursues romantic and/or sexual relationships with a particular type of person within the queer community.

"A chaser can be a bear chaser, chicken chaser, daddy chaser, chub chaser . . . the list goes on. They like what they like."

A person who has a sexual fetish for transgender people. Not to be confused with TRANS ATTRACTED, where a person's intent is to pursue an intimate relationship with a transgender person, not just sex.

SEE ALSO
TRANSAMOROUS

"Honey, I've had chasers send me dick pics online and stalk me at parties. They're just no good. Stay away from them."

 WANT MORE INFO? *THINK:* **A PERSON WITH A SPECIFIC APPETITE.**

 This term often implies a person who has fetishes based on harmful stereotypes. In the trans community, the word *chaser* is considered pejorative.

CHEMSEX

▼ *noun*

See PNP

CHERRY

▼ *noun*

A hymen.

"She thrust so hard it popped my cherry!"

 WANT MORE INFO? *THINK:* **THE MAIDENHEAD.**

CHICKEN

▼ *noun*

A young or youthful-looking gay, bisexual, or queer man.

SEE ALSO
TWINK, "Help! What's My Gay Type?," *p. 152*

"Geez, all these chickens in here, they must have fake IDs."

 WANT MORE INFO? *THINK:* **QUEER YOUNGINS AND SPRING CHICKENS.**

 This term may be considered a stereotype or derogatory.

C

CHICKEN QUEEN

▼ *noun*
An older gay man who is attracted to younger gay men. The terms PINK PANTHER, "chicken chaser," or "chicken hawk" can also be used.

SEE ALSO
CHASER, QUEEN

"You mean the chicken queen and his twink lover?"

 WANT MORE INFO? *THINK:* **HE LIKES 'EM YOUNG AND FUN.**

 This term originated in white gay male culture. It may be considered a stereotype or derogatory.

CHILD

▼ *exclamation*
A term used to express dissatisfaction or dismissal of an action or thought. Alternate spellings include "chile" or "churld."

Mr. Robinson: *We're scheduled for more overtime next week.*
Mrs. Jenkins: *Child, I'm not working another hour without being paid a real overtime rate.*
Mr. Robinson: *Churld, you know it!*

 WANT MORE INFO? *THINK:* **"UH-UH, NO WAY!"**

 This term originated in Black American culture. It has been appropriated by the LGBTQIA+ community and mainstream culture.

Child ▲

CHILD BOO

▼ *idiom*

Used to signal a disagreement or lack of interest with a particular matter. The term "child, please" can also be used.

Miguel: *Do you see that piece of trade over there?*
Ricky: *Child boo, only if you are looking for meat in the fish market.*

 WANT MORE INFO? *THINK:* **A DISAPPROVING SHAKE OF THE HEAD.**

 USAGE NOTE This term originated in Black American culture and is commonly used in the Black gay and queer community. It has been appropriated by mainstream culture.

CHILDREN, THE

▼ *noun*

Young gay and trans members of the ballroom scene.

Young members of the LGBTQIA+ community.

> **SEE ALSO**
>
> **THE KIDS, "History Lesson: The Ballroom Scene,"** *p. 232*

"The children were cutting up the runway at the Latex Ball."

 WANT MORE INFO? *THINK:* **YOUNG, WILD, AND FREE QUEER REVOLUTIONARIES.**

USAGE NOTE This term originated in ballroom culture. It has been appropriated by the larger LGBTQIA+ community and mainstream culture.

CHOP

▼ *verb*

To dismiss, eliminate, or reject.

"You just got chopped, Miss Girl! You are the weakest link. Goodbye!"

 WANT MORE INFO? *THINK:* **REJECTED.**

USAGE NOTE This term is commonly used in ballroom culture.

DID YOU KNOW In ballroom culture, categories were created to give gay and trans people of color the opportunity to embody unique identities—Butch Queens, Femme Queens, Butches, Women, Drag Queens, Trans Men, Female Figures, and Male Figures—and walk in popular categories like Realness, Realness with a Twist, Runway, Vogue Femme, Face, Bizarre, and Body. "Chop" is used when judges decide to eliminate a walker from the competition. The term can be used by judges, opposing contestants, or members of the audience to provoke D-R-A-M-A.

C

65

CHOSEN FAMILY

▼ *noun*
Individuals who are not biologically or legally related who deliberately choose to support and nurture each other like family. The word CIRCLE is also sometimes used.

SEE ALSO
DRAG FAMILY, HOUSE CULTURE

"Coming out as nonbinary can be a very confusing process. But I was really able to feel rooted, energized, and supported by my chosen family." ▸ Dariel Fernández

 WANT MORE INFO? *THINK:* **FAMILY NOT BY BLOOD, BUT BY HEART.**

DID YOU KNOW Many gay and queer people have experienced rejection from their biological families, making chosen families an important part of the LGBTQIA+ community. This social family unit plays a vital role in providing love, mentorship, and support to a queer person, as well as providing access to LGBTQIA+ history and community resources.

CHOSEN NAME

▼ *noun*
A name chosen by an individual that differs from their given name at birth. In the LGBTQIA+ community, a chosen name often helps in affirming an individual's gender identity and expression.

SEE ALSO
GIVEN NAME, DEADNAME

Registrar: *Hello, Office of the Registrar. How may I help you?*
Student: *Hi, I would like to request a name change on my student account.*
Registrar: *All requests must be made in writing and emailed to our office using our name change form. After five business days we'll send your updated ID with your chosen name.*

 WANT MORE INFO? *THINK:* **A PERSON'S NAME. PERIOD.**

USAGE NOTE This term is commonly used in the transgender, nonbinary, and gender nonconforming communities. Some queer people are unable to legally change their name because of cost, court fees, and legal issues. Regardless, an individual's chosen name is their rightful name.

C

CHUB

▼ *noun*

A body label used to refer to a gay man who is overweight. The term "chubby" may also be used. This person may also identify as being part of the gay chub subculture.

SEE ALSO
"Help! What's My Gay Type?," *p. 152*

"Hell yeah, I am a chub! I'm an adorable big boy with a heart of gold."

 WANT MORE INFO? *THINK:* **A MAN WITH MORE CUSHION FOR THE PUSHIN'.**

 This term originated in the white gay male community.

Semi-erection of a penis.

"No, I don't want no chubs. If it comes at me half-mast, we're not going at it."

 WANT MORE INFO? *THINK:* **IT ONLY GOT HALF UP.**

CHUB CHASER

▼ *noun*
SEE CHASER

CIRCLE

▼ *noun*
See CHOSEN FAMILY, FAMILY

CIRCUIT BOY

▼ *noun*

A gay, bisexual, or queer man who frequently attends circuit parties. The term "circuit queen" can also be used.

Tristan: *Hey look at that guy trying to chat up DJ Shane. Didn't we see him in Palm Springs?*
Nigel: *Yeah, he's a circuit boy. He's at every White Party.*

 WANT MORE INFO? *THINK:* **GAY POSTER CHILD FOR EVERY HOT DANCE PARTY ON THE SCENE.**

 This term originated in the white gay male community.

CIRCUIT PARTY

▼ *noun*

A gay dance party and supporting events characterized by dancing all night into the day, DJs, raves, shirtless men, and sex. Recreational drugs are often used.

"From the groovy 1970s disco parties to the bass-thumping circuit parties of today, the gays have always loved to dance all night!"

 WANT MORE INFO? *THINK:* **A WEEKEND-LONG SWEATY GAY DANCE PARTY.**

 This term originated in the white gay male community.

C

CISGENDER

▼ *adjective*
Describing a person whose gender identity matches the gender they were assigned at birth. The term can be shortened to "cis."

"Many cisgender people assume that everyone experiences gender identity in the same way. After talking about it with my boss, I bought a copy of Julia Serano's Whipping Girl *and asked him to check it out."*

 WANT MORE INFO? *THINK:* **GENDER IDENTITY IS THE SAME AS ONE'S BIRTH CERTIFICATE.**

CISGENDER PRIVILEGE

▼ *noun*
The inherent rights and immunities granted to cisgender people. Can be abbreviated as "cis privilege."

SEE ALSO
MALE PRIVILEGE, PRIVILEGE, STRAIGHT PRIVILEGE, WHITE PRIVILEGE

"Cisgender privilege shows its true self when dealing with health insurance. Even though laws are put in place making it illegal to discriminate against trans people, I go through hell to get the health care I need."

 WANT MORE INFO? *THINK:* **THE ENTITLEMENT OF CISGENDER PEOPLE.**

CISHET

▼ *adjective*
An abbreviation for "cisgender heterosexual." The term "cishetero" can also be used.

Raquel: *Well, well, well . . . look at all these supportive cishet men discussing diversity, sexuality, and gender equality! I'm impressed.*
Misaki: *Gag me with a spoon. Good for you, Mark and Tom. I'll be looking forward to seeing you bring more diversity on board and make real change around here.*

 WANT MORE INFO? *THINK:* **CIS AND STRAIGHT.**

CISSEXISM

▼ *noun*
The belief that there are only two genders (male and female), that these genders are assigned at birth and are immutable. This belief results in the oppression of gender nonconforming, nonbinary, and transgender people.

"We are speaking out against cissexism. Equality is equality. Period."

 WANT MORE INFO? *THINK:* **SOCIAL BELIEF THAT ONLY MALE AND FEMALE SEXES EXIST AND THEY CANNOT BE CHANGED.**

CIVIL UNION

▼ *noun*
See DOMESTIC PARTNERSHIP

CLAPBACK

▼ *noun*
A quick, witty response to criticism.

Hadiyah: *You know tattoos are supposed to last a lifetime, right? Why did you get that?*
Lisa: *You know marriages are supposed to last a lifetime, right? Why are you divorced?*
Nikki: *Oop, clapback!*

 WANT MORE INFO? *THINK:* **A SOCK-IT-TO-YA REBUTTAL.**

USAGE NOTE This term originated in Black American culture and is commonly used in the Black gay and queer community. It has been appropriated by mainstream culture.

CLEAN

▼ *adjective*
Having no sexually transmitted diseases.

"Clean and tight keeps the boys coming right."

 WANT MORE INFO? *THINK:* **STD-FREE.**

USAGE NOTE This term can be considered a harmful stereotype, unfairly implying that a person who has an STD is "dirty" and only those without STDs are "clean."

Having no present body content of drug or alcohol use.

"I am trying to stay clean, man. I've been clean for 319 days and counting."

 WANT MORE INFO? *THINK:* **SAYING NO TO DRUGS AND ALCOHOL.**

CLIT

▼ *noun*
An abbreviation for clitoris.

"Don't forget to stimulate the clit. That's the best foreplay."

 WANT MORE INFO? *THINK:* **ORGASM BUTTON.**

C

CLOCK

▼ *verb*
To take notice of someone or something.

"I clocked him as soon as he came in the door with that loud-ass yellow shirt."

 WANT MORE INFO? *THINK:* **DO A DOUBLE TAKE.**

To take notice of someone and identify them as gay. The term READ can also be used.

"My gay psych professor totally clocked me when this month's Out *magazine fell out of my book bag."*

 WANT MORE INFO? *THINK:* **TO PEG SOMEONE AS QUEER.**

To recognize a transgender person as trans, usually when they are trying to appear cisgender. The term SPOOK can also be used.

SEE ALSO
PASSING

"The bartender clocked her when he saw her Adam's apple."

 WANT MORE INFO? *THINK:* **TO BE SEEN AS TRANS, DESPITE TRYING TO BLEND IN AS CIS.**

 USAGE NOTE This term may have negative connotations for many queer, transgender, and gender nonconforming people.

DID YOU KNOW Due to the abuse trans people have endured and the cultural pressure to appear cisgender, being clocked can often be a disappointing or scary experience for a trans person. Not all trans and gender nonconforming people, however, feel the need to "pass" as cisgender, and many are comfortable shaking up others' perceptions of gender norms.

CLOSET

▼ *idiom*
Mostly used in the phrase "in the closet" as a metaphor to describe individuals who do not publicly disclose their sexual identity or orientation.

RELATED
CLOSETED *adjective*

SEE ALSO
COME OUT, "Coming Out 101," *p. 26*

"Freedom is too enormous to be slipped under a closet door."
▶ Harvey Milk

 WANT MORE INFO? *THINK:* **UNABLE TO EXPRESS OR EMBRACE ONE'S QUEERNESS IN PUBLIC.**

C

CLOSET CASE

▼ *noun*

An individual who denies their sexuality or gender identity. The terms "closet queen" or "closet queer" can also be used.

SEE ALSO
"Coming Out 101," *p. 26*

"That closet case is never going to come out."

 WANT MORE INFO? *THINK:* **COMPLETELY HIDING FROM ONE'S QUEERNESS.**

 This term can be considered derogatory.

CLOWN BOTTOM

▼ *noun*

A gay man who claims to prefer bottoming but actually prefers being a top.

"Look, I know you love Joe, but two tops don't make good sex. You've got to stop lying to him, or you're gonna be a clown bottom all your life."

 WANT MORE INFO? *THINK:* **A BAIT-AND-SWITCH TOP.**

 This term originated in the gay male community.

CLOWN TOP

▼ *noun*

A gay man who claims to prefer topping but actually prefers being a bottom.

"I run a bar and there are two things I can spot: a bottom who lies about being a top, and the vers bottom who lies about being all top. Ain't nothing but clown tops in this bar!"

 WANT MORE INFO? *THINK:* **A BAIT-AND-SWITCH BOTTOM.**

 This term originated in the gay male community.

CLUTCHING MY PEARLS

▼ *idiom*

Demonstrating a ladylike look of surprise, either favorable or discomforted. The phrase is usually accompanied by putting a hand close to the neckline where pearls would lie.

"Every time I look at Dwayne Johnson's body, I just have to close my eyes, take a deep breath, and clutch my pearls!"

 WANT MORE INFO? *THINK:* **GASP!**

 This term is commonly used in the gay male and drag communities.

The Queens' English

C

COCK

▼ *noun*
A penis.

"Cock, dick, schlong, knob, snake, soldier, rod? Should I continue?"

 WANT MORE INFO? *THINK:* **A WARM CORN DOG.**

COCK BLOCK OR COCKBLOCK

▼ *verb*
To obstruct the possibility of another person engaging in sexual activity. When referring to a femme-identifying person, the term TACO BLOCK can also be used.

Choi: *Here Jonas, drinks are on me tonight. So, where are you from?*
Jonas: *I'm from Denver, but I've lived here for a while now.*
Kace: *Did I hear you're from Denver? Me too! And you're cute.*
Choi: *Are you really gonna cockblock me? Really?*

 WANT MORE INFO? *THINK:* **A TOTAL BONER KILL.**

To hinder someone's achievement.

"Listen, no one can mess up this promotion for me. His attempts to cockblock me are shameless and weak. He will not get in my way."

 WANT MORE INFO? *THINK:* **TO SABOTAGE.**

USAGE NOTE This term originated in Black American culture. It has been appropriated by the larger LGBTQIA+ community and mainstream culture.

COCK RING

▼ *noun*
A sexual device placed around the base of a penis to prevent flaccidity.

"He loves to have me slip on the cock ring when he's ready to release."

 WANT MORE INFO? *THINK:* **USE ONE AND YOUR SEXUAL PARTNERS WILL THANK YOU.**

COCKSTRUCTION WORKER

▼ *noun*
A gay, bisexual, or queer man who is employed in the construction industry.

"Those cockstruction workers really know how to handle hard labor."

 WANT MORE INFO? *THINK:* **A BABE WHO LOOKS GOOD HAULING LONG WOOD.**

 USAGE NOTE This term originated in the gay male community.

COERCIVE PASSING

▼ *noun*
The coercion of a queer individual by an outside force to pass as or claim a gender or sexual preference that might not align with the individual's identity.

SEE ALSO

INVISIBILITY, ERASURE

Bobbi: *How am I supposed to explain to my parents that you are trans? Can't I just tell them you're butching it up for an acting gig?*
Campbell: *Wow, coercive passing, much? I didn't think you of all people would be uncomfortable with my identity.*

 WANT MORE INFO? *THINK:* **ACTIVELY PUSHING SOMEONE TO APPEAR AS SOMETHING THEY ARE NOT.**

COERCIVE SURGICAL GENDER REASSIGNMENT

C

▼ *noun*
The forcible alteration of someone's phenotype (the physical expression of an individual's sexual organs) without the individual's consent or because the person was misinformed and/or denied the proper medical services. This tends to happen to intersex children.

"Coercive surgical gender reassignment is an unnecessary procedure that forces the surgical reshaping of a person's body when there is absolutely nothing wrong with being intersex."

 WANT MORE INFO? *THINK:* **SURGICALLY ASSIGNING A GENDER TO AN INTERSEX PERSON WHO HAS NO AGENCY.**

COIFFED

▼ *adjective*
Carefully fashioned and exquisite in presentation. The term is most commonly used in reference to lavishly styled hair but can also be used in other contexts.

SEE ALSO

DONE, LAID

"Honey, Mrs. Fernanda always leaves my hair silky and coiffed. She has the magic touch, child."

 WANT MORE INFO? *THINK:* **STYLE SO DIVINE IT'S EASY, BREEZY, AND BEAUTIFUL.**

C

COIN

▼ *noun*
Money.

"Girl I need to get to work and make this coin!"

 WANT MORE INFO? *THINK:* **CASH.**

 USAGE NOTE This term originated in the Black American culture and is commonly used in the Black gay and queer community. It has been appropriated by mainstream culture.

COME FOR

▼ *verb*
To point out someone's faults or flaws.

"Mama is about to come for you! You still haven't cleaned your room yet?"

 WANT MORE INFO? *THINK:* **"I'LL GET YOU, MY PRETTY!"**

 USAGE NOTE This term originated in the Black gay community and is commonly used in the larger queer and trans people of color (QTPOC) community. It has been appropriated by mainstream culture.

COME OUT

▼ *idiom*
In the LGBTQIA+ community, this phrase is most commonly used in reference to a person sharing their sexual orientation or gender identity publicly. The phrase "come out of the closet" can also be used.

SEE ALSO
CLOSET, OUT, "Coming Out 101," *p. 26*

"The most important thing is for you to come out when you feel ready."

 WANT MORE INFO? *THINK:* **"I'M COMING OUT! I WANT THE WORLD TO KNOW, I GOT TO LET IT SHOW!"**

DID YOU KNOW National Coming Out Day (NCOD) is observed each year on October 11. It was first celebrated in 1988 to observe the anniversary of the 1987 National March on Washington for Lesbian and Gay Rights. Robert Eichberg and Jean O'Leary are credited as the founders of this day of awareness. Artist Keith Haring designed the first poster for NCOD—an image that is still highly recognized.

COME THROUGH

▼ *idiom*
An accolade used to affirm something fabulous.

"Come THROUGH with this baked mac and cheese! This is so good!"

 WANT MORE INFO? *THINK:* **VERY IMPRESSED.**

 USAGE NOTE This term originated in the Black gay community and is commonly used in the larger queer and trans people of color (QTPOC) community. It has been appropriated by mainstream culture.

COMMENTATOR

▼ *noun*
The emcee for a ballroom ball or other event. This person uses creativity, leadership, and improvisational skills to keep the ball competition energized and organized.

Commentator: (into bejeweled microphone) *Walk for meeee. Destroy for meeee. Eat it! Kat! Kat! Kat to kat to kat! Kitty kat! Hold that pose for me!*

 WANT MORE INFO? *THINK:* **ANNOUNCER OF A BALL COMPETITION.**

 DID YOU KNOW A commentator is often considered the crown jewel of a ball because of the dynamic level of showmanship the host position requires. They are usually a leader within the ballroom community and set the tone for competitions. Most commentators are skilled freestylers and DJs. Well-known commentators include Jack Mizrahi, Selvin Khan, Kevin Prodigy, and Jay Blahnik, to name a few.

COMMITTED

▼ *adjective*
Dedicated to presenting a particular behavior or style.

"She is committed to that bubble gum pink lipstick, giving Miss Piggy realness, child."

 WANT MORE INFO? *THINK:* **"I PLEDGE MY HONOR TO THIS CHOICE AND ONLY THIS CHOICE, SO HELP ME."**

CONSENT

▼ *noun*
Permission to do something
or an agreement to act. Sexual
consent should be affirmed before
and during sexual activity. It is
a particularly important form of
setting boundaries practiced in
BDSM, leather, kink, and fetish play.

RELATED
CONSENSUAL *adjective*

SEE ALSO
BDSM, NEGOTIATION

*"Negotiation, consent, and
contracts are all a must! Playing
safe is the true beauty of sexual
liberation."*

 WANT MORE INFO? *THINK:*
**NO MEANS NO. YES MEANS
YES. COMMUNICATION IS
NECESSARY.**

USAGE NOTE This term is commonly
used in the BDSM, leather,
and kink community. For
all BDSM-related terms, the power
exchange is a part of sadomasochistic
play and should be consensual between
all partners involved.

C

CONTOUR

▼ *verb*
To enhance or sharpen the structure and features of one's face with the aid of cosmetics.

Toddy: *Do you know how to contour?*
Miss Perfect Palette: *Honey, I will transform your face from a dumpling to a Frank Lloyd Wright structure in under a minute.*

 WANT MORE INFO? *THINK:* **CHEEKBONES FOR DAYS.**

CONVERSION THERAPY

▼ *noun*
A social, pseudo-scientific, and sometimes religious approach that attempts to forcibly change a person's sexuality and/or gender expression from anywhere on the queer spectrum to heterosexual and/or cisgender.

"If the American Psychological Association is against conversion therapy because it is harmful and actually doesn't work, then we should actively listen."

 WANT MORE INFO? *THINK:* **A "MEDICAL" TREATMENT USED TO "MAKE QUEER PEOPLE STRAIGHT."**

CROSS-DRESSER

▼ *noun*
A person who dresses in clothing associated with another sex.

RELATED
CROSS-DRESS *verb*

SEE ALSO
TRANSVESTITE

"Dan is a cross-dresser not because he is gay or wants to change his gender, but because he feels pretty as a woman."

 WANT MORE INFO? *THINK:* **"I AM SINCERE IN MY PREFERENCE FOR MY MEN'S CLOTHES—I DO NOT WEAR THEM TO BE SENSATIONAL. I THINK I AM MORE ALLURING IN THESE CLOTHES."**
▶ Marlene Dietrich

USAGE NOTE It should not be assumed that cross-dressing and sexual orientation or gender identity are related.

DID YOU KNOW In the late 1800s, public decency laws banned citizens from appearing publicly in clothes that did not align with their assigned gender at birth. By the 1960s, cross-dressing laws allowed police officers to actively target the gay community. Women were arrested for wearing less than three pieces of "female" clothing, and men faced jail time if caught in dresses or skirts.

C

CROSS-SEX HORMONE THERAPY

▼ *noun*
See HORMONE REPLACEMENT THERAPY

CROTCH GAZING

▼ *verb*
See BASKET SHOPPING

CRUISE

▼ *verb*
To check someone out with an interest to pursue them sexually.

"Tim is definitely cruising. I saw him look over here three times."

 WANT MORE INFO? *THINK:* **LOOKING TO HOOK UP.**

USAGE NOTE This term is commonly used in the gay male community.

CUB

▼ *noun*
A young gay, bisexual, or queer man with a large or stocky body and visible facial and body hair.

SEE ALSO
"Help! What's My Gay Type?," *p. 152*

"Ooh, yum. I'll probably date that cub when he gets a little older and graduates to a bear."

 WANT MORE INFO? *THINK:* **YOUNG GAY BOY WHO WILL GROW UP TO BE A BEAR.**

 USAGE NOTE This term originated in the white gay male community.

CULTURAL APPROPRIATION

▼ noun
The adoption of a marginalized culture's styles, traditions, and/or words by members of a more dominant culture without permission or acknowledgment of their origin.

SEE ALSO
APPROPRIATE, MISAPPROPRIATE, REAPPROPRIATE

"Amandla Stenberg's 'Don't Cash Crop on My Cornrows' video is a lesson in Black Cultural Appropriation 101. Basically, if you ain't Black but want to rock braids, twerk something, shake something, and rap to every popular song, remember what Amandla said."

 WANT MORE INFO? *THINK*: VIOLATION OF INTELLECTUAL AND ARTISTIC PROPERTY OF A PARTICULAR CULTURE.

CUNNILINGUS

▼ noun
The performance of oral sex on a person with a vagina.

SEE ALSO
EAT OUT

Saanvi: *Eat my pussy, now!*
Eleven: *Damn, babe. You can be a little more polite.*
Saanvi: *May I have some cunnilingus, please?*

 WANT MORE INFO? *THINK*: PUSSY-LICKING.

CUNT

▼ noun
A synonym for vagina.

"My cunt is in need of some major TLC."

 WANT MORE INFO? *THINK*: VAJAYJAY.

 This term can be considered a slur or derogatory.

A derogatory slur, typically directed at a woman.

George: *Why are you such a cunt?*
Sarah: *If by cunt you mean I have warmth and depth—thank you!*

 WANT MORE INFO? *THINK*: BITCH, BUT NASTIER.

 This term can be considered a slur or derogatory.

▼ adjective
Emphasizing extreme femininity.

"Feeling cunt, looking cunt, acting cunt, walking cunt." ▶ "C.U.N.T. (She's Cunt, She's Pussy)" by Robbie Tronco

 WANT MORE INFO? *THINK*: A SEXY, QUEER LIONESS QUALITY.

 This term is commonly used in ballroom culture.

CUNTY

▼ *adjective*
A soft and delicate display of confidence.

"She is so cunty and soft. I love the way she vogues!"

 WANT MORE INFO? *THINK:* **MIRANDA PRIESTLY IN** *THE DEVIL WEARS PRADA.*

 USAGE NOTE This term originated in ballroom culture and is commonly used in the drag community. It has been appropriated by mainstream culture.

Bitchy, extremely unpleasant.

"Baby, please don't be cunty right now—I'm PMSing, and I can't take it."

 WANT MORE INFO? *THINK:* **MEAN AND NASTY.**

Refers to a transgender person who is perceived as cisgender.

SEE ALSO
PASSING, STEALTH

"Honey, look at that waist, that beat, the forty-eight-inch Raw Virgin Indian bundles. You are serving cunty fish tuna on a platter!"

 WANT MORE INFO? *THINK:* **UNCLOCKABLE, NEVER BEEN SPOOKED!**

 USAGE NOTE This term may be considered a slur or derogatory.

CUT

▼ *verb*
To speak with sharpness or harshness intended to hurt feelings.

SEE ALSO
READ

"Why are you always trying to cut someone on Twitter? Say it to my face!"

 WANT MORE INFO? *THINK:* **TO VERBALLY ASSAULT.**

▼ *adjective*
Describing a circumcised penis or a man whose penis is circumcised.

"He was cut, clean, and ready for some fun."

 WANT MORE INFO? *THINK:* **A PENIS WITHOUT FORESKIN.**

CUTE FOR YOU

▼ *idiom*
A phrase used as a compliment or affirmation that something—be it related to style, attitude, or some other decision—suits a particular person. This can be said in a snarky tone, making it either a playful tease or a backhanded compliment.

"Oh, black is cute for you, but I like the dress better in gold."

 WANT MORE INFO? *THINK:* **NICE FOR YOU, BUT NOT FOR ME.**

 USAGE NOTE This term is commonly used in the Black gay and queer community.

COMMON PRO-NOUNS 101

Pronouns are personal identifiers that validate and support a person's gender expression. The pronouns listed below are singular pronouns—pronouns that refer to a single individual.

While this list is not exhaustive, the pronouns below are commonly used to represent a range of gender expressions including male, female, transgender, genderqueer, genderfluid, nonbinary, gender nonconforming, and other identities.

SUBJECT	OBJECT	POSSESSIVE	REFLEXIVE
he	him	his	himself
she	her	hers	herself
they	them	theirs	themselves
sie	sie	hirs	hirself
ze	hir	hirs	hirself
zie	zir	zirs	zirself
xe	xem	xyrs	xemself
ey/e	em	eirs	emself

Physical characteristics do not determine a person's pronouns, so it is always best to respectfully ask someone's pronouns if you are unsure. Do not feel ashamed to ask! Your thoughtfulness is appreciated. Pronouns are powerful identifiers, and misgendering someone is problematic and taken very seriously. Let's all continue to encourage, learn about, and celebrate the myriad ways human identity is expressed.

i really feel
our connection,
it's so strong

Demisexual ▲

Dd

D

▼ *noun*
A common abbreviation for "dick."

"Give me that D."

 WANT MORE INFO? *THINK:* **A SAUSAGE.**

DADDY

▼ *noun*
A mature masculine man (regardless of sexuality) who plays the role of provider and protector in a relationship. This partner stereotypically has a physically strong, muscular body, exhibits a sexy, confident attitude, and is the dominant one in the partnership.

> **SEE ALSO**
> **ZADDY**

"Guillermo Díaz!! Now, that's a daddy. Have mercy on me!"

 WANT MORE INFO? *THINK:* **A FREAKIN' GORGEOUS MAN.**

A masc-of-center woman or nonbinary person who plays the role of provider and protector in a queer relationship. Typically, this partner exhibits a confident attitude and is the dominant one.

> **SEE ALSO**
> **BUTCH/FEMME RELATIONSHIP, MAMA AND PAPA RELATIONSHIP**

Ashira: *Hey, Daddy—did you have a good day at work?*
Joslyn: *Yeah, but it's even better now that I see you!*

 WANT MORE INFO? *THINK:* **QUEEN LATIFAH IN** *SET IT OFF.*

An older gay, bisexual, or queer man who is financially established. The term "sugar daddy" can also be used.

"I need a sponsor. I am definitely looking for a new daddy."

 WANT MORE INFO? *THINK:* **THE GOOD-LOOKING AND KIND SOUL WHO ALWAYS PAYS MY WAY.**

DADDY DOM

▼ *noun*

A male or masc Dominant who facilitates power dynamic and scene play, both sexual and nonsexual. In the context of BDSM, leather, and kink cultures, a Daddy Dom acts as a protector, a guide, and a disciplinarian to his submissive. The term SIR can also be used.

> SEE ALSO
>
> **BDSM, DOM/SUB RELATIONSHIP, LEATHER DADDY**

"Look who's getting jealous because he got too attached to his Daddy Dom. Seems like you don't like that other boys are servicing him, do you?"

 WANT MORE INFO? *THINK:* **IDENTIFIER USED FOR BDSM ROLE-PLAY.**

 USAGE NOTE This term originated in the BDSM, leather, and kink communities. For all BDSM-related terms, the power exchange is a part of sadomasochistic play and should be consensual between all partners involved. The *D*s in Daddy and Dom should always be capitalized when referring to D/s, or power dynamic, relationships.

DAIRY

▼ *adjective*

Describing a Caucasian gay, bisexual, or queer male.

"Almost ninety degrees and sunny today, huh? I'm gonna need extra SPF 50 for this dairy skin."

 WANT MORE INFO? *THINK:* **WHITE.**

 USAGE NOTE This term may be considered a stereotype or derogatory.

DANDY

▼ *adjective*

Stylish and well-groomed. This term was originally used to describe fashionable men who were thought to be gay or queer in some capacity. The term has since evolved to also include stylish, buttoned-up butch lesbians.

▼ *noun*

A dandy person, regardless of gender.

"I'm a sucker for a well-dressed dandy. Suspenders and a bow tie? Yes, please!"

 WANT MORE INFO? *THINK:* **WELL-GROOMED, MASCULINE PEOPLE WHO FAVOR SUITS AND TIES.**

DAPPER

▾ *adjective*
Well-groomed and trim in style and appearance. Traditionally used to describe men, this term has been adopted by the lesbian community as well.

"It's time for the WNBA All-Stars Orange Carpet event! Dap, dap to them dapper girls looking so nice and so right in those fitted suits."

 WANT MORE INFO? *THINK:* **BUTTONED-UP AND HANDSOME.**

DEAD

▾ *adjective*
Not important; over, done.

"You are still on that topic? Girl, it's dead."

 WANT MORE INFO? *THINK:* **IRRELEVANT.**

Disbelieving or shocked.

SEE ALSO
DIE

"North Korea's doing a nuclear test? I am literally dead."

 WANT MORE INFO? *THINK:* **STUNNED.**

 This term originated in Black American culture and is used in the Black gay and queer community. It has been appropriated by mainstream culture.

DEADNAME

▾ *noun*
The former name of a transgender, nonbinary, or gender nonconforming person who has changed their name to affirm their gender identity.

▾ *verb*
To publicly use a transgender person's birth name instead of their chosen name.

SEE ALSO
DOXX

"Aunt Alice, I know you've known me for twenty years as Patrick, but I need you to stop using my deadname. That is not who I am. Deadnaming is like a stab."

 WANT MORE INFO? *THINK:* **TO USE THE FORMER NAME OF A TRANS OR NONBINARY PERSON.**

 This term has negative connotations for many queer and trans people. Please ask for and use a person's chosen name and pronouns.

DEATHDROP

▾ *noun*
See DIP

DEMI

▼ *adjective*
A French prefix meaning "half" or "partial."

"'Demi' is often used as a signifier to describe a sexuality or gender expression that is not solely on one end of the spectrum but floats somewhere in between the binary."

 WANT MORE INFO? *THINK:* **PART, SEMI, SORT OF.**

DEMIBOY

▼ *noun*
Gender identity label for people who only partially identify with the terms "boy," "man," or "male." They may or may not identify with another gender in addition to feeling partly male. The terms DEMIMAN and DEMIMALE can also be used.

"Every time I fill out a health form, I have to mark my gender as 'other' and I write in 'demiboy.'"

 WANT MORE INFO? *THINK:* **A PERSON WHO IDENTIFIES PARTLY AS BOY/MAN/MALE.**

 This term is used in the transgender, nonbinary, and gender nonconforming communities.

DEMIFEMALE

▼ *noun*
See DEMIGIRL

DEMIGENDER

▼ *adjective*
An umbrella term for nonbinary gender identities. When "demi" is used as a prefix to a particular gender identity, it creates a new label for people who only identify partially with that gender identity.

"Growing up you're told to be a boy or a girl. I wish I knew then that I could identify as demigender."

 WANT MORE INFO? *THINK:* **DESCRIBING SOMEONE WITH A PARTIAL CONNECTION TO A SPECIFIC GENDER.**

 This term is used in the transgender, nonbinary, and gender nonconforming communities.

DEMIGIRL

▼ *noun*
Gender identity label for people who only partially identify with the terms "girl," "woman," or "female." They may or may not identify with another gender in addition to feeling partly female. The terms DEMIWOMAN and DEMIFEMALE can also be used.

"I felt empowered when I learned about demigirls because 'female' does not represent who I am."

WANT MORE INFO? *THINK:* **A PERSON WHO IDENTIFIES PARTLY AS GIRL/WOMAN/ FEMALE.**

 USAGE NOTE This term is used in the transgender, nonbinary, and gender nonconforming communities.

DEMIMALE

▼ *noun*
See DEMIBOY

DEMIMAN

▼ *noun*
See DEMIBOY

DEMINONBINARY

▼ *adjective*
Gender identity label for people who only partially identify as nonbinary. They may or may not identify with another gender in addition to feeling partly nonbinary.

"As deminonbinary, I have the ability to release myself from trying to fit in."

 WANT MORE INFO? *THINK:* **A PERSON WHO IDENTIFIES AS PARTLY NONBINARY.**

 USAGE NOTE This term is used in the transgender, nonbinary, and gender nonconforming communities.

DEMISEXUAL

▼ *adjective*
Experiencing sexual attraction only when a strong emotional connection is present.

▼ *noun*
A demisexual person.

"I'm definitely demisexual. I can't be intimate unless I have a trusting and open connection."

 WANT MORE INFO? *THINK:* **"IF YOU REALLY WANT TO DO ME, YOU GOT TO KNOW THE TRUE ME!"**

DEMIWOMAN

▼ *noun*
See DEMIGIRL

DEN

▼ *noun*
See BATH HOUSE

DENTAL DAM

▼ *noun*
Latex or rubber barrier that can be used while participating in oral sex, protecting the mouth from the genitals or anus. Often used for protected lesbian sex.

"Excuse me ma'am, is that a dental dam?"

 WANT MORE INFO? *THINK:* **A CONDOM FOR YOUR MOUTH.**

D

D

DETRANSITION

▼ *verb*
To reverse the process of transitioning from one gender to another. A transgender person may stop any medications or reverse surgery in order to return—in some capacity—to a previously assigned gender.

"After a late-night walk home from work, three men shouted at me that I was a tranny. They would go on to physically assault me. After that, I detransitioned. I did not detransition because I wasn't trans. I detransitioned because cisgender people physically and mentally beat me down until I gave in."
▸ Robyn Kanner

 WANT MORE INFO? *THINK:* **RETURN TO PRE-TRANSITION GENDER.**

 USAGE NOTE The process of detransitioning may not always indicate that the person does not identify as transgender or gender nonconforming. The decision may have been made to ensure a person's well-being and safety.

DICK

▼ *noun*
A penis.

"Veronica, why are you pulling my dick?" ▸ Heather Chandler, *Heathers*

 WANT MORE INFO? *THINK:* **A CUCUMBER.**

DIE

▼ *verb*
To be extremely surprised, happy, or shocked. Often used in the phrases "I die," "I would die," or "I'm dying."

SEE ALSO
DEAD

Sharon: *I heard someone is going to pull the fire alarm at fifth period so we can get early dismissal from school today!*
Deon: *Oh my goddess, I would diiiiie! That means we'll miss Mrs. Mackintosh's biology exam!*

 WANT MORE INFO? *THINK:* **TO BE THUNDERSTRUCK!**

DIESEL DYKE

▼ *noun*
An overtly masculine lesbian who is characterized by an occupation or hobby involving machinery.

"Hands down, the hottest diesel dykes are Dykes on Bikes."

 WANT MORE INFO? *THINK:* **A LESBIAN IN WORK BOOTS WHO'S GOOD WITH HER HANDS.**

 USAGE NOTE This term originated in the white lesbian community. The term "dyke" originated as a derogatory slur for lesbians but has been reclaimed by some of the LGBTQIA+ community. It may still have negative connotations for some people.

DILDO

▼ *noun*
A device or toy used for sexual pleasure. It is most often a phallic shape and varies in color, size, and texture.

"That dildo was on point! What's the brand?"

 WANT MORE INFO? *THINK:* **LATEX, RUBBER, OR SILICONE FAUX PENIS.**

Diesel dyke ▶

DID YOU KNOW Dykes on Bikes (DOB) is a lesbian motorcycle club that was founded during the San Francisco Pride Parade in 1976. DOB now has twenty-two chapters around the world, and these women bikers take particular pride in their strength and masculinity. DOB is the annual riding leader in the San Francisco Pride Parade as well as many other Pride parades and festivals around the world.

Dip ▼

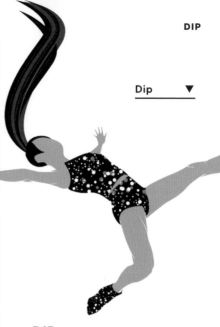

DIP

▼ *noun*
An elemental part of vogue dance, popular in ballroom culture, when a walker drops to the floor while maneuvering their body—keeping time with the music—into a pose with the back arched and one leg tucked beneath them. The term DEATHDROP is often used in mainstream and commercial dance settings.

"Oh, girl, she did the fiercest dip! Even her ponytail levitated!"

 WANT MORE INFO? *THINK:* **LOOK UP LEIOMY MALDONADO—THE WONDER WOMAN OF VOGUE—IT'LL CHANGE YOU.**

 USAGE NOTE This term originated in ballroom culture. It has been appropriated by mainstream culture.

D

DISCREET

▼ *adjective*
Being private with one's sexuality or sexual behaviors.

SEE ALSO
CLOSET

A common online dating profile descriptor for a person who does not want to publicly acknowledge their sexual acts.

"Look, this has to be discreet. I don't want anyone to know that I was with you. I have a reputation I have to keep, you know?"

 WANT MORE INFO? *THINK:* **ONLY BEHIND CLOSED DOORS.**

DISHONORABLE DISCHARGE

▼ *noun*
The dismissal of someone from the armed forces because of immoral behavior. In the past, many gay, bisexual, and queer service people were discharged because of their sexuality. The term DONALD DUCK can also be used.

"Did you read about the men who were kicked out of the army back in the sixties who are fighting to change their dishonorable discharges to 'honorable'? Their lives were ruined. They deserve to be recognized."

 WANT MORE INFO? *THINK:* **NO GAY SAILORS ALLOWED.**

▼ *verb*
To masturbate after attempting (and failing) to orgasm during sexual activity.

Erin: *Last night, the sex with Jaden was amazing but he failed to cum after our first round.*
Chris: *What happened?*
Erin: *I went to take a shower, and when I got back to his room, I caught him during his, uh . . . dishonorable discharge.*

 WANT MORE INFO? *THINK:* **"I'M GONNA BUST THIS NUT SOMEWAY, SOMEHOW."**

DIVA

▼ *noun*
A person who is recognized for being extraordinary, fabulous, and unapologetically fierce. While this term was originally used for women, it can be used to describe people of all gender identities.

"The gays love divas: Whitney! Cher! Madonna! Beyoncé! Gaga!"

 WANT MORE INFO? *THINK:* **SINGING CHAKA KHAN'S SONG "I'M EVERY WOMAN!"**

Someone who is demanding, conceited, or high-maintenance.

"Gray is being a diva. I know they are the project leader, but this bossy I-don't-care-what-anyone-thinks attitude needs to go!"

 WANT MORE INFO? *THINK:* **A DIG FOR SOMEONE WHO IS DIFFICULT.**

DIVA FEMME

▼ *noun*
See HIGH FEMME

DOING SHOWS

▼ *idiom*
Blatantly acting out of character.
The term STUNT can also be used.

"Oh, please hide me! Here comes my ex doing shows! It's like watching a melodrama in three acts."

 WANT MORE INFO? *THINK:* **BEING EXTRA.**

 This term originated in ballroom culture.

DO IT

▼ *verb*
To encourage someone to continue to display greatness or to pay a compliment.

"You got accepted into all eight Ivy Leagues? Oh, do it, girl! Talk about brain power!"

 WANT MORE INFO? *THINK:* **TO GIVE A VERBAL HIGH FIVE.**

 This term originated in Black American culture and is used in the Black gay and queer community. It has been appropriated by mainstream culture.

DOM

▼ *noun*
See DOMINANT

DOM/SUB RELATIONSHIP

▼ *adjective*
A consensual relationship based on power and role-play, where one partner acts as the Dominant and one as the submissive. This relationship may be both sexual and nonsexual in nature. Often abbreviated as "D/s."

SEE ALSO
BDSM, DOMINANT, SUBMISSIVE

"In the D/s exchange of power, if you are submissive, you are giving someone power. And if you are the Dom, you have to respect the power you've been given."

 WANT MORE INFO? *THINK:* **POWER AND CONSENT.**

 USAGE NOTE This term originated in the BDSM community and is commonly used in the leather and kink communities. For all BDSM-related terms, the power exchange is a part of sadomasochistic play and should be consensual between all partners involved. The *D* in the word "Dom" should always be capitalized and the *s* in the word "sub" should always be lowercase when referring to D/s, or power dynamic, relationships.

DOMESTIC PARTNERSHIP

▼ *noun*
A relationship between two people who live and share a domestic life together but are not married. The term CIVIL UNION can also be used.

"Before marriage equality, the only option for same sex couples was a domestic partnership."

 WANT MORE INFO? *THINK:* **COMMON-LAW SKIM-MILK MARRIAGE FOR THE GAYS.**

DOMINANT

▼ *noun*
The authoritative or influential role in a relationship. Often abbreviated as DOM.

SEE ALSO
BDSM, DOM/SUB RELATIONSHIP, SUBMISSIVE

"My Dom blindfolded me, tied me to the bed, and spanked me like the bad boy I am."

 WANT MORE INFO? *THINK:* **THE BOSS.**

▼ *adjective*
Performing as the authoritative figure in an intimate or sexual partnership.

"Some people think the dominant partner has to be masculine, supporting traditional gender roles, but that isn't necessarily the case. Femininity can be just as dominant."

WANT MORE INFO? *THINK*: THEY WHO "WEAR THE PANTS" IN A RELATIONSHIP.

 USAGE NOTE This term is commonly used in the BDSM, leather, and kink communities. For all BDSM-related terms, the power exchange is a part of sadomasochistic play and should be consensual between all partners involved. The *D* in the word "Dom" should always be capitalized when referring to D/s, or power dynamic, relationships.

DOMINATRIX

▼ *noun*
A female or femme Dominant who facilitates power dynamic and scene play, both in a sexual and/or nonsexual manner. In the context of BDSM, a Dominatrix acts as a stern disciplinarian to her submissive, often using humiliation as a form of play. The term "Domme" can also be used.

SEE ALSO
BDSM, DYKE DADDY, FEMME DADDY, SIR

"A Dominatrix has special mixology skills and makes a great drink of pain, endorphins, and desire, with a splash of humiliation and degradation."

 WANT MORE INFO? *THINK*: A FEMME DISCIPLINARIAN.

USAGE NOTE This term originated in the BDSM community and is commonly used in the leather and kink communities. For all BDSM-related terms, the power exchange is a part of sadomasochistic

play and should be consensual between all partners involved. The *D* in the word "Dominatrix" should always be capitalized when referring to D/s, or power dynamic, relationships.

DONALD DUCK

▼ *noun*
See DISHONORABLE DISCHARGE

DONE

▼ *adjective*
Being completely over an idea, person, or situation.

"I am done. I am not about to wait another two hours in this DMV line."

 WANT MORE INFO? *THINK*: IRRITATED.

A refined and polished state.

"Gurl! That brownstone we saw in Chelsea was done! I think the old CEO of Barneys used to live there."

SEE ALSO
LAID

 WANT MORE INFO? *THINK*: FANCY.

 USAGE NOTE This term is commonly used in the Black gay community and the larger queer and trans people of color (QTPOC) community.

DON'T DO ME

▼ *idiom*

A phrase used to tell someone in a playful or sarcastic way to not openly insult or judge you. The phrases "don't come for me" and "don't do it" can also be used.

"Look, don't do me, Alex. I'm going to eat this chocolate cake. Actually, two pieces, and I dare you to say something about my diet."

 WANT MORE INFO? *THINK:* **"BACK OFF!"**

 USAGE NOTE This term originated in ballroom culture. It has been appropriated by the larger LGBTQIA+ community and mainstream culture.

DON'T GO THERE

▼ *idiom*

An expression used to tell someone not to expose unwarranted information or to avoid a particular subject or situation. The phrase "don't even" can also be used.

"Don't go there. Mind your business, Miss Thing!"

 WANT MORE INFO? *THINK:* **"DON'T PUSH MY BUTTONS."**

 USAGE NOTE This term originated in Black American culture and is commonly used in the Black gay and queer community. It has been appropriated by mainstream culture.

DOPPELBANGER

▼ *noun*

A play on the word "doppelgänger," this term is for a queer person who dates partners who look like them.

SEE ALSO

DOUBLE HOMO

"Major doppelbanger moment: when you realize that your fiancé is your long-lost twin!"

 WANT MORE INFO? *THINK:* **WHEN YOUR PARTNER LOOKS JUST LIKE YOU.**

DOUBLE GOLD STAR

▼ *noun*
See PLATINUM STAR

DOUBLE HOMO

▼ *idiom*
A gay couple who look alike and may even wear each other's clothes. The term DYKE ALIKE can also be used for lesbian couples.

SEE ALSO
DOPPELBANGER

"She only dates femmes with strawberry blonde hair like hers, a true double homo."

 WANT MORE INFO? *THINK:* **"WAIT, IS THAT THEIR LOVER OR THEIR TWIN?"**

DOUCHE

▼ *noun*
A vagina or anus cleanse using water or a mixed fluid base to eliminate odor and/or body waste.

▼ *verb*
To wash the vagina or anus.

"Douche until clear, foreplay until comfortable, rim, then lube, then perform the magic!"

 WANT MORE INFO? *THINK:* **GIVING THE VAJAYJAY OR BACK DOOR A SPA TREATMENT.**

DOWN

▼ *idiom*
An intensifier that makes anything increase in value or priority.

"Louboutins on the feet? Rollie on the wrist? Oh, he is dressed down and giving executive realness. Dooowwwwn!"

 WANT MORE INFO? *THINK:* **A DEGREE OF EMPHASIS.**

 USAGE NOTE This term originated in ballroom culture and is commonly used in the larger queer and trans people of color (QTPOC) community.

▼ *adjective*
In agreement.

Ibinabo: *Ladies, who's down to drink, make horrible decisions, and be home no later than midnight?*
Dash: *I'm down.*
Brittany: *I'm down, too. But can we stop by Popeyes before it closes?*

 WANT MORE INFO? *THINK:* **ALL IN.**

 USAGE NOTE This term originated in Black American culture. It has been appropriated by mainstream culture.

DOWN LOW OR DL

▼ *noun*
To intentionally hide one's queerness. A person "on the down low" strives to appear as heterosexual to the public. Often used in the phrases "on the down low" or "on the DL."

SEE ALSO
CLOSET, DISCREET, SWEET'N LOW

"Meet me at my car when you're done with your workout. You know I can't bring you to the crib, though. Gotta keep things on the DL."

 WANT MORE INFO? *THINK:* **DESIRING SAME-SEX INTIMACY—BUT ONLY BEHIND CLOSED DOORS.**

USAGE NOTE This term originated in the Black gay male community. It has been appropriated by mainstream culture.

DID YOU KNOW "On the down low" was coined as a way to identify a gay Black male who was living as heterosexual, possibly with a wife and children, but was involved in male-to-male sexual relationships without his primary partner's knowledge. Author J. L. King wrote a *New York Times* bestseller about this called *On the Down Low: A Journey into the Lives of "Straight" Black Men Who Sleep with Men.*

DOXX

▼ *verb*
Exposing someone's personal and/or confidential information online without permission.

SEE ALSO
DEADNAME

"I can't believe Terry doxxed me online. She outed me as trans using my deadname on Facebook. It's a nightmare."

 WANT MORE INFO? *THINK:* **THE MALICIOUS ACT OF DROPPING DOCS.**

DID YOU KNOW Doxxing is short for "dropping documents," which is computer hacker shorthand for revealing an individual's or business's sensitive documents. It was brought into the queer community when a lawsuit was filed by feminist activist Cathy Brennan against a journalist working for lesbian media website AfterEllen. Brennan believed she was defamed in an article saying she harassed, outed, and "doxxed" transgender women.

DRAG

▼ *noun*

The art of dressing up in clothing or costume that embodies an exaggerated portrayal of gender stereotypes. Drag is frequently performed for entertainment purposes, honoring femininity, masculinity, and queerness. Often used in the phrase "in drag."

"Sean's first time in drag was incredible, but his five o'clock shadow stole the show."

 WANT MORE INFO? *THINK:* **CAMPY CROSS-DRESSING FOR ENTERTAINMENT.**

▼ *verb*

To insult someone harshly.

"He called Mrs. Anderson a hippo in front of the entire class! Why did he have to drag her like that?"

 WANT MORE INFO? *THINK:* **TO DRAG THROUGH THE MUD.**

To feel sluggish and tired.

"I am dragging today, but I can't sleep until I finish this paper. It's due by midnight!"

 WANT MORE INFO? *THINK:* **MUST. GET. SLEEP.**

DRAG PAGEANT

▼ *noun*

A form of pageantry—typically for female impersonators and transgender women—that mimics the traditional beauty pageant. In recent years, pageants have become more inclusive for male impersonators and transgender men, as well.

"When I do drag pageants, I transform into my alter ego Valencia Diamond. She always wins the crown."

 WANT MORE INFO? *THINK:* **BEAUTY CONTEST FOR QUEER GENDER-BENDERS.**

DID YOU KNOW Drag pageants started out as small events held at local gay bars and clubs. In 1971, Nashville began the Miss Gay America Pageant—a pageant for female impersonators themed after the Miss America contest.

DRAG DAUGHTER

▼ *noun*

A drag performer who has been taken under the wing of a more experienced drag queen mentor, called a DRAG MOTHER.

"Laganja Estranja and Shangela Laquifa Wadley are drag daughters of the incredible queen Alyssa Edwards."

 WANT MORE INFO? *THINK:* **JOHN LEGUIZAMO IN** *TO WONG FOO, THANKS FOR EVERYTHING! JULIE NEWMAR.*

The Queens' English

D

DRAG FAMILY

▼ *noun*
An intimate community of drag queens, typically comprised of a family tree of queens: a drag mother and all of her drag daughters. Roles within a drag family are used to imply close friendship between drag performers.

SEE ALSO
CHOSEN FAMILY, DRAG MOTHER, DRAG DAUGHTER, HOUSE CULTURE

"I wouldn't know how to pad, tuck, lip-sync, or contour without my loving drag family. These girls are my life."

 WANT MORE INFO? *THINK:* **A QUEEN AND ALL OF HER DRAG DAUGHTER MENTEES.**

DRAG MOTHER

▼ *noun*
An experienced drag queen who supports and educates an amateur queen and teaches her about drag culture (and how to slay).

"My drag mother showed me the ropes of the business, and I vow to do the same for someone else someday."

 WANT MORE INFO? *THINK:* **A MENTOR FOR YOUNG DRAG QUEENS.**

Drag king ▲

DRAG KING

▼ *noun*
A person—typically a woman—who entertains while dressed in masculine drag, personifying and/or exaggerating masculine stereotypes.

"She puts on her trousers, suspenders, blazer, and top hat and tap dances like Fred Astaire. This drag king is my favorite."

 WANT MORE INFO? *THINK:* **ANNIE LENNOX AT THE 1984 GRAMMY AWARDS.**

 DID YOU KNOW American drag king performance can be traced back to 1868, when male impersonator Annie Hindle rose to fame. In the 1920s, blues singer Gladys Bentley performed as a drag king with a chorus line of drag queens. In the 1950s, Stormé DeLarverie was a popular drag performer at the first racially integrated drag establishment in America. In the modern drag community, performing in male drag is often seen as an homage to masculinity.

DRAG QUEEN

▼ *noun*

A person—typically a man—who entertains while dressed in feminine drag, personifying and/or exaggerating feminine stereotypes.

"Bianca Del Rio, Bob the Drag Queen, Lady Bunny, Alaska Thunderfuck, and Divine are iconic drag queens. These girls don't play around when it's time to beat, tuck, and strut."

 WANT MORE INFO? *THINK:* **RUPAUL, THE FIRST QUEEN TO BE HONORED WITH A STAR ON HOLLYWOOD'S WALK OF FAME.**

DRAG SHOW

▼ *noun*

A live performance or show featuring drag performers who typically entertain through dancing, singing, or lip-syncing to popular songs. Other performance components include stand-up comedy, skits, visual art, and political activism.

"You've never been to a drag show? Honey, your gay card is revoked! Just turn your TV to LOGO or VH1!"

 WANT MORE INFO? *THINK:* **MUSIC + DRAG QUEENS + COMEDY = PURE ENTERTAINING JOY.**

DRAG SISTER

▼ *noun*

One of more than one drag daughters who are supported by the same drag mother.

A friend within the drag community who uses "sister" as an indicator of a close relationship.

"Queen Mayhem Miller has a squad of drag sisters who are not to be messed with."

 WANT MORE INFO? *THINK:* **BESTIES WITHIN THE DRAG COMMUNITY.**

D

Drag queen

DID YOU KNOW Drag is often associated with the history of theater, dating back to classical Chinese theater and Shakespearean productions. Theater was considered unfit for women and they were banned from performing, so men played both male and female characters. In the modern drag community, performing in female drag is often seen as an homage to femininity.

DRAMA

▼ *noun*
An extreme level of emotion or scandal.

"Mr. McAllister's wife caught him cheating with his new male secretary. The drama!"

 WANT MORE INFO? *THINK:* **EXTRA, EXTRA, READ ALL ABOUT IT!**

DRAMA AND KAFLAMA

▼ *idiom*
A heightened version of DRAMA.

"Miss Thing came to the ball getting her tens with drama and kaflama!"

 WANT MORE INFO? *THINK:* **DOING WAY TOO MUCH!**

 This term originated in ballroom culture.

DRESSED TO THE NINES

▼ *idiom*
An expression describing someone who is dressed exquisitely. This person usually demonstrates exceptional taste in fashion and style.

"Yes, mother queen! The sight of André Leon Talley dressed to the nines always leaves me so satisfied!"

 WANT MORE INFO? *THINK:* **IN FLAWLESS ATTIRE.**

DUCKWALK

▼ *verb*
A vogue dance move that emphasizes a deep squat walk.

"Omari teaches a fierce vogue class. We learn vogue femme, and you know we have a duckwalk battle."

 WANT MORE INFO? *THINK:* **DANCING LIKE A DUCK— BUT LOOKING FABULOUS.**

 This term originated in ballroom culture.

DUST

▼ *noun*
A term used to dismiss someone or something completely.

"He cheated on me twice. I paid him dust."

 WANT MORE INFO? *THINK:* **ERASED.**

 This term originated in Black American culture and is commonly used in ballroom culture.

DUSTED

▼ *adjective*
To be chic, refined, or perfect. Often used to refer to makeup.

"Stepping out tonight with my boo looking dusted. Our selfies are about to flood your timelines."

 WANT MORE INFO? *THINK:* **THE OPPOSITE OF BUSTED.**

DYKE

▼ *noun*
A lesbian, bisexual, or queer woman.

A masculine, aggressive lesbian, bisexual, or queer woman.

RELATED
DYKEY *adjective*

SEE ALSO
"The Lesbian Spectrum," *p. 194*

"I love sports bars on the weekend—so many dykes yelling at soccer games on TV. I swoon!"

 WANT MORE INFO? *THINK:* **A LESBIAN.**

USAGE NOTE This term originated as a slur but has been reclaimed by some of the LGBTQIA+ community. It may still have negative connotations for some people.

DID YOU KNOW Dyke, traditionally meaning butch lesbian, dates back to as early as the 1920s. It originated as a slur directed toward masculine lesbians but has since been reappropriated by many in the lesbian community as an empowering descriptor for queer women or gender nonconforming people who are typically attracted to women.

DYKE ALIKE

▼ *noun*
See DOUBLE HOMO

DYKE DADDY

▼ *noun*
In the BDSM, leather, and kink communities, this term refers to a lesbian who facilitates power dynamic and scene play as the Dominant. While this woman is typically thought of as butch, she may also identify somewhere else on the butch/femme spectrum. The term MOMMY can also be used.

SEE ALSO
DOMINATRIX, FEMME DADDY, SIR

"My Dyke Daddy has created a family of girls and bois who she disciplines and loves in equal measure."

 WANT MORE INFO? *THINK:* **A LEZ DOM.**

USAGE NOTE For all BDSM-related terms, the power exchange is a part of sadomasochistic play and should be consensual between all partners involved. The *D*s in Dyke and Daddy should always be capitalized when referring to D/s, or power dynamic, relationships.

D

ST. JOHN PARISH LIBRARY

D

DYKE DRAMA

▼ *noun*
Drama that is the result of stereotypical lesbian behavior.

"Look over there! Cassie just sat down at the bar with a girl in a 'FUTURE IS FEMALE' tee and her ex is here, giving crazy eyes! We are about to witness some serious dyke drama!"

 WANT MORE INFO? *THINK:* **LESBIAN DRAMA THAT IS BOTH ENJOYABLE AND MAYBE EMBARRASSING.**

 USAGE NOTE This term is commonly used in the lesbian community. The term "dyke" originated as a derogatory slur for lesbians but has been reclaimed by some of the LGBTQIA+ community. It may still have negative connotations for some people.

DYKE IN DENIAL

▼ *noun*
A woman who fits the stereotype of a lesbian through behavior or appearance but does not identify as gay. The term "syke-a-dyke" can also be used.

"Denise is such a dyke in denial. When will she ever accept that she is a big lezzie?"

 WANT MORE INFO? *THINK:* **"ARE YOU SURE YOU'RE NOT A LESBIAN?"**

USAGE NOTE The term "dyke" originated as a derogatory slur for lesbians but has been reclaimed by some of the LGBTQIA+ community. It may still have negative connotations for some people.

DYKIE FIT

▼ *noun*
See LP

DYKON

▼ *noun*
A woman—usually gay, but not always—who is considered an icon within the lesbian community.

"Dykons? Clea DuVall, Sarah Paulson, k.d. lang, Wanda Sykes, Jenny Shimizu—shall I go on? Oh, well I can include the straight dykons like Hillary Clinton, Oprah, and Pink, too."

SEE ALSO
BICON, GAY ICON

 WANT MORE INFO? *THINK:* **QUEER (OR QUEER-FRIENDLY) WOMEN WHO ARE GAME CHANGERS.**

 The term "dyke" originated as a derogatory slur for lesbians but has been reclaimed by some of the LGBTQIA+ community. It may still have negative connotations for some people.

DYSPHORIA

▼ *noun*
A state of feeling unhappy, uneasy, and/or insecure with one's personal state of being.

SEE ALSO
GENDER DYSPHORIA

"Be gentle and encourage Cam when you see them. They're dealing with some serious dysphoria and have been super-stressed lately."

 WANT MORE INFO? *THINK:* **THE OPPOSITE OF EUPHORIA.**

D IS FOR DICTIONARY...
LOOK AT YOU HAVING FUN READING ONE!

The Queens' English

Ee

EARTHY-CRUNCHY DYKE

▼ *noun*

A lesbian, bisexual, or queer woman who is eco-conscious and may also practice veganism, vegetarianism, or pescetarianism.

SEE ALSO
GRANOLA

"Babe, I love that you are my earthy-crunchy dyke, but I don't think your lavender and baking soda natural deodorant is working today."

 WANT MORE INFO? *THINK:* **ALL-NATURAL, EARTH-FRIENDLY LESBIAN.**

USAGE NOTE The term "dyke" originated as a derogatory slur for lesbians but has been reclaimed by some of the LGBTQIA+ community. It may still have negative connotations for some people.

EAT IT

▼ *idiom*

Sexual expression used to request or demand oral sex.

"Eat it good, sugar!"

 WANT MORE INFO? *THINK:* **GETTING SOME OF THAT PEACHES AND CREAM.**

In ballroom culture, this phrase is used to display confidence or to be exceptional. The phrase "oh, you ate that" can also be used.

"I'm serving fresh hot tilapia tonight, hunties! Eat it allllll up!"

 WANT MORE INFO? *THINK:* **SHINING YOUR LIGHT OH, SO BRIGHT!**

EAT OUT

▼ *verb*
To perform oral sex. Often used in the phrase "eat you/her/them out." The phrase "eat pussy" can also be used.

> SEE ALSO
> **CUNNILINGUS, BLOW**

"She eats me out so good. I swear she never comes up for air."

 WANT MORE INFO? *THINK:* **GOING DOWN BETWEEN THE LEGS.**

EDGE

▼ *verb*
Practice of personal or mutual sexual stimulation bringing an individual close to climax, then ceasing stimulation. This is often repeated multiple times in order to eventually experience a deeper and fuller orgasm.

> RELATED
> **EDGING** *noun*

"I'm so horny! I can't wait to get home and edge."

 WANT MORE INFO? *THINK:* **STOP-AND-GO MASTURBATION.**

ENBY

▼ *adjective*
The phonetic pronunciation of the abbreviation for nonbinary, or "nb," a gender identity that is open to a full spectrum of gender expressions, not limited by masculinity and femininity. An enby person may express masculinity, femininity, both, or neither.

> SEE ALSO
> **GENDER NONCONFORMING, GENDERQUEER, NONBINARY**

"This enby baby is ready to embrace a queerer, more androgynous wardrobe. Going to do some online shopping at the Phluid Project and Bindle and Keep."

 WANT MORE INFO? *THINK:* **NON-HETERONORMATIVE GENDER EXPRESSION.**

USAGE NOTE The term "enby" is commonly used in the nonbinary, gender-fluid, and gender nonconforming communities, though some people may find it offensive. The abbreviation "nb" is not often used because it was once a common reference for a "non-Black person."

E

ENDO

▼ *noun*
An abbreviated form of endocrinologist, a doctor who specializes in medical interventions for patients who need assistance with hormone balance, including, but not limited to, transgender patients.

"I take great pride in being an endo for the queer community. My patients are important to me and their happiness is my priority."

 WANT MORE INFO? *THINK:* **A KEY HEALTH PROVIDER SUPPORTING THE MEDICAL CARE OF QUEER AND TRANS BODIES.**

E

ENDOWED

▼ *adjective*
Having a large penis. The term HUNG can also be used.

"Let's just say he is very well endowed."

 WANT MORE INFO? *THINK:* **HE'S GOT A THIRD LEG.**

EQUALITY

▼ *noun*
The quality or state of being equal—having equal rights, opportunities, and status.

"The fight for equality has been relentless and exhausting, but we will not give up!"

 WANT MORE INFO? *THINK:* **EQUAL TREATMENT FOR ALL PEOPLE.**

Equality ▲

DID YOU KNOW The Human Rights Campaign (HRC) is America's largest organization that advocates for lesbian, gay, bisexual, transgender, and queer equality while educating the public on LGBTQIA+ issues. HRC's mission is to improve the lives of queer people and their families by encouraging more inclusive policies in laws, work environments, ideological spaces, and other supportive avenues worldwide.

ERASURE

▼ *noun*
Elimination or absence from data or history.

SEE ALSO
INVISIBILITY

"Queer theory very rarely engages with bisexuality, and textbooks have neglected to include important trans history, thus supporting—whether intentional or not—queer erasure."

 WANT MORE INFO? *THINK:* **LACK OF REPRESENTATION.**

DID YOU KNOW Karla Rossi created a magazine called *Anything That Moves: Beyond the Myths of Bisexuality* to confront the issues of bi-erasure and biphobia in America. The magazine was published from 1990 to 2002 as an extension of the San Francisco Bay Area Bisexual Network. Rossi used the publication to promote bisexual visibility by highlighting diverse voices and experiences while redefining the traditional concepts of sexuality and gender.

EVERYTHING

▼ *adjective*
Describing something or someone fabulous, and giving 100 percent approval.

"Ooh la la! Girl, that lipstick is everything!"

 WANT MORE INFO? *THINK:* **TENS ACROSS THE BOARD!**

USAGE NOTE This term originated in the Black gay community and is commonly used in the larger queer and trans people of color (QTPOC) community. It has been appropriated by mainstream culture.

Everything ▲

EX-GAY

▼ *noun*
A person who identified as gay at one point in time, but no longer identifies as such.

SEE ALSO
YESTERGAY

"New Jersey, Colorado, Maine, Oregon, Illinois, New Mexico, and so many other states have signed their gay conversion therapy ban! Therapy will not turn someone into an ex-gay."

WANT MORE INFO? *THINK*: NOT GAY ANYMORE.

 This term has negative connotations as it limits sexuality to a hetero/homo binary, denying the reality of sexual fluidity.

EXTRA

▼ *adjective*
Displaying excessive behavior. Often seen as XTRA.

"Just putting your business out there for all to see? Not couth at all. Xtra, xtra, read all about it!"

 WANT MORE INFO? *THINK*: DRAMATIC, NARCISSISTIC, AND/OR OVER THE TOP.

 This term originated in Black American culture and is commonly used in the Black gay and queer community. It has been appropriated by mainstream culture.

EYEBALL QUEEN

▼ *noun*
A gay, bisexual, or queer man who enjoys watching other people have sex. Other names for this include "watch queen," "lookie freak," and "peer queer."

"I should let Jonathan film us being kinky tonight; he is an eyeball queen."

 WANT MORE INFO? *THINK*: VOYEUR.

EQUALTIY AND JUSTICE FOR ALL LGBTQIA+ QUEENS!

#stonewall #marriageequality
#transrights #blacklivesmatter
#daca #genderequality
#LGBTQEmployeesAreProtected

Friend of Dorothy ▲

Ff

FAB

▼ *adjective*
An abbreviation of "fabulous."

RELATED
FABULOUSNESS *noun*
FABULOSITY *noun*

"Trader Joe's is just as fab as Whole Foods but it's so much better for your bank account."

 WANT MORE INFO? *THINK:* **WONDERIFIC.**

FACE

▼ *idiom*
An acknowledgment of beauty and fierceness. Often used in the phrase "giving face."

"Avery is giving face in these pictures. Those cheekbones, those lashes, yas!"

 WANT MORE INFO? *THINK:* **GORGEOUS.**

▼ *noun*
In ballroom culture, a prominent competition category where a competitor is judged on the smoothness, symmetry, and beauty of their face. The term CARTA can also be used.

"An agent from Wilhelmina saw him slay face last night at the ball and the bitch got signed!"

 WANT MORE INFO? *THINK:* **COMPETITION CATEGORY THAT IS A MUST-SEE AT A BALL.**

 USAGE NOTE This term originated in ballroom culture. It has been appropriated by mainstream culture.

FACIAL FEMINIZATION SURGERY (FFS)

▼ *noun*
A series of surgical procedures that alters masculine facial features to make them appear more feminine.

"FFS can be rewarding but it is not for everyone. Being part of a support group was an important part of finding the right surgeon and preparing myself emotionally."

 WANT MORE INFO? *THINK:*
SPECIALIZED COSMETIC FACIAL SURGERY FOR PEOPLE TO APPEAR MORE FEMININE.

 USAGE NOTE This term is commonly used in the transgender, nonbinary, and gender nonconforming communities.

FAG BAG

▼ *noun*
See BEARDED LADY, FISHWIFE

FAGGOT

▼ *noun*
A gay man. While it originated as a slur, some members of the LGBTQIA+ community have reclaimed the insult, using it as a term of endearment or powerful personal identifier. Often shortened to "fag."

"Look at those fags over there kissing! I love gay PDA!"

 WANT MORE INFO? *THINK:*
AN OFFENSIVE TERM FOR A GAY MAN.

USAGE NOTE This term originated as a derogatory slur for gay men but has been reclaimed by some of the LGBTQIA+ community. It may still have negative connotations for some people.

DID YOU KNOW The use of the word "faggot" in American English slang goes back to 1914 and was popularized in the Black culture of New York during the 1920s and 1930s. Many people referred to the popular Hamilton Lodge Ball—a Harlem Renaissance-era party known for celebrating gay love and freedom of expression—as the "Faggots Ball."

FAG HAG

▼ *noun*
A woman—usually straight—who enjoys the friendship of and spends great amounts of time with gay men. The term FRUIT FLY can also be used.

SEE ALSO
FAGGOT, FAG STAG, GOLDILOCKS

"The fag hag pledge: Every girl needs a gay best friend!"

 WANT MORE INFO? *THINK:*
LADY BEST FRIEND TO GAY MEN.

 USAGE NOTE Like the word "fag," "fag hag" originated as a derogatory slur but has since been reclaimed by some of the LGBTQIA+ community. It may still have negative connotations for some people.

F

FAG STAG

▼ *noun*

A man—usually straight—who enjoys the friendship of and spends great amounts of time with gay men. Also known as FRUIT FLY.

> SEE ALSO
>
> **FAGGOT, FAG HAG, SAPPHO DADDY-O**

"I'm obsessed with my sister's gay friend Matt. My sister says I'm a fag stag, but I'm cool with that. His fashion advice has gotten me tons of dates with hot girls."

 WANT MORE INFO? *THINK:* **STRAIGHT MAN WHO WATCHES** *QUEER EYE* **WITH HIS GAY BFF.**

USAGE NOTE The term "fag" originated as a derogatory slur for gay men but has been reclaimed by some of the LGBTQIA+ community. It may still have negative connotations for some people.

FAIRY

▼ *noun*

A gay, bisexual, or queer man who has a light and airy demeanor and deeply identifies with feminine expression.

"I like nail polish, Britney Spears, and flying high in the sky with my glittery butterflies. Yes, I live the fairy life."

 WANT MORE INFO? *THINK:* **A QUEER MALE WHOSE INTERESTS ARE CONSIDERED STEREOTYPICALLY FEMININE.**

USAGE NOTE The term "fairy" originated as a derogatory slur for gay men but has been reclaimed by some of the LGBTQIA+ community. It may still have negative connotations for some people.

FAMILY

▼ *noun*

Used to acknowledge and refer to members within the lesbian, gay, bisexual, transgender, and queer community, and those in supporting social communities.

> SEE ALSO
>
> **CHOSEN FAMILY**

"Wow, I'm reading Zuri's blog on Black history and she is shouting out family! It mentions gay literary powerhouse James Baldwin, acclaimed journalist Don Lemon, trans media mogul Janet Mock, lesbian comedian Danitra Vance, and bisexual activists Billy S. Jones-Hennin and Angela Davis. That's so fly!"

 WANT MORE INFO? *THINK:* **TOGETHERNESS, SUPPORT, AND LOVE WITHIN THE LGBTQIA+ COMMUNITY.**

DID YOU KNOW "Family" was first popularized by the Black gay community and was used as a coded word to ask if someone was homosexual. Today, "family" is used widely among the LGBTQIA+ community, regardless of race or ethnicity.

F

The Queens' English

F

FANNY BELLHOP

▼ *noun*

A gay, bisexual, or queer man who is employed in the hospitality industry.

"Oh, I bet Mr. Fanny Bellhop would be able to tell us how to get to Nashville's gay district."

 WANT MORE INFO? *THINK:* **A GAY HOTEL WORKER.**

FATHER OF THE HOUSE

▼ *noun*

See HOUSE FATHER

FAUX QUEEN

▼ *noun*

A woman who entertains, either professionally or recreationally, while dressed in exaggerated female attire and makeup. The term BIO QUEEN can also be used.

"I was addicted to drag culture. The only thing I watched for two years was RuPaul's Drag Race, *so I became a faux queen."*

 WANT MORE INFO? *THINK:* **A FEMALE FEMALE IMPERSONATOR.**

 The term "faux queen" is typically preferred over the term "bio queen," as the implication of biology may be considered derogatory to transgender, nonbinary, and gender nonconforming queens.

FEATURE

▼ *verb*

To give attention to something.

SEE ALSO
NOT FEATURING

"She is featuring that sixteen-carat ring! Good lawd, three million dollars is a lot of money. Hell, I would say yes, too!"

 WANT MORE INFO? *THINK:* **TO SHOW OFF.**

 This term originated in ballroom culture and is commonly used in the larger queer and trans people of color (QTPOC) community.

FEELING IT

▼ *idiom*

To have a self-confident demeanor. The phrases "feeling yourself" or "feeling myself" can also be used.

Exploring the deepest and most honest part of yourself.

"You're feeling it now that your braces are off, huh? Keep smiling, boo!"

 WANT MORE INFO? *THINK:* **A STRONG DOSE OF SELF-ADMIRATION.**

 This term originated in Black American culture. It has been appropriated by the larger LGBTQIA+ community and mainstream culture.

FELLATIO

▼ *noun*
The act of giving oral pleasure to a person with a penis. The terms BLOWJOB and HEAD can also be used.

RELATED
FELLATE *verb*

"These dudes can't take me! My fellatio game is on point. My milkshake brings all the boys to the yard—damn right it's better than yours!"

 WANT MORE INFO? *THINK:* **SUCKING A DICK.**

FEMALE

▼ *adjective*
A biological sex or identity expression often associated with the display of feminine physicality, demeanor, and behavior.

▼ *noun*
A female-identifying person.

SEE ALSO
"The Genderbread Person," *p. 56*

"The future is female. The world is nothing without her."

 WANT MORE INFO? *THINK:* **ASSOCIATED WITH GIRLS AND WOMEN.**

FEMALE FIGURE

▼ *noun*
A competition category in ballroom culture. This competition involves any individual who represents the femme form in their performance, and may include cisgender women, transgender women, and drag queens.

"The Female Figure performance prize is going for two thousand dollars tonight. Get that money!"

 WANT MORE INFO? *THINK:* **BALLROOM CATEGORY FOR FEMMES.**

FEMALE-TO-MALE

▼ *noun*
A person who is assigned female at birth but has transitioned or is in the process of transitioning to male. The term is often abbreviated as "FTM."

▼ *adjective*
Describing a person who has undergone an FTM transition.

SEE ALSO

AFAB, FEMALE-TO-NONBINARY/GENDER NEUTRAL/NEUTROIS, MALE-TO-FEMALE, MALE-TO-NONBINARY/GENDER NEUTRAL/NEUTROIS, STP, TRANSMASCULINE

"Laith Ashley, Ian Harvie, Lucas Silveira, and Buck Angel are all proud FTM transgender power-houses."

 WANT MORE INFO? *THINK:* **A TRANS MAN.**

 This term may be considered outdated by many members of the LGBTQIA+ community. The use of "AFAB," or "Assigned Female at Birth," is widely accepted because it does not imply an individual's gender identity has changed, instead acknowledging the binding nature of being assigned a specific gender at birth. The use of this term relies on an individual's preference. Please ask for a person's chosen name and pronouns.

FEMALE-TO-NONBINARY/GENDER NEUTRAL/NEUTROIS

▼ *noun*
A person who is assigned female at birth and identifies as nonbinary, gender neutral, or neutrois. The term is often abbreviated as "FTN."

▼ *adjective*
Describing a person who has undergone an FTN transition.

SEE ALSO

AFAB, FEMALE-TO-MALE, MALE-TO-FEMALE, MALE-TO-NONBINARY/GENDER NEUTRAL/NEUTROIS

"I may look femme to you, but 'woman' is not my identity. I don't feel like a man either. I identify as FTN or nonbinary."

 WANT MORE INFO? *THINK:* **A PERSON WHO IDENTIFIES AS NONBINARY, GENDER NEUTRAL, OR NEUTROIS.**

 This term may be considered outdated by many members of the LGBTQIA+ community. The use of "AFAB," or "Assigned Female at Birth," is widely accepted because it does not imply an individual's gender identity has changed, instead acknowledging the binding nature of being assigned a specific gender at birth. The use of this term relies on an individual's preference. Please ask for a person's chosen name and pronouns.

FEMINISM

▼ *noun*
Political theory supporting equality
of the sexes, often advocating for
equal pay, respect, and opportunity
for all people, regardless of gender.

RELATED
FEMINIST *noun*

*"Feminism ensures our young girls
will grow up knowing their value—
knowing that their strength,
beauty, and voices are just as
important as anyone else's."*

 WANT MORE INFO?
THINK: **"FEMINISM
IS A MOVEMENT TO
END SEXISM, SEXIST
EXPLOITATION, AND
OPPRESSION."**
▶ **bell hooks**

FEMINIZING HORMONE THERAPY

▼ *noun*
A process in which hormones are
used to produce physiological
changes within the body to exhibit
physical female attributes. The
term HORMONE REPLACEMENT
THERAPY can also be used.

SEE ALSO
BLOCKERS, MASCULINIZING HORMONE THERAPY

*"The doctor said that estrogen,
testosterone blockers, and
progesterone are certain types
of medicine used for feminizing
hormone therapy."*

 WANT MORE INFO? *THINK:*
**MEDICAL THERAPY USED
FOR FEMALE GENDER
AFFIRMATION.**

 This term is used in the
transgender, nonbinary,
and gender nonconforming
communities.

FEMME

▼ adjective
Denoting the vast and dynamic representation of feminine characteristics, regardless of gender. Both "femme" and "butch" are often paired with adjectives soft/hard or high/low as a means of distinction.

SEE ALSO
BUTCH

"He rocked that 'FEMME VIBE' crop top. I saw it at H&M last week. Yes, kween!"

 WANT MORE INFO? *THINK:* **ACTING, DRESSING, OR BEHAVING IN A TRADITIONALLY FEMININE MANNER.**

In the lesbian community, denoting a queer woman who possesses a feminine appearance and behaviors.

SEE ALSO
HIGH FEMME, LIPSTICK LESBIAN

"Just because I'm a femme lesbian and I like to wear high heels, doesn't mean I'm less queer than a stud in flannel."

 WANT MORE INFO? *THINK:* **THE OPPOSITE OF BUTCH.**

 USAGE NOTE This term originated in the lesbian community. It has been appropriated by the larger LGBTQIA+ community and mainstream culture.

DID YOU KNOW *The Oxford English Dictionary* credits bisexual poet Lord Byron with one of the earliest uses of the word "femme" in 1814. By the mid-twentieth century, the term was used widely in working-class bar culture to label and identify lesbian women—it became the feminine counterpart to "butch." By the 1980s, "femme" was widely used to describe gay men in addition to lesbians.

FEMME DADDY

▼ *noun*

In the BDSM, leather, and kink communities, this term refers to a female or femme-identifying person who facilitates power dynamic and scene play as the Dominant. The terms FEMME DOM, MISTRESS, or MOMMY can also be used.

> **SEE ALSO**
>
> **DOMINATRIX, DYKE DADDY**

"A Femme Daddy is sexy, is powerful, and will whip you into shape. She earns the title 'Daddy' by pushing, disciplining, and protecting her submissive."

 WANT MORE INFO? *THINK:* **A KINKY WOMAN IN CHARGE.**

USAGE NOTE For all BDSM-related terms, the power exchange is a part of sadomasochistic play and should be consensual between all partners involved. The *F* in Femme and the *D* in Daddy should always be capitalized when referring to D/s, or power dynamic, relationships.

FEMME DOM

▼ *noun*

See FEMME DADDY

FEMME FLAGGING

▼ *verb*

A coded system used by female or femme queers to subtly signal their queerness to others. The act of painting particular fingernails symbolic colors is most commonly used. The term FINGER FLAGGING can also be used.

Cait: *I'm femme flagging my fucking fingers.*
André: *So, you mean all of them, right?*

 WANT MORE INFO? *THINK:* **HOW TO SPOT A FEMME IN THIS WILD, WILD WORLD.**

FEMME FOR FEMME

▼ *idiom*

Expression referring to intimate relationships between two queer femmes. This also can be referred to as "femme on femme" or abbreviated as "F4F."

> **SEE ALSO**
>
> **BUTCH/FEMME RELATIONSHIP, BUTCH-ON-BUTCH CRIME, MASC FOR MASC**

"Femme for femme relationships should be respected. Please lose the stereotypical view of a butch/ femme relationship. That goes for you, too, heteros!"

 WANT MORE INFO? *THINK:* **A PARTNERSHIP BETWEEN TWO LIPSTICK LEZZIES.**

 This term originated in the lesbian community.

F

FEMME-OF-CENTER

▼ *adjective*
Referring to gender identities that lean toward femininity.

SEE ALSO
MASC-OF-CENTER

"Femme and femme-of-center, butch, and masc are labels queer people use to support our gender expressions and identities. I cannot deal with straight cis people using our words—they don't need to call themselves femme or masc to be understood and accepted."

 WANT MORE INFO? *THINK:* **ON THE FEMININE SIDE.**

 USAGE NOTE This term is used in the transgender, nonbinary, and gender nonconforming communities.

FEMMEPHOBIA

▼ *noun*
Aversion, fear, or hatred toward femmes.

RELATED
FEMMEPHOBIC *adjective*   **FEMMEPHOBE** *noun*

SEE ALSO
ACEPHOBIA, BIPHOBIA, HOMOPHOBIA, LESBO-PHOBIA, MISOGYNY, QUEERPHOBIA, TRANSPHOBIA

"You hate me because I'm femme? Well, I hate to tell you that your femmephobia is stifling your character and you should really work on that!"

 WANT MORE INFO? *THINK:* **DISLIKE OF OR PREJUDICE AGAINST FEMMES.**

FEMME QUEEN

▼ *noun*
A category competition in the ballroom scene for transgender women.

SEE ALSO
BUTCH QUEEN, CATEGORY, QUEEN

Refers to a drag queen or femme-presenting person.

"Sheila is working it in that slinky little dress! Tits out, shoulders back, get it! Yaaas, you're giving me iconic femme queen, darling!"

 WANT MORE INFO? *THINK:* **A TRANS OR FEMME-PRESENTING WOMAN.**

 USAGE NOTE This term originated in ballroom culture. It has been appropriated by the larger LGBTQIA+ community.

F

FEMME TOP

▼ *noun*
A feminine gay, bisexual, or queer man who prefers topping over bottoming.

> *SEE ALSO*
> ## BLOUSE, TOP

A queer, femme-identifying person who prefers topping or being the sexual pursuer.

Hollis: *Hey, sis! I'm about to go slide to this boy's house.*
Vincent: *What boy? That queen from last night? The femme top?!*

 WANT MORE INFO? *THINK:* **FEMME AND CUTE IN THE STREETS, BOSSY IN THE SHEETS.**

USAGE NOTE This term originated in the gay male community.

FETISH

▼ *noun*
A fixation or obsession. While a fetish is typically thought of as sexual, it can also be nonsexual.

"My fetishes? I like to be restrained. I'm into bondage— leather cuffs and harnesses."

 WANT MORE INFO? *THINK:* **SOMETHING KINKY THAT TURNS YOU ON.**

FIERCE

▼ *adjective*
Exceptional, powerful, intense.

"Snap, snap, snap, snap! FIERCE! FIERCE! FIERCE!"

 WANT MORE INFO? *THINK:* **SPECTACULAR.**

USAGE NOTE This term originated in ballroom culture. It has been appropriated by the larger LGBTQIA+ community and mainstream culture.

FINGER

▼ *verb*
The sexual act of inserting a finger or multiple fingers into the vagina or anus. The terms "finger fuck" and "fingerbang" can also be used.

"I got to third base last night. She wanted me to finger her."

 WANT MORE INFO? *THINK:* **THE OTHER SEXUAL POWER TOOL. SMALL, BUT MIGHTY.**

FINGER FLAGGING

▼ *verb*
See FEMME FLAGGING

FIRE

▼ *adjective*
Outstanding, energetic, hot. The terms NASTY and "fiyah" can also be used.

"That model is fire walking down the runway! Absolutely stunning."

 WANT MORE INFO? *THINK:* **SIZZLING.**

 USAGE NOTE This term originated in Black American culture and is used in the Black gay and queer community. It has been appropriated by the larger LGBTQIA+ community and mainstream culture.

FISH

▼ *adjective*
Looking super-femme. In the ballroom scene and drag community, it identifies a person who looks like a woman. The term "fishy" can also be used.

"You mean Galaxy? She's so fish, sexy as hell."

SEE ALSO
SERVE FISH

▼ *noun*
A woman.

"I'm gay. I definitely don't want that fish."

 WANT MORE INFO? *THINK:* **LE POISSON EST LA FEMME.**

 USAGE NOTE This term originated in Black American culture. It has been appropriated by the larger LGBTQIA+ community. The term may be considered derogatory.

FISHWIFE

▼ *noun*
The wife of a gay man.

SEE ALSO
BEARDED LADY, BEARD

"Allen is totally gay and closeted. Pam is his fishwife!"

 WANT MORE INFO? *THINK:* **FEMALE MARRIAGE PARTNER FOR A GAY MALE.**

FIST

▼ *verb*
A sexual act of inserting all five fingers or the entire hand into the vagina or anus for sexual pleasure.

SEE ALSO
FINGER

"Two fingers didn't cut it, so Taylor asked me to fist."

 WANT MORE INFO? *THINK:* **A LITTLE LUBE AND EVERY FINGER.**

F

FIVE-YEAR TUNE-UP

▼ *idiom*
A rare urge of a lesbian woman to have a sexual experience with a man.

Megan: *Bradley Cooper makes me want a five-year tune-up. Mmmf!*
Lauren: *Don't judge me, but my trainer offered me a tune-up . . . and did he ever* tune *it up.*

 WANT MORE INFO? *THINK:* **A LESBIAN'S HETEROSEXUAL CRAVING.**

 USAGE NOTE This term originated in the lesbian community.

FLAGGING

▼ *verb*
The use of color-coded symbols to show membership to the LGBTQIA+ community as well as sexual desires.

SEE ALSO
FEMME FLAGGING, HANKY CODE

"*A dark blue bandana was in his left pocket, so he was flagging—he's a gay top.*"

 WANT MORE INFO? *THINK:* **SYSTEM OF COLORED BANDANAS USED TO COMMUNICATE QUEER SEXUAL PREFERENCES.**

FLAMING

▼ *adjective*
Extremely flamboyant.

RELATED
FLAMER *noun*

"*She is fierce, flaming, and on fiyah! Jeans tighter than ballet tights and a cloak as plush as a velvet throne. I bow down, kween!*"

 WANT MORE INFO? *THINK:* **ALL HAIL THE QUEENS JONATHAN VAN NESS AND BILLY PORTER!**

 USAGE NOTE This term may be considered a stereotype or derogatory.

FLANNEL

▼ *noun*
A garment—usually a button-up shirt—using soft plaid or tartan material. A stereotypically lesbian piece of clothing.

▼ *adjective*
Describing a plaid piece of clothing.

"*I looked in my girlfriend's closet and all she owns are flannels, jeans, hiking boots, and Birkenstocks.*"

 WANT MORE INFO? *THINK:* **THE UNOFFICIAL DYKE DRESS CODE.**

F

The Queens' English

F

FLIP

▼ *verb*
To influence a sexual partner to switch from sexually domineering to submissive. The term "flip flop" can also be used.

SEE ALSO
SWITCH

"By some miracle I was able to get my partner to flip. She's always on top, but I convinced her she needed some extra TLC last night."

 WANT MORE INFO? *THINK:* **TO TOUCH A STONE BUTCH SEXUALLY OR FLIP A GAY TOP TO A BOTTOM.**

FLIPCOLLAR FAIRY

▼ *noun*
A gay priest. The term comes from the formal garment called the flip collar, which is worn at the priest's neck. The term MARY OF THE CLOTH can also be used.

SEE ALSO
"Religion and LGBTQIA+ Believers," *p. 266*

"As a gay Christian leader, I don't believe your sexuality affects your calling to do God's work. Some call me a flipcollar fairy and that nickname is okay with me."

 WANT MORE INFO? *THINK:* **A QUEER PRIEST.**

 USAGE NOTE This term may be considered derogatory.

FLIT

▼ *noun*
A homosexual.

RELATED
FLITTY *adjective*

"Ah, at last, we have arrived. The gay beach, where every flit is wearing a Speedo and holding a cocktail."

 WANT MORE INFO? *THINK:* **GAY, BANANA, HOMO, FAG.**

DID YOU KNOW The word "flit" as it is defined here first appeared in print in J. D. Salinger's *Catcher in the Rye*: "A flitty-looking guy with wavy hair came out and played the piano."

FLOWER

▼ *noun*
An effeminate male or delicate queer person.

"I'm a dainty flower and prefer to be the lady in this relationship. So, would you be a gentleman and kindly pay for this meal?"

 WANT MORE INFO? *THINK:* **AN ELEGANT FEMME.**

The anus. The terms "bloom" and "rose bud" can also be used.

"Oh my, he poked my flower."

 WANT MORE INFO? *THINK:* **THE BACK DOOR.**

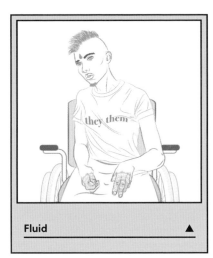

Fluid ▲

FLUID

▼ *adjective*

An identity descriptor that expresses the fluctuating nature of one's sexual orientation and/or gender expression over time.

"I'm fluid. I change. I float. I move along the spectrum of self-expression in every way."

 WANT MORE INFO? *THINK:* **NOT FIXED; CHANGING OVER TIME.**

FOLX

▼ *noun*

A way to write "folks" that implies inclusivity and celebrates queerness, similar to the use of the letter *X* in the terms LATINX and WOMXN.

"It's almost time for One Magical Weekend! Epcot, circuit parties, and swimming pools. Oh, dreams really do come true for queer folx!"

 WANT MORE INFO? *THINK:* **AN INCLUSIVE IDENTIFIER FOR THE QUEER COMMUNITY.**

FOOLISHNESS AND DEBAUCHERY

▼ *idiom*

Describes someone acting in an outlandish or comical way for others' amusement.

"You are foolishness and debauchery! My stomach hurts from laughing so hard."

 WANT MORE INFO? *THINK:* **COMIC RELIEF.**

 USAGE NOTE This term originated in Black American culture and is commonly used in the Black gay and queer community.

FOR BLOOD

▼ *idiom*

To go to the extreme; to do something full out, with no regrets. This term is most often used in the phrase "go for blood."

"The kids go for blood at AfroPunk: piercings, mohawks, dashikis, and tattoos. Unapologetically Black and beautiful. Brooklyn, stand up!"

 WANT MORE INFO? *THINK:* **ALL OUT.**

 USAGE NOTE This term originated in ballroom culture. It has been appropriated by the larger LGBTQIA+ community and mainstream culture.

FOR POINTS

▼ *idiom*
An emphatic phrase used to acknowledge something or someone highly exceptional.

"Churl, I been watching old episodes of Noah's Arc *all day! I forgot season two went for points like that. Why is this so my life?"*

 WANT MORE INFO? *THINK:* **SCORING BIG POINTS FOR A JOB WELL DONE.**

 USAGE NOTE This term originated in ballroom culture and is commonly used in the larger queer and trans people of color (QTPOC) community.

FOR THE BIRDS

▼ *idiom*
A response to an undesirable situation, experience, or comment.

"There's no alcohol here? This party is for the birds."

 WANT MORE INFO? *THINK:* **AN EXPRESSION OF DISTASTE.**

FOR THE GODS OR TO THE GAWDS

▼ *idiom*
A phrase used to praise something exceptional.

"This one right here is for the kids who slay. We be up on YouTube talking makeup all day. Slay to the gawds! Slay, slay to the GAWDS!"
▶ Tatiana Ward, "Beat Face Honey"

 WANT MORE INFO? *THINK:* **BOW DOWN TO THE BEST.**

 USAGE NOTE This term originated in ballroom culture and is commonly used in the larger queer and trans people of color (QTPOC) community.

FRAME

▼ *noun*
A cisgender heterosexual man who entertains an attraction to men but does not typically engage in same-sex relationships or hookups.

SEE ALSO
FRUIT PICKER, SWEET'N LOW

"He has been making passes at me all night. Do you think he's out or just a frame?"

 WANT MORE INFO? *THINK:* **A GAY WINDOW SHOPPER.**

FREE AGENT

▼ *noun*
In ballroom culture, this is a person who performs in ball competitions without being represented by a house or team. The term "007" can also be used.

"You know she doesn't perform as Infiniti anymore; she is a free agent now."

 WANT MORE INFO? *THINK:* **A FREELANCER IN THE BALLROOM SCENE.**

FRIEND OF DOROTHY

▼ *idiom*
A dated expression used to inconspicuously identify another gay or queer person.

"Hey Ralph, the friends of Dorothy are coming over for tea at noon. Care to join?"

 WANT MORE INFO? *THINK:* **CODE FOR A MEMBER OF THE LGBTQIA+ COMMUNITY.**

USAGE NOTE This term originated in the gay male community.

F

DID YOU KNOW The term "Friend of Dorothy" gained contemporary usage as a reference to actress Judy Garland's role of Dorothy in *The Wizard of Oz*. Garland was adored by the gay community and remains a gay icon.

FRUIT

▼ *noun*
Used to refer to a gay man, but can be used to identify a lesbian, bisexual, transgender, and/or other queer individual. The terms "fruitcake" and "fruit basket" can also be used.

RELATED
FRUITY *adjective*

Sebastian: *Fruits come in all different shapes and sizes.*
Anna: *Yeah, no two are exactly alike!*

 WANT MORE INFO? *THINK:* **A GAY.**

USAGE NOTE The term "fruit" originated as a derogatory slur for a homosexual man but has been reclaimed by some of the LGBTQIA+ community. It may still have negative connotations for some people.

FRUIT FLY

▼ *noun*
See FAG HAG, FAG STAG

FRUIT PICKER

▼ *noun*
Refers to a man who may identify as heterosexual but has occasional male-to-male sexual relationships.

SEE ALSO
FRAME

"You will find a few fruit pickers at the Pride parade willing to taste your rainbow."

 WANT MORE INFO? *THINK:* **A STRAIGHT MAN WHO IS NOT STRICTLY HETEROSEXUAL.**

USAGE NOTE This term may be considered offensive or derogatory.

FTM

▼ *adjective*
See FEMALE-TO-MALE

FTM ▲

FTN

▼ *adjective*
See FEMALE-TO-NONBINARY/ GENDER NEUTRAL/NEUTROIS

FULL HOUSE

▼ *noun*
Someone who has a sexually transmitted disease.

"Stop, look, and listen! That one is a full house."

 WANT MORE INFO? *THINK:* **"YES THIS BODY PROVIDES A COMFORTABLE HOME TO THE ACQUIRED IMMUNE DEFICIENCY SYNDROME."**
▶ Angel Dumott Schunard, *Rent*

FULL OUT

▼ *idiom*
Giving maximum output.

"You have to dance the routine full out, with feeling! Kick your face! Leave it all on the floor! Don't you want to win top solo?"

 WANT MORE INFO? *THINK:* **GO HARD OR GO HOME.**

 USAGE NOTE This expression originated in ballroom culture. It has been appropriated by the larger LGBTQIA+ community and mainstream culture.

Full spectrum ▲

FULL SPECTRUM

▼ *adjective*
Total, intergenerational, culturally diverse inclusion within the LGBTQIA+ community across gender and sexuality spectrums. Typically used in the phrase "full spectrum community," the term is used to create space for marginalized groups within the gay community.

SEE ALSO
RAINBOW

"We need language and spaces dedicated to bringing everyone in our queer family—in all its diverse glory—together in an effort to create and support a full spectrum community."

 WANT MORE INFO? *THINK:* **ALL-INCLUSIVE.**

FUTCH

▼ *noun*
A lesbian, bisexual, or queer woman who presents herself as a mix of feminine and masculine; a portmanteau of "femme" and "butch."

SEE ALSO
SOFT STUD, SOFT BUTCH, "The Lesbian Spectrum," *p. 194*

"A futch lesbian is the dopest!"

 WANT MORE INFO? *THINK:* **A BUTCH GIRL WHO PRESENTS WITH SOME FEMININITY.**

 USAGE NOTE This term originated in the lesbian community.

TUCKING & BINDING 101

Here are a few do-it-yourself practices for producing an appearance that matches your gender expression or desired drag performance persona. A few friends created these easy-to-follow, step-by-step tutorials to tucking and binding.

ALWAYS TALK TO YOUR DOCTOR BEFORE YOU START TUCKING OR BINDING. PLEASE RESEARCH THE BENEFITS AND RISKS OF THESE PRACTICES.

HOW DO YOU EXPRESS *YOUR* GENDER?

HOW TO BIND

Binding is the practice of flattening or concealing one's breasts/chest with constricting materials, commonly used by transgender men or nonbinary and gender nonconforming people. It can also be used by cisgender women who perform masculine drag. A binder is the healthiest and safest way to bind. Take a look below at some tips on how to bind from our friend, Ryen.

1 Based on your body type, select a properly sized binder. You can buy a binder online or apply for a program that gives away free binders. Do not use tape or bandages.

2 Step into the binder as opposed to pulling it over your head. It's much easier! If you feel uncomfortable with the binder on your skin, wear a shirt underneath it.

3 Adjust your chest/breast outward and down for a natural and flat look in the binder.

4 Put a shirt on over your binder and double-check everything is adjusted.

PRO-TIP: Dark-colored shirts mask a lot!

5 To ensure safety, inform your doctor that you are wearing binders. Also, do not sleep in or wear a binder for long periods of time, because it may cause lack of oxygen, bruising, or tissue damage.

HOW TO TUCK

Tucking to hide the penis and scrotum is commonly used by transgender women, nonbinary and gender nonconforming people, and cisgender men who perform in drag. Take a look below for some tips on tucking from Genderosity and Brenda Darling.

OLD WAY, *courtesy of Genderosity*

1 Shave the genitals with a good-quality razor. You want the area nice and smooth.

2 Put testicles in hip cavities and pull the penis back between your legs.

3 Put napkin over shaft of penis to protect it from the tape.

4 Take duct tape strips and tape the covered penis using a front-to-back taping technique.

5 Repeat until satisfied.

NEW WAY, *courtesy of Brenda Darling*

1 Shave genitals with a good razor and make sure you use a shaving cream or gel. Get that hair off!

2 Put testicles in hip cavities. Here is where the tucking begins. If it's your first time, it may feel uncomfortable. But you will get the hang of it over time.

3 Pull penis back to anus. Remember, tight, tight, tight.

4 Pull up gaff/tucking pants. Make sure you choose a pair that works best for you. Spandex and microfiber are a good choice to keep everything nice and tight.

★★★★
★ ★ ★
HISTORY
LESSON
★ ★ ★
★★★★

GAYS

IN THE

MILITARY

Homosexuality was illegal in all branches of the American military and subject to severe punishment dating back as early as the Revolutionary War. Men were discharged from the armed forces for homosexual acts throughout the eighteenth and nineteenth centuries. By the mid-1940s, women who served in the Women's Army Corps (WAC) were also discharged if found engaging in intimate same-sex affairs.

In 1975, Sergeant Leonard Matlovich—a gay man who dedicated his life to the air force and received a Bronze Star and a Purple Heart—became the face of the gay rights movement with his groundbreaking *TIME* magazine interview and cover. The cover of the magazine showed Matlovich in his U.S. Air Force military uniform with a caption reading, "'I Am a Homosexual': The Gay Drive for Acceptance." This marked the beginning of a broader cultural conversation around equal rights in the military.

The U.S. military banned openly gay, lesbian, bisexual, and transgender people from service until 1993, insisting "Homosexuality is incompatible with military service." President Bill Clinton signed Don't Ask Don't Tell (DADT) into law, allowing gay, lesbian, and bisexual people to serve in the military, as long as they kept their sexual orientation to themselves.

In 2011, President Barack Obama repealed DADT, asserting that any person, regardless of sexual orientation or gender identity, could serve openly and freely in the U.S. military without limitation. However, under President Donald Trump's administration and the Transgender Military Ban, the fight for transgender and intersex equality in the armed forces is an ongoing battle.

Gg

GAFF

▼ *noun*
A clothing item used for people with penises to smooth out the appearance of their genitals, especially when wearing slim-fitting clothing or practicing tucking.

> **SEE ALSO**
> **TUCK, "Tucking & Binding 101," *p. 130***

"I need ten more minutes! I just finished beating my face and putting my gaff on. They are going to have to hold the show."

 WANT MORE INFO? *THINK:* **TIGHT UNDERGARMENT USED TO TUCK A DICK.**

USAGE NOTE This term is commonly used in the transgender, nonbinary, gender nonconforming, and drag communities.

GAG

▼ *verb*
To be in a state of total surprise or disbelief. The terms SCREAM or DIE can also be used.

> **RELATED**
> **GAGGED** *adjective*

"I had them gagging when I pulled up to the club in a crimson Ferrari."

 WANT MORE INFO? *THINK:* **CHOKING ON EMOTION.**

USAGE NOTE This term originated in ballroom culture. It has been appropriated by the larger LGBTQIA+ community and mainstream culture.

GAGA

▼ *noun*
See WHAT'S THE GAGA?

GAL PAL

▼ *noun*
A term typically used by people outside of the queer community to describe two women in what they view as a "close" relationship without acknowledging them as lesbians.

"Kristen Stewart always has a close gal pal for some reason—Soko, Alicia, Annie, Stella. She must be such a good friend."

 WANT MORE INFO? *THINK:* **THE WAY A STRAIGHT PERSON MIGHT REFER TO A LESBIAN COUPLE.**

GAWD

▼ *exclamation*
A nonreligious and nonblasphemous spelling of the word "God." Most times used as an intensifier to show a supreme reaction.

> **SEE ALSO**
> **LAWD; YES, GAWD!**

Jamal: *GAWD! Look at me!*
Tyrone: *Yes queen! Didn't I tell you you'd look good in this?!*

 WANT MORE INFO? *THINK:* **EXCLAMATION POINT, EXCLAMATION POINT, EXCLAMATION POINT!**

GAY

▼ *adjective*
Homosexual.

Queer, not completely heterosexual.

▼ *noun*
A homosexual person. Often used to describe a male, but it's an identifier for many others.

"Being gay is natural. Hating gay is a lifestyle choice."
▶ John Fugelsang

 WANT MORE INFO? *THINK:* **A PERSON WHO EXISTS SOMEWHERE ON THE GENDER AND SEXUALITY SPECTRUM OTHER THAN HETEROSEXUAL.**

USAGE NOTE This term is commonly used as an inclusive identifier for anyone who does not strictly identify as heterosexual. The use of this term relies on an individual's preference.

 DID YOU KNOW The first recognized gay organization in America was the Society for Human Rights, founded in 1924 by Henry Gerber in Chicago, Illinois, to reform anti-homosexual laws. In 1950, Harry Hay and other gay men in Los Angeles founded the Mattachine Society to protect and improve the rights of homosexuals. Both organizations added momentum to the gay rights movement and inspired other organizations and activists to join the fight for equality.

Gay ▲

GAY AFTER THREE

▼ *idiom*
A phrase used to describe someone who engages in same-sex flirtation or sexual activity, but only after having three beers. The terms BEER BI or THREE-BEER QUEER can also be used.

Jessica: *Is that Max making out with Oliver by the bathroom?*
Aubree: *Ha, typical Max. Gay after three every time.*

 WANT MORE INFO? *THINK:* **WHEN ALCOHOL LUBES SOMEONE UP FOR GAY ENCOUNTERS.**

GAY-BASHING

▼ *noun*
The harassment and mistreatment of LGBTQIA+ people. Verbal, physical, and emotional mistreatment all fall under the umbrella of gay-bashing.

SEE ALSO
"Violence & Hate Crime Epidemic," *p. 310;* **HOMOPHOBIA**

▼ *verb*
Engaging in the activity of mistreating gay, lesbian, or queer people.

"What do people get out of gay-bashing? It's a cowardly act of insecurity."

 WANT MORE INFO? *THINK:* **QUEER BULLYING AND HATE CRIMES.**

G

135

The Queens' English

Gay Christian ▲

GAYBIE OR GAYBY

▼ *noun*
A young gay or queer person.

"We are having an online discussion for gaybies who need support and guidance on how to come out to their parents."

 WANT MORE INFO? *THINK:* **LGBTQIA+ YOUTH.**

A child of a gay or queer parent or parents.

"We are so emotional right now! Kurt and I just got our adoption papers finalized. We're getting our gayby!"

 WANT MORE INFO? *THINK:* **A KID WITH LGBTQIA+ PARENTS.**

A close friend who identifies as gay or queer.

"I love a good debate with my gaybies. Everyone's opinion is always respected."

 WANT MORE INFO? *THINK:* **YOUR LGBTQIA+ BESTIE.**

GAYBORHOOD

▼ *noun*
A neighborhood primarily made up of LGBTQIA+ residences, businesses, and entertainment.

> **SEE ALSO**
> **"U.S.A. Gayborhoods,"** *p. 310*

"Philadelphia has a great gayborhood. Its motto is 'Get your history straight and your nightlife gay!'"

 WANT MORE INFO? *THINK:* **THE CASTRO, WEST HOLLYWOOD, BOYSTOWN, AND NEW YORK'S TRIFECTA: THE VILLAGE, CHELSEA, AND HELL'S KITCHEN.**

GAY CHRISTIAN

▼ *noun*
A queer person who practices Christianity.

SEE ALSO

"Religion and LGBTQIA+ Believers," *p. 266*

"Churches that welcome gay Christians believe it is unjust to close their doors to anyone in search of God's word."

 Want more info? *Think:* **A GOD-LOVING GAY.**

GAY DAD

▼ *noun*
A gay man or masc-identifying person who is supportive in the development and well-being of younger LGBTQIA+ people. The term "gay father" can also be used.

Aaliyah: *Let's throw a party at the Center to celebrate our gay dads.*
Marquis: *Man, if it wasn't for James stepping up and being a father to me, I'd be so lost.*

 WANT MORE INFO? *THINK:* **A GAY MENTOR.**

 This term originated in the gay male community. It has been appropriated by the larger LGBTQIA+ community.

GAYDAR

▼ *noun*
The perceived ability to intuitively identify if a person is gay, bisexual, or queer. The term "queerdar" can also be used.

Ye: *How did you know Jim Parsons was gay?*
Corey: *My gaydar is 20/20.*

 WANT MORE INFO? *THINK:* **A SKILL FOR IDENTIFYING GAYS.**

GAY FOR PAY

▼ *idiom*
When a heterosexual performer takes on a queer role in some form of entertainment, whether it's on film or on stage.

Rhett: *Ooooh, Brokeback Mountain. I'd be Jake Gyllenhaal's trusty steed any day.*
Jenn: *Sorry honey, I'm pretty sure he was gay for pay.*

 WANT MORE INFO? *THINK:* **STRAIGHTS ACTING GAY FOR MONEY.**

Nonqueer employee in a queer establishment.

Gio: *Damn, that bartender is hot. I'm getting his Insta so I can slide into his DMs tonight.*
Eduardo: *Bro, don't waste your time. He's only gay for pay.*

 WANT MORE INFO? *THINK:* **STRAIGHT WORKER INVASION IN THE GAY CLUB.**

G

GAY GAMES

▼ *noun*
International sporting events that celebrate LGBTQIA+ people.

"My uncle participated in the 1986 Gay Games in San Francisco, and he came to watch me in the 2018 Gay Games in Paris. He told me how proud he was that I'm continuing the legacy."

 WANT MORE INFO? *THINK:* **THE GAY OLYMPICS.**

GAY HUSBAND

▼ *noun*
A gay man or masc-identifying person who has formed a close platonic friendship with a woman or femme-identifying person and has playfully been adopted as a "husband."

Sandra: *Wait, I'm confused. Your dinner date is with Juan? I thought he was gay!*
Kelly: *Oh, he absolutely is. He's my gay husband.*

 WANT MORE INFO? *THINK:* **A GAL'S MASC GAY BESTIE.**

GAY ICON

▼ *noun*
A public figure—queer or not— who is exalted by the LGBTQIA+ community.

"We salute our gay icons for their individuality, their fabulosity, and for supporting our queer community with a little extra love each and every day."

SEE ALSO

BICON, DYKON

 WANT MORE INFO? *THINK:* **DEAR VILLAGE PEOPLE, THANK YOU FOR "Y.M.C.A." LOVE, QUEER NATION.**

GAY LITERATURE

▼ *noun*
A genre of literature written for and by the LGBTQIA+ community. Themes, characters, and plots are centered on queer lives. The terms "queer literature" and "lesbian literature" can also be used.

"Go stick your nose into books by Leslie Feinberg, Edmund White, or Essex Hemphill for some good queer literature. Or try classics by Oscar Wilde and Virginia Woolf."

 WANT MORE INFO? *THINK:* **QUEER FICTION, NONFICTION, ROMANCE, SCI-FI, YA, AND HORROR BOOKS.**

GAY MARRIAGE

▼ *noun*
See MARRIAGE EQUALITY

GAYMER

▼ *noun*
A queer individual who is part of the gaming community—one who plays video-, tabletop, and/or computer games. The term "gay gamer" can also be used.

"Hey, are you going to the GaymerX convention this year? I can't wait to see Sonic Fox, Heather Alexandra, and Nick Scratch."

 WANT MORE INFO? *THINK:* **GAYS WHO LOVE** *CALL OF DUTY, THE SIMS,* **AND** *MINECRAFT.*

> **DID YOU KNOW** Gaming has a history of misogyny and homophobia. GaymerX, a nonprofit organization, was created in 2012 to champion queer gamers and game developers, with the goal of creating a safer space within the gaming community for LGBTQIA+ players.

GAY MOTHER

▼ *noun*
A lesbian or femme-identifying person who is supportive in the development and well-being of younger LGBTQIA+ people. The term "gay mom" can also be used.

"My gay moms are the best at giving dating advice. I would still be dating self-centered Leos and critical Virgos if it wasn't for them."

 WANT MORE INFO? *THINK:* **A GAY MENTOR.**

GAY PRIDE

▼ *noun*
See PRIDE

GAYSIAN

▼ *noun*
A gay, bisexual, or queer person of Asian descent.

"High five to Vicky Du and her short documentary Gaysians! It tells the stories of five queer and trans Asian-American people navigating life, family, and culture. It's incredible representation!"

 WANT MORE INFO? *THINK:* **BD WONG AND MARGARET CHO.**

 USAGE NOTE This term may be considered a stereotype or derogatory.

Gaysian ▲

GCS

▼ *noun*
See GENDER AFFIRMATION SURGERY

GENDER

▼ *noun*
In a historical context, this refers to the characteristics associated with masculinity and femininity.

"I went to Sophie's gender reveal party. She's having a boy! I can't wait to buy him his first baseball bat and mitt!"

 WANT MORE INFO? *THINK:* **BLUE FOR BOYS. PINK FOR GIRLS.**

In a modern context, this refers to a broader range of characteristics that go beyond the gender binary.

SEE ALSO

GENDER EXPRESSION, GENDER IDENTITY, "The Genderbread Person," *p. 56*

"Gender and sex are often used interchangeably, but they are not synonymous! Gender relates to a person's identity and self-expression, while sex relates to a person's reproductive organs. The two do not have to be aligned in a traditional sense to be legit."

 WANT MORE INFO? *THINK:* **A MULTIFACETED EXPRESSION OF A PERSON.**

▼ *verb*
To assign masculine or feminine characteristics to a person, place, or thing.

"Drew likes pink, but he never feels comfortable wearing it because society has gendered the color as feminine. Just let colors be colors!"

 WANT MORE INFO? *THINK:* **TO IMPOSE MALE-NESS OR FEMALE-NESS ON SOMEONE OR SOMETHING.**

GENDER AFFIRMATION SURGERY

▼ *noun*

A medical procedure for a transgender person that alters the physical body in order for the physical appearance to reflect their gender identity. The terms "gender confirmation surgery," GCS, SEX REASSIGNMENT SURGERY, and SRS can also be used. The trans, nonbinary, and gender nonconforming communities often use the words PRE-OP and POST-OP when referring to gender affirmation surgery.

"Toni had his gender affirmation surgery last week. He's in recovery but says he already feels more aligned with his gender identity."

 WANT MORE INFO? *THINK:* **A WAY OF CONNECTING THE MIND AND THE BODY TO AFFIRM A PERSON'S GENDER.**

USAGE NOTE Using the terms "gender confirmation surgery" or "gender affirmation surgery" over "sex reassignment surgery" may be more affirming for transgender, nonbinary, and gender nonconforming people.

DID YOU KNOW In America, evidence of gender affirmation surgery (then called sex reassignment surgery) was apparent as early as the 1940s. Transgender women Virginia Prince and Christine Jorgensen were some of the first documented people to undergo the procedure.

GENDERBEND

▼ *verb*

To go against, or "bend," expected gender norms physically, behaviorally, or otherwise. The term GENDERFUCK can also be used.

RELATED
GENDERBENDER *noun*

"Genderbending is using one's outward expression to actively disagree with and subvert society's old-fashioned ways of thinking about gender."

 WANT MORE INFO? *THINK:* **TO EMBRACE MASCULINITY, FEMININITY, AND ANDROGYNY, BLURRING THE LINES BETWEEN "MAN" AND "WOMAN."**

GENDER BINARY

▼ *noun*

The enforced societal system of male and female gender identities—two distinct identities that each come with a set of expected, gendered roles.

RELATED
GENDER BINARISM *noun*

SEE ALSO
BINARY

"The gender binary is so limiting. I love wearing glittery nail polish and a three-piece suit or a flowy dress and my facial hair. I am beyond the binary."

 WANT MORE INFO? *THINK:* **A WAY OF THINKING ABOUT GENDER IN BLACK AND WHITE.**

G

141

The Queens' English

GENDER DYSPHORIA

▼ *noun*

A profound dissatisfaction with one's physical and/or mental state, caused by discrepancies between one's gender identity and gender assigned at birth.

SEE ALSO
DYSPHORIA

"Signs of gender dysphoria may include social isolation, depression, and anxiety in addition to being super-uncomfortable in one's body. Here at the clinic, we offer outpatient therapy to help you unpack these complicated feelings."

 WANT MORE INFO? *THINK:* **A DEEP DISCONNECT BETWEEN BODY AND GENDER IDENTITY.**

GENDER EXPRESSION

▼ *noun*

Outward characteristics—such as appearance, behaviors, and attitudes—that communicate a person's identity to society.

SEE ALSO
"The Genderbread Person," *p. 56*

"Gender expression is fluid. It's a bit of this and a dash of that. Just ask the Genderbread Person."

 WANT MORE INFO? *THINK:* **THE EXTERNAL EXPRESSION OF A PERSON'S GENDER.**

GENDER-FLUID OR GENDERFLUID

▼ *adjective*

Not confined to a fixed gender expression or presentation.

"Identifying as gender-fluid— not limited by masculinity and femininity—is so empowering!"

 WANT MORE INFO? *THINK:* **GENDER EXPRESSION AND/OR IDENTITY THAT FLOWS BACK AND FORTH AND ALL AROUND THE GENDER SPECTRUM.**

 USAGE NOTE This term is commonly used in the transgender, nonbinary, and gender nonconforming communities.

GENDERFLUX

▼ *adjective*

An identifier for people who experience a range of intensity within a particular gender identity.

"I am genderflux. I identify mostly as female, but the intensity of my femininity changes over time. I have felt ultrafeminine, I have felt nonbinary and femme, and I've also felt super-butch, but still female."

 WANT MORE INFO? *THINK:* **YOUR GENDER IS A LAMP WITH A DIMMER SWITCH—THE LIGHT ITSELF DOESN'T CHANGE, BUT THE DIMNESS AND BRIGHTNESS FLUCTUATE OVER TIME.**

 USAGE NOTE This term is commonly used in the transgender, nonbinary, and gender nonconforming communities.

GENDERFUCK

▼ *noun*
See GENDERBEND

GENDER IDENTITY

▼ *noun*
The internal understanding of one's gender and the self. This identity may or may not correlate with one's assigned sex at birth and may not be directly correlated to one's outward gender expression.

SEE ALSO
"The Genderbread Person," *p. 56*

"Gender identity isn't about the gender, which is socially constructed, it's about my sense of self. My sense of: Am I a boy or a girl? How do I feel about who I am?"
▶ Rikki Arundel

 WANT MORE INFO? *THINK:* **THE INTERNAL FEELINGS A PERSON HAS ABOUT THEIR GENDER.**

GENDERISM

▼ *noun*
Grouping individuals into distinct masculine and feminine categories based on the belief that there are or should be only two genders. The term "gender binarism" can also be used.

SEE ALSO
GENDER BINARY

"We are taught genderism as early as kindergarten, where name tags and bathrooms are separate based on kids' male-ness and female-ness."

 WANT MORE INFO? *THINK:* **A PERVASIVE BELIEF THAT THE WORLD IS MADE UP OF TWO INHERENTLY DIFFERENT GROUPS OF PEOPLE: MEN AND WOMEN.**

GENDERLESS

▼ *adjective*
Not identifying with any gender. The terms AGENDER or NONGENDER can also be used.

SEE ALSO
NEUTROIS, NULL GENDER

"To avoid the gender binary, I like to teach my students to incorporate genderless language in our discussions. This aids in having a more inclusive environment for productive learning and growth."

 WANT MORE INFO? *THINK:* **NOT FEMALE, NOT MALE, NOT BOTH OR NEITHER.**

 This term is commonly used in the transgender, nonbinary, and gender nonconforming communities.

GENDER-NEUTRAL DRESS CODE

▼ *noun*
A dress code policy in a school or other institution without gender-specific rules.

G

"A gender-neutral dress code supports body positivity and a feminist cause—allowing everybody to wear what they want without being targeted for being 'distracting' or 'provocative.'"

 WANT MORE INFO? *THINK:* **A DRESS CODE THAT DOESN'T REPRIMAND STUDENTS FOR WARDROBE CHOICES.**

GENDER NEUTRALITY

▼ *noun*
The movement to end gender discrimination through means of gender-neutral language, the end of gender-based segregation, and other social causes.

"Gender neutrality is practiced by having more gender-neutral restrooms, a gender-neutral option on state ID cards, and fewer gender-specific job titles. These initiatives will get us to build a more equal and loving society."

 WANT MORE INFO? *THINK:* **"A GENDER-EQUAL SOCIETY WOULD BE ONE WHERE THE WORD 'GENDER' DOES NOT EXIST: WHERE EVERYONE CAN BE THEMSELVES."**
▶ Gloria Steinem

GENDER NONCONFORMING

▼ *adjective*
Expressing one's gender in a way that does not fit neatly into the gender binary. Often abbreviated as "GNC."

SEE ALSO
GENDERQUEER, NONBINARY

144

The Queens' English

Cole: *May I ask how you identify? What are your pronouns?*
Kiyoshi: *I'm femme-of-center GNC. I use she/her or they/them. Thanks for asking!*

 WANT MORE INFO? *THINK:* **NOT BOUND TO A MALE OR FEMALE GENDER IDENTITY.**

USAGE NOTE "Gender nonconforming" is an umbrella term for people who identify outside of the gender binary. It is important to ask how a person identifies, because every person's preference is unique.

GENDERQUEER

▼ *adjective*

Not identifying with the conventional labels of female or male. This person may relate to both genders, express gender ambiguity, or refrain from expressing any gender at all.

SEE ALSO
GENDER NONCONFORMING, NONBINARY

"Genderqueer Taurus Sun, Pisces rising seeks ultra-femme, bossy Capricorn who can whip my ass into shape. Must love dogs and hiking."

 WANT MORE INFO? *THINK:* **NOT BOUND BY THE GENDER BINARY.**

 USAGE NOTE The term is commonly used in the transgender, nonbinary, and gender nonconforming communities.

GET INTO THIS

▼ *idiom*

To bring attention to something— a specific idea, attitude, or item.

"Why yes, this is a complete Louis Vuitton luggage set. GET INTO THIS!"

 WANT MORE INFO? *THINK:* **"COME ON, DON'T YOU LOVE IT?!"**

 USAGE NOTE This term is commonly used in the Black gay community and the larger queer and trans people of color (QTPOC) community.

GET IT

▼ *idiom*

Giving a compliment or pushing someone to do something great.

"GET IT, GET IT, GET IT, POP IT. Yes, girl! You betta tweeerrrk!"

 WANT MORE INFO? *THINK:* **"DO IT!"**

To imply a desire for sexual activity.

"His sexy ass can get it. Anytime!"

 WANT MORE INFO? *THINK:* **"DO ME."**

 USAGE NOTE This term originated in Black American culture and is commonly used in the Black gay and queer community.

GIG

▼ *noun*

A short-term job.

"Damn! I double-booked myself for two gigs tonight. CoCo, you wanna do a show for me at Lucky's?"

 WANT MORE INFO? *THINK:* **A PLACE TO MAKE DEM COINS!**

 USAGE NOTE The term is commonly used in the LGBTQIA+ community.

An emphatic word used to enhance the phrase "Get into this."

Carlos: *Well, is this Versace?*
Jacob: *Get into this gig, girl! We eat it up!*

 WANT MORE INFO? *THINK:* **THIS IS THE SHIT.**

GILLETTE BLADE

▼ *noun*
A dated term that originated in the 1950s referencing a bisexual woman, implying that her sexuality cuts both ways.

Barbra: *Some lesbians won't date Gillette blades because they are still open to being with men.*
Darlene: *Well that's not very nice. What's the word the kids are using now? Oh right—"biphobic." That's biphobic, Barb!*
Barbra: *Hey, don't kill the messenger, Darlene!*

 WANT MORE INFO? *THINK:* **AN OLD EUPHEMISM FOR "BISEXUAL."**

 This term may have negative connotations as it limits bisexuality to the gender binary. It is inappropriate to use this label if a person has not self-identified as such.

GIRL OR GURL

▼ *noun*
A term of endearment for a friend or loved one, regardless of gender. Often used in conversation to grab someone's attention. The terms BABY GIRL, "gurr," or "girrrl" can also be used.

> **SEE ALSO**
> ## BITCH; GIRL, PLEASE; SISTER

"Girrrl! My day was so long! Come meet me at this happy hour downtown."

  WANT MORE INFO? *THINK:* **PAL, CUTIE, FRIEND, OR A VERBAL EXCLAMATION POINT.**

USAGE NOTE This term originated in Black American culture and is commonly used in the Black gay and queer community. It has been appropriated by the larger LGBTQIA+ community and mainstream culture.

In the BDSM, leather, and kink communities, the term refers to a submissive female or femme role within a D/s, or power dynamic relationship.

> **SEE ALSO**
> ## DOM/SUB RELATIONSHIP, BDSM

 "In D/s, a 'girl' will generally have a Mommy or Daddy Dom, but I'm not beholden to that. I identify as a baby girl and have played with several Doms."

 WANT MORE INFO? *THINK:* **A FEMALE SERVICE ROLE IN SCENE PLAY.**

USAGE NOTE For all BDSM-related terms, the power exchange is a part of sadomasochistic play and should be consensual between all partners involved. The *g* in the word "girl" should always be lowercase when referring to D/s, or power dynamic, relationships.

G

GIRL CRUSH

▼ *noun*
A straight girl's intense, platonic admiration for another woman. Girl crushes are typically not sexual by nature and tend to be between straight women.

"Wesley is such a badass. Her nuclear energy research project was flawless, and she always has the funkiest style. I have such a girl crush!"

 WANT MORE INFO? *THINK:* **#WCW FOR STRAIGHT GIRLS.**

GIRLFAG

▼ *noun*
A cisgender woman who is attracted to gay men.

Cliff: *I have a girlfag!*
Morris: *Shut up, no, you don't.*
Cliff: *I do! Johanna told me last night, 'Cliff, I know you're gay, but I want you sooooo bad!'*
Morris: *I'm screaming!*

 WANT MORE INFO? *THINK:* **A STRAIGHT WOMAN CRUSHING ON A MAN-LOVING MAN.**

 USAGE NOTE This term originated in the gay male community. The term "fag" originated as a derogatory slur for gay men but has since been reclaimed by some of the LGBTQIA+ community. It may still have negative connotations for some people.

GIRL, PLEASE

▼ *idiom*
A term of dismissal to show disinterest. The phrase, "girl, bye" can also be used.

"Girl, please. I am not about to get up at five a.m. to work out with you. Don't mess with my beauty sleep."

 WANT MORE INFO? *THINK:* **ABSOLUTELY NOT.**

 USAGE NOTE This term originated in Black American culture and is used in the Black gay and queer community. It has been appropriated by the larger LGBTQIA+ community and mainstream culture.

GIRL, WHA?

▼ *idiom*
A response to express misunderstanding. The phrase "bitch, wha?" can also be used.

"Girl, wha? I can't hear what you are saying from under this hair dryer!"

 WANT MORE INFO? *THINK:* **"COME AGAIN?"**

A phrase used to express surprise.

"Girl, wha? You're lying! You won the lottery? WE RICH, BITCH!"

 WANT MORE INFO? *THINK:* **A FLABBERGASTED RESPONSE.**

 USAGE NOTE This term originated in Black American culture and is used in the Black gay and queer community. It has been appropriated by the larger LGBTQIA+ community and mainstream culture.

G

The Queens' English

GIRLS, THE

▼ *noun*
Good friends. This term is often used by gay men to refer to their closest friends.

"The girls are going to Mexico next month for Kendrick's thirtieth! We are going to lose our minds!"

 WANT MORE INFO? *THINK:* **THE BESTIES.**

G

GIVEN NAME

▼ *noun*
A person's legal name that was assigned at birth.

> SEE ALSO
> **CHOSEN NAME, DEADNAME**

"On these official documents you are required to use your given name."

 WANT MORE INFO? *THINK:* **THE NAME ON SOMEONE'S BIRTH CERTIFICATE.**

GIVING FACE

▼ *idiom*
See FACE

GIVING ME LIFE

▼ *idiom*
An expression used to announce extreme excitement.

> SEE ALSO
> **GOT MY LIFE**

"The Golden Girls are giving me life! That Blanche. I bet she and I would kiki all day."

 WANT MORE INFO? *THINK:* **EXTRAORDINARY ENTHUSIASM.**

USAGE NOTE This term is commonly used in the Black gay community and the larger queer and trans people of color (QTPOC) community.

GLAMAZON

▼ *noun*
A tall and beautiful woman or femme.

"Look at all these glamazons on America's Next Top Model!"

 WANT MORE INFO? *THINK:* **ULTRA-GLAM, ULTRA-FEMININE, TALL GLASS OF WATER.**

GNC

▼ *noun*
See GENDER NONCONFORMING

GO BE WITH HER OR GO BE WITH IT

▼ *idiom*
An expression jokingly suggesting that someone go and connect with who or whatever attracts their attention.

"I can't believe you have been watching Netflix for more than twelve hours. Jeez, go be with it!"

 WANT MORE INFO? *THINK:* **TWO MAGNETS CONNECTING.**

GO DOWN ON

▼ *idiom*
See BLOW, CUNNILINGUS, EAT OUT, FELLATIO

GOLDEN RULE

▼ *noun*
See ABSOLUTE CODE

GOLDILOCKS

▼ *noun*
A woman who enjoys the company of gay men who identify as bears.

"Aw, look at Goldilocks and the three bears."

 WANT MORE INFO? *THINK:* **A GIRL WHO LOVES HER GAY TEDDY BEARS.**

GOLD STAR

▼ *adjective*
A gay person who only has had sex with members of the same gender. The specific term "gold star lesbian" is often used.

Elle: *We are gold star homos till the day we die!*
Chase: *That's right. Never been with the opposite sex and proud of it, babe.*

 WANT MORE INFO? *THINK:* **A LESBIAN WHO'S NEVER BEEN WITH A MAN; A GAY MAN WHO'S NEVER BEEN WITH A WOMAN.**

G

GO OFF

▼ *idiom*
A command to deliver a top-quality presentation. The superlative phrase is "go all the way off."

SEE ALSO
EAT IT

"I need you to go off on the last four measures of this song. Sing every riff and run you know."

 WANT MORE INFO? *THINK:* **"GIVE ME ALL YOU'VE GOT!"**

To get upset.

"I am about to go off if that damn dog doesn't stop barking!"

 WANT MORE INFO? *THINK:* **TO TURN INTO THE HULK.**

USAGE NOTE This term is commonly used in ballroom culture and the queer and trans people of color (QTPOC) community.

GOT MY LIFE

▼ *idiom*
An expression of total happiness, enjoyment, and fulfillment.

"When Rihanna came out with Fenty Beauty, I got my life. Launching forty shades of foundation—for all skin tones—was legendary!"

 WANT MORE INFO? *THINK:* **TOTALLY EUPHORIC.**

USAGE NOTE This term originated in the Black gay community.

GRANOLA

▼ *adjective*
Super health-conscious and environmentally aware—may practice a holistic lifestyle. This term is not limited to queer people.

SEE ALSO
EARTHY-CRUNCHY DYKE

"Berkeley, California, is the promised land for granola gays."

 WANT MORE INFO? *THINK:* **HIPPIE-DIPPY.**

GRAY-ASEXUAL OR GRAYSEXUAL

▼ *noun*
A sex-positive asexual person who is not sexually averse but may not have sexual feeling or attraction toward others. Often referred to as "a grace," "a gray ace," or "being gray-A."

"I identify as being straight and graysexual. I'm thirty-nine years old and have only ever been sexually attracted to two people."

 WANT MORE INFO? *THINK:* **AN UMBRELLA TERM FOR THOSE WHO IDENTIFY AS SOMEWHERE ON THE ASEXUAL SPECTRUM.**

 USAGE NOTE This term originated in the asexual community.

GRAY QUEEN

▼ *noun*
A gay, bisexual, or queer man in the financial services industry.

"Out *magazine featured a list of LGBTQIA+ leaders in finance. I bet half those gray queens work for Goldman Sachs.*"

 WANT MORE INFO? *THINK:* **QUEERS ON WALL STREET.**

 This term originated in gay male culture in the 1950s, when professional attire in the financial district was a gray flannel suit.

GUG

▼ *noun*
See LUG

GUYDYKE

▼ *noun*
A cisgender, heterosexual man who fetishizes lesbians or queer women.

Brad: *I don't know why, man, but I'm attracted to lesbians. I can be their guydyke and give them babies!*
Spencer: *Come on, dude. They're lesbians for a reason.*

 WANT MORE INFO? *THINK:* **A STRAIGHT MAN WHO CRUSHES ON GAY WOMEN.**

 This term may be considered offensive.

GYM BUNNY

▼ *noun*
A gay, bisexual, or queer man who spends excessive time in the gym. The terms MUSCLE MARY and "gym rat" can also be used.

"Welcome to California! The home of beautiful gym bunnies!"

 WANT MORE INFO? *THINK:* **SOMEONE WHO IS AT THE GYM SEVEN DAYS A WEEK.**

 This term originated in the gay male community.

GYNESEXUAL OR GYNOSEXUAL

▼ *adjective*
Experiencing sexual attraction toward femininity.

RELATED
GYNESEXUALITY *noun*

SEE ALSO
ANDROSEXUAL

▼ *noun*
A gynesexual person.

"This gynesexual's hands can not resist a supple breast."

 WANT MORE INFO? *THINK:* **ATTRACTED TO FEMMES.**

G

Help! WHAT'S MY GAY TYPE?

Many gay men use a specific set of animal identifiers based on body type and age to identify other gay men. It is sometimes referred to as *The Animal Kingdom*. These are playful labels based on stereotypes found within the gay male community.

Caleb

These body labels are confusing. Am I a wolf or an otter? What's the difference? What are the hair requirements again?

PLEASE NOTE

This is not an exhaustive list but represents the most commonly used body type labels in the gay male community.

Jack

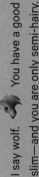 I say wolf. You have a good muscular build—not slim—and you are only semi-hairy.

GAY TYPE	BODY	HAIR	 AGE	THINK
BEAR	Big and broad, often with a belly, but sometimes built	Lots	Any	A sturdy, hairy gay man

	Build	Hair	Age	Description
CUB	Big and broad, often with a belly, but sometimes built	Lots	Young or young-looking	Young gay boy who will grow up to be a bear
OTTER	Thin and athletic	Lots	Any	Gay man who is athletic, hairy, and at the gym several times a week
PUP	Slender	None	Any	A baby gay
WOLF	Lean, muscular	Some	Any	A muscular, hairy hottie
BULL	Super-muscular	Doesn't matter	Any	A muscle man with high libido
GYM BUNNY/ GYM RAT	Sculpted	Doesn't matter	Bunny is under fifty; rat can be any age	Someone who works out at the gym seven days a week
JOCK	Muscular and athletic	Doesn't matter	Any	A super-athletic babe
CHUB	Very big	Doesn't matter	Any	A man with more cushion for the pushin'
TWINK	Slender	None	Young	Baby-faced skinny gay boy
TWUNK	Slender	None	Young	A twink with muscle

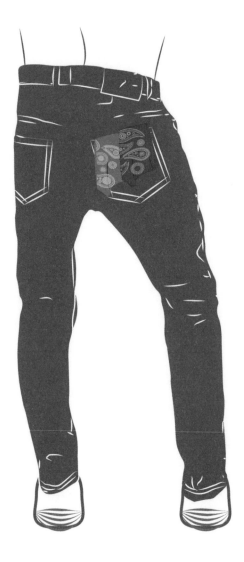

KNOW THE CODE

LEFT IS TOP
———
RIGHT IS BOTTOM

FIST TOP
———
FIST BOTTOM

PISSER
———
PISS FREAK

DADDY
———
ORPHAN BOY

BONDAGE TOP
———
FIT TO BE TIED

WANTS HEAD
———
GIVES HEAD

TIT TORTURER
———
TIT TORTUREE

Hanky code ▲

Hh

HANKY CODE OR HANDKERCHIEF CODE

▼ *noun*

A code used by members of the queer community to communicate a particular sexual desire. This color-coded system of handkerchiefs—including placement of the hanky—indicates preferred sexual acts and positions. The term BANDANA CODE can also be used.

> SEE ALSO
>
> **FEMME FLAGGING, FLAGGING**

"The hanky code was made popular by the gay male community in the 1970s and has since been adopted by queer people across the gender spectrum."

 WANT MORE INFO? *THINK:* **POCKET SQUARE CODE FOR GAY SEXUAL PLAY.**

HARD FEMME

▼ *noun*

A queer person whose appearance is feminine and presents as strong, tough, and/or resilient.

"I've put together every piece of furniture my wife and I have purchased from IKEA, all while in a Michael Kors skirt suit and pumps. It's called the hard femme membership club, baby!"

 WANT MORE INFO? *THINK:* **FEMININITY WITH A KISS OF TOUGHNESS.**

 USAGE NOTE This term originated in the lesbian community. It has been appropriated by the larger LGBTQIA+ community.

HASBIAN

▼ *noun*
A tongue-in-cheek term for a female who has dated or sexually dabbled with women but does not identify as a lesbian.

"Anne Heche's breakdown in the nineties definitely qualifies her as a hasbian."

 WANT MORE INFO? *THINK:* **FORMER LEZZIE.**

 USAGE NOTE This term has negative connotations as it limits sexuality to the gender binary, negating any notion that a person could be bisexual, queer, or any number of sexually fluid identifiers.

HATE CRIMES

▼ *noun*
Crimes, typically violent, committed against a particular identity or group because of prejudice.

SEE ALSO
ACEPHOBIA, BIPHOBIA, FEMMEPHOBIA, HOMO-PHOBIA, QUEERPHOBIA, LESBOPHOBIA, TRANS-PHOBIA, "Violence & Hate Crime Epidemic," *p. 310*

"The violence committed against queer people—especially trans women of color—is a national epidemic. Hate crimes? No, these are death sentences."

 WANT MORE INFO? *THINK:* **HATE TURNED PHYSICAL AND, OFTEN, DEADLY.**

DID YOU KNOW In 2009, President Barack Obama signed the Matthew Shepard and James Byrd Jr. Hate Crimes Prevention Act into law. The act expanded upon the existing federal hate crime law to further protect Americans from crimes committed on the basis of gender, sexual orientation, or disability. Unfortunately, hate crimes are still prevalent in society today. On June 12, 2016, the Pulse nightclub shooting in Orlando, Florida, marked the deadliest hate crime committed on the LGBTQIA+ community in U.S. history. A shooter opened fire on club patrons on a Latin-themed night, killing forty-nine people and wounding fifty-three others.

HAVE A SEAT

▼ *idiom*
A phrase expressing dissatisfaction with a person or action. The superlative phrase is "have several seats."

"I am going to need for you to fall back and have several seats."

 WANT MORE INFO? *THINK:* **"STOP WHAT YOU ARE DOING, IMMEDIATELY."**

 USAGE NOTE This term is used in the Black gay community and the larger queer and trans people of color (QTPOC) community.

H

HAWK

▼ *noun*
A gay man or lesbian who prefers partners considerably younger in age. Also known as "chicken hawk."

"That hawk can teach you a few lessons, you know."

 WANT MORE INFO? *THINK:* **QUEER CRADLE ROBBER.**

HEAD

▼ *noun*
See FELLATIO

HE/HIM/HIS

▼ *pronouns*
A set of pronouns typically used for masculine-identifying people.

SEE ALSO
"The Genderbread Person," *p. 56*, **"Common Pronouns 101,"** *p. 81*

"Hi, I'm Clark. It's nice to meet you. I use he/him/his pronouns. What are your pronouns?"

 WANT MORE INFO? *THINK:* **MASC IDENTIFIERS.**

HENNY

▼ *noun*
See HONEY

HERMAPHRODITE

▼ *noun*
A dated, problematic term used for intersex individuals. See INTERSEX.

Mom: *Hermaphrodites are people born with both male and female sexual organs, right?*
Joshua: *The proper word is "intersex," and it's a little more complicated than that.*

 WANT MORE INFO? *THINK:* **A STIGMATIZING SYNONYM FOR "INTERSEX."**

 USAGE NOTE This term is considered derogatory.

HERSTORY

▼ *noun*
A feminization of the word "history."

"Queer Herstory 101: The Daughters of Bilitis was the first lesbian civil and political rights organization in America."

 WANT MORE INFO? *THINK:* **WOMEN'S HISTORY.**

DID YOU KNOW The Daughters of Bilitis formed in San Francisco in 1955 as a reaction to police raids targeting lesbian bars and harassing queer patrons. Lesbian couple Del Martin and Phyllis Lyon founded the club in an effort to create a safe social setting for lesbians to find community and empowerment. They also created *The Ladder*—the first nationally distributed lesbian publication.

HETEROFLEXIBLE

▼ *adjective*

Describing a person who is predominantly heterosexual but is open to experiencing gay or queer relationships and sexual encounters. This person is not likely to identify as bisexual.

SEE ALSO

HOMOFLEXIBLE, LESBIFLEXIBLE

"I haven't had a same-sex or queer relationship yet, but I do consider myself to be open and heteroflexible."

 WANT MORE INFO? *THINK:* **OPEN TO EXPLORING NONHETERO RELATIONSHIPS.**

 USAGE NOTE The use of this term relies on an individual's preference. Do not assume that an individual wants to be identified by this term.

HETERO-NORMATIVITY

▼ *noun*

A belief that people are given specific gendered roles within a societal binary and that these roles, along with heterosexuality, are automatically assumed as the norm.

"Even after the legal recognition, marriage equality continues to be a difficult fight. People have to understand that heteronormativity is not actually the norm. Love is love."

 WANT MORE INFO? *THINK:* **A SYSTEM OF PERVASIVE SOCIETAL NORMS ROOTED IN HETEROSEXUALITY.**

HETEROSEXUAL

▼ *adjective*

Sexually attracted to people of "the opposite sex." This term relies on the gender binary and assumes there are only two genders: male and female. This term can be abbreviated as "het," "hetty," or "hetero."

▼ *noun*

A heterosexual person.

RELATED

HETEROSEXUALITY *noun*

"My best friend is hetero, and he supports my gay ass no matter what."

 WANT MORE INFO? *THINK:* **STRAIGHT.**

HIGH FEMME

▼ *noun*
A queer person whose appearance is extremely feminine. In the Black lesbian community, the term DIVA FEMME can also be used.

> **SEE ALSO**
>
> **"The Lesbian Spectrum,"** *p. 194*

"I have to wear makeup for this photo shoot, and Lord knows I don't know how to contour or put on fake lashes. Where are my high femmes when I need them?!"

 WANT MORE INFO? *THINK:* **A SUPER-GIRLY LESBIAN.**

 USAGE NOTE This term originated in the lesbian community. It has been appropriated by the larger LGBTQIA+ community.

HIJRA

▼ *noun*
A third gender specifically identified in the country of India. A person whose identity is neither male nor female or is transitioning to another gender.

"Many hijras live in communities in north India where gender nonconforming people support one another like family."

 WANT MORE INFO? *THINK:* **INDIA'S RESPECTED KINNAR AND ARAVANI COMMUNITIES.**

HITACHI

▼ *noun*
See MAGIC WAND

HIV/AIDS

▼ *noun*
Acquired immunodeficiency syndrome (AIDS) is a spectrum of conditions caused by infection with human immunodeficiency virus (HIV). Over time, this results in the complete failure of the immune system and an inability to fight infections.

> **SEE ALSO**
>
> **A-WORD, "History Lesson: HIV/AIDS,"** *p. 160*

"Fight against AIDS by testing for HIV."

 WANT MORE INFO? *THINK:* **A GLOBAL HEALTH CARE EPIDEMIC.**

◀ **Hijra**

 DID YOU KNOW Laxmi Narayan Tripathi, a hijra and activist for minority sexualities, was instrumental in advocating in India for gender recognition beyond male and female. In April 2004, the Indian Supreme Court officially recognized transgender rights.

H

HIV/AIDS

The HIV/AIDS pandemic is one of the most serious public health challenges in modern history. America announced its first findings of HIV in June of 1981. The Centers for Disease Control and Prevention reported that five young men in Los Angeles had a rare lung infection, and within a short period of time, they had all died. The disease spread rapidly across the country and seemed to be afflicting scores of gay men in metropolitan areas.

As HIV spread, so did discrimination against the gay community. The Reagan administration delayed its response to the crisis. At one point, a proposal was made to quarantine HIV victims, but the proposal was denied. The Gay Men's Health Crisis (GMHC) was one of the first and few organizations that provided immediate assistance to gay men living with HIV/AIDS and raised funds for research. People lived in fear and a harsh stigma was placed on those living with the disease due to the lack of publicly available information about HIV/AIDS.

As medical research began to catch up, understanding that AIDS was the result of an HIV infection that could only be contracted in distinct ways, activists began a dynamic movement to change the scope and stigma of HIV/AIDS in America. Education about the disease, safe sex, and other preventative measures and treatments became widely available. HIV testing was offered in medical clinics and gay community centers. Activists and organizations like ACT UP demanded that pharmaceutical companies, medical researchers, and government officials understand the consequences of the disease and work harder to find treatment.

More than 76 million people have been infected with HIV worldwide, and the disease has taken over 35 million lives. While there is still no cure, through the efforts of activists, educators, medical research, pharmaceutical advancements, and government assistance, most people living with HIV are able to enjoy long and healthy lives. Groundbreaking antiretroviral therapy can prevent sexual HIV transmission and help preserve the health of people living with HIV.

National HIV Testing Day is celebrated annually on June 27, during Pride Month. This is a campaign to encourage people to get tested for HIV and know their status.

World AIDS Day is celebrated annually on December 1. This day is dedicated to bringing international awareness to the ongoing crisis.

HIV-NEGATIVE

▼ *adjective*
See NEG

HIV-POSTIVIE

▼ *adjective*
See POZ

HOMO

▼ *noun*
See HOMOSEXUAL

HOMOFLEXIBLE

▼ *adjective*
Describing a person who is gay or lesbian but open to experiencing relationships and sexual encounters with people of other gender expressions. This person is not likely to identify as bisexual.

SEE ALSO
HETEROFLEXIBLE, LESBIFLEXIBLE

Nate: *Dee, you were staring at her lips the whole time.*
Dee: *She was so sexy. As gay as I am, I wouldn't push her outta bed. I must be homoflexible.*

 WANT MORE INFO? *THINK:* **GAY BUT OPEN TO SEXUAL EXPERIENCES WITH PARTNERS OF A DIFFERENT SEX.**

 USAGE NOTE The use of this term to describe someone relies on that individual's preference. Do not assume that a person wants to be identified by it.

HOMONORMATIVITY

▼ *noun*
A term that addresses the problems of privilege and erasure within the LGBTQIA+ community as its members intersect with race, capitalism, sexism, transmisogyny, and cissexism.

"The queer community claims to be inclusive and intersectional, but homonormativity begs to differ. According to the media, queer people are all white, middle-class, cisgender, gay males."

 WANT MORE INFO? *THINK:* **IGNORANCE TOWARD MINORITY GROUPS WITHIN THE LGBTQIA+ COMMUNITY.**

HOMOPHOBIA

▼ *noun*
Aversion, fear, or hatred toward homosexuality and queerness.

RELATED
HOMOPHOBE *noun* **HOMOPHOBIC** *adjective*

SEE ALSO
ACEPHOBIA, BIPHOBIA, FEMMEPHOBIA, LESBO-PHOBIA, QUEERPHOBIA, TRANSPHOBIA

"Did you see that sign? 'Homos are possessed by demons.' Okay, homophobe, that's extreme."

 WANT MORE INFO? *THINK:* **DISLIKE OF OR PREJUDICE AGAINST GAY AND QUEER PEOPLE.**

HOMOROMANTIC

▼ *adjective*
Describes a person who has a romantic or emotional attraction to people of the same gender.

▼ *noun*
A homoromantic person.

"I am a woman, a pansexual, and a homoromantic. I'll have sex with men and women and enbies, whoever. But my heart only truly beats for women—cis or trans—I just love women."

 WANT MORE INFO? *THINK:* **A PERSON SEEKING SAME-GENDER LOVE.**

USAGE NOTE This term is commonly used in the asexual community.

HOMOSEXUAL

▼ *adjective*
Sexually attracted to the same sex or gender. As with HETEROSEXUAL, this term relies on the gender binary, and assumes there are only two genders: male and female. Many LGBTQIA+ people prefer using broader identifiers such as "gay" or "queer" as a means of acknowledging genders outside of the gender binary.

▼ *noun*
A homosexual person.

RELATED
HOMOSEXUALITY *noun*

"Everybody's journey is individual. If you fall in love with a boy, you fall in love with a boy. The fact that many Americans consider it a disease says more about them than it does about homosexuality."
▶ James Baldwin

 WANT MORE INFO? *THINK:* **ADAM AND STEVE OR ALLY AND EVE.**

HONEY

▼ *noun*
A term of endearment. The term HENNY can also be used.

SEE ALSO
CHILD, GIRL, HUNTY, MISS THING

"Listen, honey, always choose jewel tones, not the yellows."

 WANT MORE INFO? *THINK:* **DARLING.**

HOOKUP

▼ *noun*
A casual sexual encounter.

RELATED
HOOK UP *verb*

Skylar: *I love that we are here in Cannes together. I feel like we never get to see each other back at home, since you got your new job.*
Aidan: *Totally . . . omigod that boy is hot. Oui, oui!*
Skylar: *Aidan! This trip is about us! No hookups!*

 WANT MORE INFO? *THINK:* **A LIL SEX ADVENTURE.**

DID YOU KNOW In 2009, the gay dating app Grindr revolutionized the idea of gay and bi male hookups and lifestyle. Joel Simkhai, creator of the cruising app, provided an opportunity for queer men to instantly connect with each other. Many men have found their life partners, formed travel groups, and built a supportive queer family network using Grindr.

HORMONE REPLACEMENT THERAPY

▼ *noun*
Medical treatments where doses of hormones are administered to individuals to assist in affirming a person's gender identity. Often abbreviated as HRT. The terms CROSS-SEX HORMONE THERAPY or TRANSGENDER HORMONE THERAPY can also be used.

SEE ALSO
FEMINIZING HORMONE THERAPY, MASCULINIZING HORMONE THERAPY

"Feminizing hormone therapy and masculinizing hormone therapy are two of the most common HRTs used with transgender or nonbinary individuals."

 WANT MORE INFO? *THINK:* **ADMINISTERED DOSES OF HORMONES TO SUPPORT A PERSON'S MEDICAL TRANSITION.**

USAGE NOTE This term is commonly used in the transgender, nonbinary, and gender nonconforming communities.

HORMONES

▼ *noun*
A general reference to medications used to assist in affirming a person's gender identity.

"Hey, Asa? I started hormones this month, so, I, uh, want you to know that you'll start to notice some physical changes in me. You've been such a huge support to me, and I needed to tell someone."

 WANT MORE INFO? *THINK:* **GENERIC TERM FOR MEDS USED IN HRT.**

 USAGE NOTE This term is commonly used in the transgender, nonbinary, and gender nonconforming communities.

HOUSE CULTURE

▼ *noun*
Another name for ballroom culture, referring to the social houses that provide a safe space for LGBTQIA+ people—particularly Black and Latinx—within the ballroom community. Each house adopts a family name (usually named after a fashion label or LGBTQIA+ icon) and is typically governed by a house mother and/or father who acts as a mentor and leader. House parents foster a sense of community that becomes family for queer and trans people who may have been rejected by their biological family due to their gender or sexuality.

SEE ALSO

BALL, BALLROOM SCENE/ CULTURE, CHOSEN FAMILY, "History Lesson: The Ballroom Scene," *p. 232*

"You know what a house is? I'll tell you what a house is. A house is a gay street gang. Now, where street gangs get their rewards from street fights, a gay house street fights at a ball. And you street fight at a ball by walking in the categories."
▶ Pepper LaBeija

 WANT MORE INFO? *THINK:* **MULTIGENERATIONAL CHOSEN FAMILY FOR GAY, QUEER, AND TRANS PEOPLE.**

HOUSE FATHER

▼ *noun*
In ballroom culture, this is a social patriarch of a particular house. This leader (of any gender) maintains the image of the house and presides over its members. The term FATHER OF THE HOUSE can also be used.

"My house father made me the man I am today." ▶ Sydney Baloue

 WANT MORE INFO? *THINK:* **PATRIARCH OF A CHOSEN FAMILY.**

DID YOU KNOW Legendary house father Larry Ebony founded the House of Ebony in 1978 to support Black gay youth abandoned by their biological families. The house was noted for their three-story Brooklyn brownstone that many said housed up to fifty children at a time. House Father Larry Ebony believed, "You always had our ballroom family, your house."

H

HOUSE MOTHER

▼ *noun*

In ballroom culture, this is the social matriarch of a particular house. This leader (of any gender) maintains the image of the house and presides over its members. She is usually an iconic member of the ballroom scene. The term MOTHER OF THE HOUSE can also be used.

"After walking for years and destroying every category, they finally announced her as the house mother."

 WANT MORE INFO? *THINK:* **MATRIARCH OF A CHOSEN FAMILY.**

DID YOU KNOW Legendary mother Crystal LaBeija, a prominent Latinx drag queen, founded the House of LaBeija in New York City in 1977. House of LaBeija is noted for pioneering house culture for the drag community and today Crystal LaBeija and her successor Pepper LaBeijia are considered some of the most iconic mothers in ballroom culture history.

HOUSE SYSTEM

▼ *noun*
See BALLROOM CULTURE

House mother ▲

HOW BAD ARE YOU?

▼ *idiom*
A phrase used to challenge one's opponent.

Kevin Aviance: *Your little dip at the end was cute. But it don't hold a candle to my duckwalk.*
Willie Esperanza: *Oh, really? You think you're it? How bad are you?!*

 WANT MORE INFO? *THINK:* **"BAD" BY MICHAEL JACKSON.**

 USAGE NOTE This term is commonly used in ballroom culture.

HPV

▼ *noun*
Human papillomavirus, a sexually transmitted infection. Depending on the strain, HPV may cause warts and, if left untreated, can lead to cervical cancer.

"HPV is one of the most common STDs that affect today's youth. There may be a chance, if you are sexually active, that you have been exposed to one or more strains. Definitely consult with your doctor."

 WANT MORE INFO? *THINK:* **THE MOST COMMON STD— MOST OF THE TIME IT ISN'T A BIG DEAL, BUT IT'S IMPORTANT TO GET IT CHECKED OUT.**

HRT

▼ *noun*
See HORMONE REPLACEMENT THERAPY

HUNDRED-FOOTER

▼ *noun*
A lesbian who is easy to spot from one hundred feet away, based on stereotypically butch physicality, behavior, and demeanor.

"I don't need binoculars to see that's a hundred-footer right there. Her hair is shorter than my brother's fade, and judging from those cargo shorts, I guarantee she's never seen a tube of lipstick in her life."

 WANT MORE INFO? *THINK:* **WHEN YOU CAN TELL SHE'S A DYKE FROM ACROSS A CROWDED ROOM.**

 USAGE NOTE This term originated in the lesbian community.

HUNG

▼ *adjective*
See ENDOWED

HUNTY

▼ *noun*
A portmanteau of honey and cunt/cunty. Used to simultaneously confront and compliment someone at the same time.

"Hunty, I know you are super-talented, but that high C is way out of your alto range."

 WANT MORE INFO? *THINK:* **"I LOVE YOU, BUT I'VE GOTTA CHECK YOU."**

▼ *exclamation*
An exclamation used to alert the disclosure of salacious information.

"HUN (clap) TY (clap)! You are not going to believe this!"

 WANT MORE INFO? *THINK:* **A SALUTATION BEFORE SPILLING THE T.**

 USAGE NOTE This term originated in the Black gay community and is commonly used in the larger queer and trans people of color (QTPOC) community. It has been appropriated by the larger LGBTQIA+ community and mainstream culture.

H

HYFEE

▼ *adjective*
Acting in a snooty manner.

"You're acting hyfee today. Your nose is up so high the sun might burn it off."

 WANT MORE INFO? *THINK:* **HIGHFALUTIN.**

HYPERFEMINIZATION

▼ *noun*
Exaggeration of femininity, typically characterized by sex appeal, sexual objectification, and sexual passiveness.

RELATED
HYPERFEMINIZE *verb*

SEE ALSO
HYPERSEXUALIZATION

"Hyperfeminization is so evident in professional sports. Female volleyball players wear bikinis and tennis players wear short skirts, while male athletes wear uniforms with much more coverage."

 WANT MORE INFO? *THINK:* **MARILYN MONROE, NICKI MINAJ, THE VICTORIA'S SECRET FASHION SHOW— YOU KNOW, TITTIES UP, ASS OUT.**

HYPER-MASCULINIZATION

▼ *noun*
Exaggeration of masculinity, typically characterized by physical strength, machismo, and sexual dominance.

RELATED
HYPERMASCULINIZE *verb*

SEE ALSO
HYPERSEXUALIZATION, TOXIC MASCULINITY

"Society chastises boys for crying, then turns around and is dissatisfied when they are detached from their emotions. To be honest, hypermasculinization is crippling."

 WANT MORE INFO? *THINK:* **ANGRY WWE DUDES.**

HYPERSEXUALIZATION

▼ *noun*
The act of making something extremely sexual in nature; linked to sexual objectification.

RELATED
HYPERSEXUALIZE *verb*

"So many people think all gay men do is have sex all day every day. Trans femmes are often fetishized— Black gays, too. And straight dudes are always asking lesbians if they can 'watch.' What the hell, people? Can we chill with the hypersexualization of gays?!"

 WANT MORE INFO? *THINK:* **THE REINFORCING OF SEXUAL STEREOTYPES.**

HISTORY LESSON

LGBTQIA+ YOUTH

Homelessness

Homelessness is a harsh reality for many LGBTQIA+ youth in the United States. Several hundred thousand queer youth face the hardship of homelessness each year.

Many young LGBTQIA+ people leave their homes with nowhere to turn due to family rejection or abuse because of their gender expression or sexual orientation. Some queer youth age out of foster systems and are unable to find proper housing. Transgender kids experience difficulty and are often denied admission into shelters that do not support their gender identity. During the 2020 COVID-19 pandemic, these young people encountered many obstacles that kept them from receiving the aid and care they needed.

The many challenges faced by homeless youth are extensive, but there are supportive housing agencies across the country that are passionate about protecting the young minds, bodies, and hearts of our future like Covenant House, Ali Forney Center, The Ruth Ellis Center, New Alternatives, Thrive Youth Center, Homeless Youth Alliance, the National Coalition for the Homeless, and many LGBT centers. These organizations and the activists and donors who support them understand the specific challenges endured when facing homelessness at a young age, giving our youth the safety, housing, financial, and emotional support needed to thrive.

I'm in charge of the girls ▲

Ii

I CAN'T OR I CAN NOT

▼ *idiom*
A phrase commonly used as a response of disbelief, disapproval, or annoyance. The phrase "I can't deal" can also be used.

"All these bugs flying around! I hate camping. I can't!"

 WANT MORE INFO? *THINK:* **ABSOLUTELY OVER IT.**

ICE CREAM

▼ *noun*
A person who exhibits the qualities of being sweet and desirable.

"People just released the 'Sexiest Man Alive' issue! I scream, you scream, we all scream for ice cream."

 WANT MORE INFO? *THINK:* **SOMEONE SO DELICIOUS.**

Ice cream ▲

ICON

▼ *noun*

A highly respected and influential individual who is deemed worthy of praise and reverence.

RELATED
ICONIC *adjective*

SEE ALSO
BICON, DYKON

"Sally Ride, Frank Kameny, Christine Jorgensen, and Sylvester are LGBTQIA+ icons who have stood the test of time."

 WANT MORE INFO? *THINK:* **A DEITY OF SORTS, A GODDESS, A SUPERSTAR.**

In ballroom culture, this is usually a person who has over twenty years of ballroom experience and has won numerous ball competitions; an icon is one step above a legend.

SEE ALSO
LEGENDARY

"This is a bitch that has slayed. Yolanda, my daughter, where are you, girl? The icon!" ▶ Sinia Ebony

 WANT MORE INFO? *THINK:* **ANGIE XTRAVAGANZA, DORIAN COREY, AVIS PENDAVIS, AND PEPPER LABEIJA.**

IDENTITY

▼ *noun*

The characteristics that define who or what a person is; a person's character, personality, individuality, self-expression, and core being.

SEE ALSO
GENDER IDENTITY

"Racial identity: Human. Gender identity: Nonbinary. Sexual identity: Love the world."

 WANT MORE INFO? *THINK:* **WHO YOU ARE, WHAT YOU STAND FOR, WHAT YOU'RE MADE OF.**

IDENTITY POLITICS

▼ *noun*
The tendency for people of similar backgrounds/identities to form politically focused groups, with the goal of pushing a particular agenda forward.

"We rely on identity politics because in today's world, the LGBTQIA+ community is still fighting for acceptance, understanding, equality, and respect."

 WANT MORE INFO? *THINK:* **POLITICAL ACTION ROOTED IN IDENTITY LIKE MARRIAGE EQUALITY, BLACK LIVES MATTER, AND #METOO.**

I DON'T HAVE YOU UP

▼ *idiom*
A phrase used to indicate something is unclear and could possibly be dismissed.

"I don't have you up. You're speaking nonsense."

 WANT MORE INFO? *THINK:* **"I DON'T GET WHAT YOU ARE SAYING, AND I HAVE LITTLE PATIENCE."**

 This term is commonly used in the Black gay and queer community.

I DON'T SEE YOU OR I DON'T SEE HER

▼ *idiom*
A phrase used to intentionally disregard a person, place, or thing.

"Not answering my call, huh? Well, two can play this game. You're now invisible, dust. I don't see you!"

 WANT MORE INFO? *THINK:* **"I'M IGNORING YOU."**

 This term is commonly used in ballroom culture and the larger queer and trans people of color (QTPOC) community.

I'M IN CHARGE OF THE GIRLS

▼ *idiom*
In ballroom culture, this phrase is used by a competitor at the top of the game to indicate their status. It may also turn into a competitive group chant initiated by the commentator at a ball competition.

"Who's in charge of the girls?! I'm in charge of the girls!"

 WANT MORE INFO? *THINK:* **"I'M THE BOSS."**

I'M INTO IT

▼ *idiom*
An expression indicating intrigue and support.

Cheryl: *I'm thinking about hosting a QWOC retreat next month. What you think?*
Ashanti: *I'm into it! Actually, I'm all the way into it. Girl, you know we need this. I can help with conversation topics and meditations.*

 WANT MORE INFO? *THINK:* "I LIKE THAT IDEA."

 This term is commonly used in the Black gay community and the larger queer and trans people of color (QTPOC) community.

I'M SLEEP

▼ *idiom*
A deliberate dismissal; uninterested. The phrase "I'm sleep though" can also be used.

Desiree: *Did you like the dress she wore at the Oscars?*
Jeroboam: *Child, I'm sleep.*

 WANT MORE INFO? *THINK:* AN INDICATION OF BOREDOM.

 This term originated in Black American culture and is commonly used in the Black gay and queer community.

INTERSECTIONALITY

▼ *noun*
The complex way in which varied forms of discrimination overlap or intersect; the importance of focusing on the presence of all marginalized communities within the larger framework of society.

RELATED

INTERSECTIONAL *adjective*

"[Kimberlé] Crenshaw introduced the theory of intersectionality, the idea that when it comes to thinking about how inequalities persist, categories like gender, race, and class are best understood as overlapping and mutually constitutive rather than isolated and distinct." ► Adia Harvey Wingfield

INTERSEX

▼ *adjective*
Born with variations on sex characteristics that would traditionally assign a child male or female. Variations may involve genital ambiguity and/or combinations of the chromosomal genotype and sexual phenotypes other than XY-male and XX-female.

SEE ALSO

COERCIVE SURGICAL GENDER REASSIGNMENT, GENDER NONCONFORMING, "The Genderbread Person," p. 56

YOU

ETHNICITY

GENDER

1ˢᵗ LANGUAGE

SOCIO-ECO CLASS

NATIONALITY

RELIGION

RACE

AGE

SEXUALITY

ABILITY

WANT MORE INFO? *THINK:* **LOOKING AT EQUALITY WITH EVERYONE'S UNIQUE EXPERIENCES IN MIND.**

I

"Being intersex is a naturally occurring variation of being human; it isn't a medical problem. Just because I may appear female on the outside but have male-typical anatomy on the inside doesn't mean I'm abnormal."

 WANT MORE INFO? *THINK:* **NOT AMAB OR AFAB BUT BORN WITH WHAT DOCTORS CONSIDER "ATYPICAL" SEX CHARACTERISTICS (E.G., A GIRL BORN WITH A LARGE CLITORIS OR A BOY BORN WITH A DIVIDED SCROTUM THAT LOOKS LIKE A LABIA).**

DID YOU KNOW Many intersex children are given coercive surgery to firmly place them in a traditionally male or female body. Some parents and doctors think that existing in a body that does not fit into the gender binary is too difficult for a child, so they have to "choose" one sex or the other. Because of intersex activists like Hanne Gaby Odiele, Pidgeon Pagonis, and many others, the cultural conversation around gender is evolving, giving voice to the intersex experience and making positive change in the medical treatment of intersex people. In 2018, the state of Colorado was the first to issue an intersex birth certificate.

In the Life ▼

IN THE LIFE

▼ *idiom*
Involved in or part of the LGBTQIA+ community.

SEE ALSO
"History Lesson: The Harlem Renaissance," *p. 202*

"Back in the day, Studio 54 was a place to be in the life."

 WANT MORE INFO? *THINK:* **IMMERSED IN QUEER CULTURE.**

DID YOU KNOW This term is a century old, with historical roots tracing back to the Black gay slang used in Harlem, New York, during the early 1920s. It is still used in the Black gay community and has since been appropriated by the LGBTQIA+ community and mainstream culture.

INVISIBILITY

▼ *noun*
The cultural dismissal of a particular identity or group of people due to a lack of understanding, acceptance, or representation.

SEE ALSO
ERASURE

Camila: *A gay man told me that I was too pretty to be a dyke.*
Fabi: *I get dirty looks at lesbian bars all the time. They think I'm a straight girl infringing on their gay territory or something.*
Denzel: *Well, everyone tells me I have to be gay or straight—I can't be bisexual?! Why does being bisexual or straight-passing make us invisible to the rest of the gay community?*

 WANT MORE INFO? *THINK:* **IGNORING PEOPLE WHO DON'T FIT NEATLY INTO BOXES.**

-IQUE

▼ *suffix*
A suffix used to make something extravagant and/or extra.

Billy: *Merritt was angelic at the Hendersons' house last night. I'm so proud of our baby boy.*
Maurice: *I think you mean* angel-ique. *He runs this fam and he knows it!*

 WANT MORE INFO? *THINK:* **QUEERING AN ADJECTIVE BY MAKING IT FANCY AND CHIQUE!**

IRON CLOSET

▼ *noun*
The superlative form of "closet"—refers to an individual who is extremely uncomfortable with being gay, bisexual, transgender, intersex, or otherwise queer, so much so that the individual is reluctant to publicly display any signs of their queer identity.

SEE ALSO
CLOSET, COME OUT, DISCREET, OUT, "Coming Out 101," *p. 26*

"So many of us have difficulty admitting we are gay. I'm glad that I finally came out and wasn't in the iron closet like other people I know. I see how they are unhappy and struggling with who they are."

 WANT MORE INFO? *THINK:* **THE CLOSET, BUT WITH A PADLOCK AND NO KEY.**

I SEE YOU

▼ *idiom*
A compliment given to someone, or a term that acknowledges someone's accomplishment.

"Yaasss! I see you! Congratulations on the new promotion and the new house."

 WANT MORE INFO? *THINK:* **A WHOLEHEARTED AFFIRMATION.**

 USAGE NOTE This term is commonly used in the Black gay community and the larger queer and trans people of color (QTPOC) community.

I WON'T

▼ *idiom*
An expressive, dramatic way to say no.

SEE ALSO
I CAN'T

"How many times do I have to say it? How many ways do I have to show it? I can't and I won't. And that is final."

 WANT MORE INFO? *THINK:* **"ABSOLUTELY NOT."**

Jock ▲

Jj

JACKIE

▼ *noun*

A person who seems deceptive or pretentious.

"Girl, don't trust that Jackie. She has been caught stealing!"

 WANT MORE INFO? *THINK:* AN UNTRUSTWORTHY PERSON.

JEWELS

▼ *noun*

A word to reference the penis and testicles. The term "family jewels" can also be used.

"I keep having daydreams of bananas and jewels."

 WANT MORE INFO? *THINK:* THE TWIG AND BERRIES.

JOCK

▼ *noun*

A label for a gay, bisexual, or queer man who has an athletic body type.

> **SEE ALSO**
>
> **"Help! What's My Gay Type?,"** *p. 152*

"There is nothing like a jock in a muscle tank at the Muscle Beach Party."

 WANT MORE INFO? *THINK:* ABS AND BICEPS LIKE WENTWORTH MILLER OR MATT BOMER.

A slang term for "jockstrap," an undergarment commonly worn by gay men.

 WANT MORE INFO? *THINK:* ESSENTIAL PART OF THE GAY UNIFORM TO MAKE YOUR ASS LOOK FAB.

J

J-SETTING

▼ *noun*
A style of dance that uses highly energized, rhythmic movement and structured group formations. The dancers are often in a V-shape formation, with a leader initiating movement. The phrase "eight count girls" can also be used.

"J-Setting Troupes roll call! Let me hear you, let me see you 'Salt and Pepper' and 'Strut'!"

 WANT MORE INFO? *THINK:* **AN HBCU MARCHING BAND.**

USAGE NOTE This term originated in Black American culture and is commonly used in the Black gay and queer community.

DID YOU KNOW J-Setting dates back to the 1970s with the Prancing J-Settes, an all-female dance team from Jackson State University. Gay male dancers from several Historically Black Colleges and Universities (HBCUs) adopted the style, creating competitive dance groups and bringing the dance to nightclubs, particularly in southern states like Mississippi, Georgia, Texas, and Louisiana.

JUDY

▼ *noun*
In the gay community, this term is used to acknowledge a good friend; usually refers to a gay man. The phrases "good Judy" or "my Judy" can also be used.

SEE ALSOW
FRIEND OF DOROTHY, MARY

"Headed out with my Judy. Thursday is movie night!"

 WANT MORE INFO? *THINK:* **BESTIES.**

USAGE NOTE This term originated in the gay male community.

DID YOU KNOW Actress Judy Garland has been a gay icon since her rise to fame in the 1930s. Some scholars have even called her the quintessential gay icon. Garland died on June 22, 1969, just six days before the Stonewall riots. In the years following her death, Judy's elder daughter, Liza Minnelli, followed in her footsteps, becoming a gay icon herself.

JUGS

▼ *noun*
See BOOBS

JUST BE YOURSELF

Inclusivity in the LGBTQIA+ Community

Society has been conditioned to understand gender and sexuality in a binary way. Male and female, masculine and feminine, heterosexual and homosexual, cisgender and transgender—it's all very black and white. However, binaries are limiting and are an unrealistic representation of human expression. Gender and sexuality are vast and extend beyond binary boundaries. The LGBTQIA+ community represents the dynamic idea that our gender, sexuality, and outward expression are layered and complex. Take a look below and consider the layers of your own identity.

BIPOC	European	Gay	Aromantic
QPOC	American	Lesbian	Femme
QTPOC	Immigrant	Dyke	Butch
QWOC	First-generation	Fag	Masc
WOC	Second-generation	Homo	Futch
MOC	Disabled	Hetero	Monogamous
POC	Able-bodied	Flexible	Non-monogamous
Blaqueer	Genderqueer	Fluid	Polyamorous
Gaysian	No label	Flux	Kinkster
Asian	Null gender	Straight	Dominant
Asian and Pacific Islander	Agender	Asexual	Submissive
Latinx	Gender nonconforming	Bisexual	Mommi
Latina	Nonbinary	Pansexual	Daddy
Latino	Transgender	Polysexual	
African	Trans man	Homosexual	
Hispanic	Transmasculine	Heterosexual	
Jewish	Trans woman	Homoromantic	
White	Transfeminine	Heteroromantic	
Black	Man	Biromantic	
Native American	Woman	Panromantic	
Indigenous	Androgynous	Polyromantic	

WHO ARE YOU?

The kids ▲

Kk

KAI KAI

▼ *noun*
The act of sex between two drag queens.

The act of sex between two gay men.

"Lady Lust and Sherri Pop have been flirting all night. There might be a kai kai party tonight."

 WANT MORE INFO? *THINK*: NAUGHTY NIGHT OF SEXUAL FUN WITH TWO DRAG QUEENS.

USAGE NOTE This term originated in the drag community.

KIDS, THE

▼ *noun*
The Black and Latinx gay and trans community, particularly the youth and young adults.

The young queer community.

SEE ALSO
THE CHILDREN

"The kids are everywhere! I love DC Pride Weekend!"

 WANT MORE INFO? *THINK*: "YOUNG AND BLACK AND FINE AND GAY."

 USAGE NOTE This term originated in ballroom culture. It has been appropriated by the larger LGBTQIA+ community and mainstream culture.

KIKI

▼ *noun*

A social gathering of like-minded friends. A kiki is marked by intimate, fun-filled conversations and hot gossip.

An onomatopoeia for the sound of laughter.

"We had a good kiki last night laughing about our trip last year to Vegas!"

 WANT MORE INFO? *THINK:* **"LET'S HAVE A KIKI" BY SCISSOR SISTERS.**

 This term originated in ballroom culture. It has been appropriated by the larger LGBTQIA+ community and mainstream culture.

▼ *adjective*

A dated term for a queer woman who does not identify as butch or femme, nor does she have a preference for a butch or femme partner. This term was considered derogatory when it originated in the 1940s because "kiki girls" did not fit into the butch/femme binary and were often mocked by others. Can also be seen as "ki ki."

"Hilary is a kiki girl. She's cool with dating any type of woman."

 WANT MORE INFO? *THINK:* **LESBIAN WHO DOESN'T DISCRIMINATE BASED ON THE BUTCH/FEMME SPECTRUM.**

 This term originated in the lesbian community.

KIKI SCENE

▼ *noun*

In ballroom culture, this is a subcommunity for young queer and trans people of color (QTPOC) competitors, with ages ranging from 12 to 24. The kiki scene mirrors the mainstream ballroom scene in many ways and has similar structure, including kiki houses, kiki ball competitions, and freedom to explore and express identity and sexuality.

"The kiki scene is a space for youth development, where everyone's unique. And the kiki scene is a place for everyone to explore that uniqueness." ▶ Gia Marie Love

 WANT MORE INFO? *THINK:* **KIKI, THE DOCUMENTARY FEATURING TWIGGY GARÇON.**

DID YOU KNOW The kiki scene emerged in New York City in the early 2000s, providing young QTPOC with an outlet to deal with the challenges of homelessness, disease, and lack of acceptance. Young competitors would often be found practicing their routines inside local LGBTQIA+ wellness centers because they were safe spaces to hang out. Eventually, the centers began to sponsor the kiki community, hosting competitions and raising money for their balls.

K

KINK

▼ *noun*
An unconventional sexual activity or behavior that may include fetishes and other erotic activity.

SEE ALSO
BDSM, FETISH

"Being peed on is a kink. It's called a 'golden shower.'"

 WANT MORE INFO? *THINK:* **DIRTY TALK, BONDAGE, BACK-DOOR PLAY, WHATEVER TURNS YOUR MIND ON SEXUALLY.**

A particularly strong and stimulating preference.

"You know I'm all about these bath bombs and putting orange slices in my bathwater. That self-care shit is my kink."

 WANT MORE INFO? *THINK:* **SOMETHING THAT TURNS YOU ON (IN ANY WAY).**

DID YOU KNOW Kink and erotic sex trace back to the ancient civilizations of Egypt, Greece, and Rome where cultural art depicts sexual acts of whipping, hair-pulling, and bondage.

K

KINKSTER

▼ *noun*
A kinky person.

A person who practices a lifestyle involving BDSM or other related fetish and kink play.

"Kinksters are sex-positive people seeking endorphins, fetishes, and fun."

 WANT MORE INFO? *THINK:* **AN ENTHUSIAST OF UNCONVENTIONAL SEXUAL PLAY.**

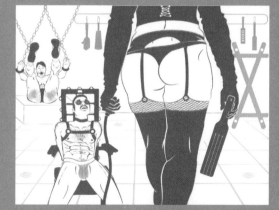

KWEEN OR KWANE

▼ *noun*
See QUEEN

CHILDREN MUST
READ!
BUT I DON'T HAVE TO TELL YOU
(BECAUSE YOU KNOW YOU'RE UGLY)
READING IS FUNDAMENTAL
I'MA READ I'MA READ I'MA READ I'MA READ
DON'T DO IT, BITCH
UGLY CONVERSATIONS WITH PEOPLE
IF YOU HAVE
NOTHING NICE TO SAY,
COME THROW SHADE WITH ME
BEAUTY MAY BE
SKIN DEEP,
BUT UGLY GOES
DOWN TO THE BONE

Ll

LABEL

▼ *noun*
An individual's gender, sexuality, appearance, and/or other expression.

"Labels are very personal. People can share the same label but interpret it differently. There is no right or wrong expression of a label."

 WANT MORE INFO? *THINK:* **A PERSON'S UNIQUE IDENTITY AND ATTRACTION LAYERS.**

LADY

▼ *noun*
A person (regardless of gender) who is mannerly and poised.

"Billy was way too trashy for me, honey. I am a lady." ▶ Lady Chablis

 WANT MORE INFO? *THINK:* **A PRIM AND PROPER FEMME.**

LAID OR LAYED

▼ *adjective*
Looking exceptionally stylish.

SEE ALSO
DONE

"I inspected her whole head and saw no bumps, no lace. That wig is laid, girl!"

 WANT MORE INFO? *THINK:* **LOOKING SO FRESH AND SO CLEAN.**

USAGE NOTE This term originated in Black American culture and is commonly used in the Black gay and trans community. It has been appropriated by the larger LGBTQIA+ community.

LALA

▼ *adjective*
See LESBIAN

LANCING

▼ *verb*
Sexual intercourse where a transgender woman penetrates a partner.

"Daddy likes lancing."

 WANT MORE INFO? *THINK:* **PENETRATION OF A MAN FROM A TRANSFEMININE TOP.**

 The term has negative connotations for many queer, nonbinary, and transgender people and may be considered offensive or derogatory.

LATE

▼ *adjective*
Not up-to-date on the current trends, events, or fashions.

"You are still wearing last year's Jordans? Ugh, late."

 WANT MORE INFO? *THINK:* **LIVING UNDER A ROCK.**

 This term is commonly used in the Black gay community and the larger queer and trans people of color (QTPOC) community.

LATINX

▼ *adjective*
A gender-neutral, inclusive alternative to Latino or Latina, identifying people of Latin American descent.

Mr. Gonzalez: *What is this here? Creo que escribió la palabra Latino incorrectamente en su document. (I think you spelled the word Latino wrong in your document.)*
Mateo: *No, deber de ser Latinx. (No, it should be Latinx.) Changing the o or a to x makes it more inclusive to all gender expressions. Inclusión es importante. (Inclusion is important.)*

 WANT MORE INFO? *THINK:* **AN EMPOWERING TERM FOR ALL PEOPLE OF LATIN AMERICAN DESCENT.**

 Pronounced \luh-TEE-neks\, this term originated in Latin American culture and has been adopted by mainstream culture.

L

The Queens' English

L

DID YOU KNOW There have been many Latinx queer icons who have made substantial changes in both the Latinx and LGBTQIA+ communities. Venezuelan and Puerto Rican trans woman Sylvia Rivera is known as the "Mother of the Movement" for her leadership in the Stonewall Riots; Colombian-American José Julio Sarria, founder of the charitable Imperial Court System, was the first openly gay American to run for office; Dennis deLeon, a former New York City human rights commissioner and president of the Latino Commission on AIDS, was one of the first officials to disclose his HIV status in 1993 and worked tirelessly to support gay equality in his community.

LAVENDER

▼ *noun*
A pale purple color often used to represent the LGBTQIA+ community.

Steven: *Come to think of it, I did go through a lavender phase in middle school.*
Jesse: *And you dressed up in your sister's witch costumes, too. The signs were all there—you were such a baby gay!*

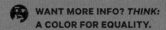 **WANT MORE INFO?** *THINK:* **A COLOR FOR EQUALITY.**

DID YOU KNOW In the 1950s, around the same time as the anticommunist movement known as McCarthyism, a series of mass firings of gay and lesbian government officials occurred, known as the Lavender Scare, claiming queer employees were both security risks and communist sympathizers. The color has since been reclaimed by the lesbian radical feminist group Lavender Menace and the larger LGBTQIA+ community.

LAVENDER LINGUISTICS

▼ *noun*
The study of jargon, expressions, and colloquial language used within the LGBTQIA+ community.

"Lavender linguistics celebrates our language, our vernacular, our story!"

 WANT MORE INFO? *THINK:* **QUEER LANGUAGE AND ETYMOLOGY.**

LAVENDER MARRIAGE

▼ *noun*
A marriage between a man and a woman used to conceal the sexual orientation of one or both partners.

"The most famous lavender marriage I know is Rock Hudson and his wife, Phyllis Gates."

 WANT MORE INFO? *THINK:* **CLOSETED MARRIED COUPLE.**

DID YOU KNOW Lavender marriages were popular in Old Hollywood because of an indecency code enforced by the Motion Picture Association of America between the 1930s and 1960s. The Hays Code prohibited "sex perversion" (read: homosexuality) on film; the MPAA censored all studios' scripts and put "morals clauses" into many actors' and directors' contracts. Big names like Marlene Dietrich, Randolph Scott, and Barbara Stanwyck were pushed to participate in publicized lavender marriages.

L

LAWD

▼ *idiom*
A nonreligious and nonblasphemous spelling of the word "Lord."

SEE ALSO
GAWD

"Lawd, no! She did not just say that!"

 WANT MORE INFO? *THINK:* "OH MY GOD!"

 USAGE NOTE This term originated in Black American culture and is used in the Black gay and queer community. It has been appropriated by mainstream culture.

LEATHER COMMUNITY

▼ *noun*
A community dedicated to a particular lifestyle denoted by leather garments and unorthodox sexual expression. Traditional themes seen within the community are hypermasculinity, sexual power and kink, BDSM, motorcycles, and leather fetishism; however, the community's evolution has embraced elements of family, safety, and empowering femininity.

RELATED
LEATHER *adjective*

SEE ALSO
FETISH, KINK, LEATHER DADDY

"There are two popular schools within the leather community: Old Guard and New Guard. Old Guard is regimented, based on militaristic traditions, and prioritizes leather in one's uniform. New Guard is more flexible in power dynamics and uses various textiles in addition to leather, like latex, neoprene, and rubber."

 WANT MORE INFO? *THINK:* **LEATHER FOLKS UNITED BY IDENTITY, RELATIONSHIP STRUCTURE, AND SEXUAL EXPRESSION.**

DID YOU KNOW The leather community in the United States originated in the 1940s and '50s as an extension of post–World War II biker culture. Thousands of gay servicemen were given blue discharges, and they began to build leather and biker communities in port cities like San Francisco and New York City. Leather bars and motorcycle clubs also began to pop up in major U.S. cities, patronized by a subcommunity of gay men who were unhappy with the mainstream gay culture of the time period. Motorcycle clubs would host weekend-long social events for their members, culminating in a dinner that would start with the Pledge of Allegiance to honor the military and veterans who fought for the safety and rights of the United States.

L

LEATHER DADDY

▼ *noun*

A man who practices the leather lifestyle and identifies as a Daddy.

SEE ALSO

DADDY DOM, LEATHER COMMUNITY, SIR

"We're headed to the Windy City for International Mr. Leather, home of the best leather Daddies in the country."

 WANT MORE INFO? *THINK*: A SEXY DOMINATOR IN LEATHER CHAPS.

USAGE NOTE This term originated in the BDSM, leather, and kink communities. For all BDSM-related terms, the power exchange is a part of sadomasochistic play and should be consensual between all partners involved. The *L* in Leather and *D* in Daddy should always be capitalized when referring to D/s, or power dynamic, relationships.

DID YOU KNOW The first American leather bar, the Gold Coast, was established in Chicago, Illinois, in 1958, making the city one of the pioneers of leather culture. In 1964, the leather community gained widespread recognition when *Life* magazine published an article called "Homosexuality in America," and mentioned San Francisco's gay and leather scene. This was one of the first mainstream publications to acknowledge gay culture. Since then, Folsom Street has been the center of San Francisco's male leather community and the annual Folsom Street Fair is one of the largest BDSM and leather events in the world, celebrating leather counterculture for over thirty years.

Lesbians ▲

LEGENDARY

▼ *adjective*
Honored and remembered for displaying the highest degree of fierceness.

In ballroom culture, this describes a person who has had five to ten years of ballroom experience and has won countless competitions.

RELATED
LEGEND *noun*

SEE ALSO
ICON

"Rick is legendary in the ballroom scene. He shows the girls exactly how to destroy the runway, winning the Legends Ball year after year. He's soft, he's pussy, he's cunt!"

 WANT MORE INFO? *THINK:* **RENOWNED FIERCENESS.**

LESBIAN

▼ *adjective*
As a woman, having a sexual and emotional attraction toward other women. The term LALA—which comes from the non-derogatory Chinese slang term 拉拉—may also be used.

▼ *noun*
A lesbian woman. Often abbreviated as LESBO, LEZ, or LEZZIE.

RELATED
LESBIANISM *noun*

SEE ALSO
"The Lesbian Spectrum," *p. 194*

"Falling in love with a lesbian was the best thing that ever happened to me."

 WANT MORE INFO? *THINK:* **DYKE, MUFF DIVER, RUG MUNCHER, SAPPHIC SISTER.**

DID YOU KNOW The word "lesbian" is derived from the Greek island of Lesbos, where the poet Sappho lived in the fifth century BCE. Much of her poetry focused on her admiration of and romances with women.

L

FEMME

HIGH FEMME

DIVA FEMME

LIPSTICK
LESBIAN

HARD FEMME

SOFT/LOW
FEMME

CHAPSTICK
LESBIAN

TOMBOY

STEMME

FUTCH

BOI

SOFT
BUTCH

AG

DYKE

SOFT STUD

BUTCH

STUD

STONE
BUTCH

BULL DYKE

BUTCH

THE *Lesbian* SPECTRUM

As early as the 1940s, when women were first
allowed to go out to bars without the company
of men, lesbian women began to establish their
own community, finding visibility and acceptance
in speakeasies and dive bars. Some queer women
preferred stereotypically feminine garb, while
others dressed in starched shirts and trousers;
thus, the butch/femme binary was born. Over time,
the binary evolved into myriad identities along
the butch/femme spectrum. While some of the
commonly used identifiers are shown at left, there
are countless ways for queer women to express
their identity.

FYI

Like a lot of language in *The Queens'
English*, the interpretations of the
Lesbian Trivia quiz at right can be
totally fluid. Have fun rearranging the
label order! That's the best part!

L

Lesbian Trivia

Please fill in the blanks using the words from the word bank. Good luck! If you get 100% on this extremely accurate and all-encompassing quiz, you can present yourself with a "DIP ME IN HONEY AND THROW ME TO THE LESBIANS" button!

_____ is a total stereotype and very far from the truth! (Just kidding, it's all true.)

Alice Walker created a historic romance between Celie and Shug Avery in *The Color* _____ .

Every lesbian has been a _____ at least once.

Lesbians love playing with a cute _____ and a sweet _____ .

Lesbians are both _____ and _____ .

Lesbian Visibility Day is celebrated on _____ every year.

We voted _____ our lesbian she-ro when she came out on TV in 1997.

Our kids tell us all the time that having two _____ rocks!

Lesbians don't hate _____ ! We ♥ you. We just don't want to sleep with you and resent those of you who struggle with _____ .

Cheers to _____ and _____ *Is the New Black* for representing our diverse community of incredible lesbians!

APRIL 26	HANDSOME	PURPLE	ORANGE	MOMS	MEN
U-HAULING	THE L WORD	ELLEN	BEAUTIFUL	VEGETARIAN	
CAT	TOXIC MASCULINITY	PUSSY			

LESBIAN BED DEATH

▼ *noun*
The decrease in sexual activity experienced over time in a committed relationship between two queer women.

"Are all lesbians doomed to lesbian bed death? McKenzie and Leona hit their five-year mark, and Leona said her vagina has turned into a giant spiderweb."

 WANT MORE INFO? *THINK*: THE LONGER-YOU-ARE-TOGETHER-THE-LESS-SEX-YOU-WILL-HAVE SYNDROME.

 This term may be considered a stereotype.

LESBIAN DAD

▼ *noun*
In a lesbian relationship with the presence of children, this is the partner who establishes the parental role that most closely resembles the social and heteronormative stereotypes of a father.

"I am absolutely Brett and Connor's lesbian dad. I feel like I can't really embrace parenthood if I have to be a conventionally feminine mother. I offer my boys balance and love in a different way—ya know?"

 WANT MORE INFO? *THINK*: LESBIAN PARENT WHO IDENTIFIES WITH THE TRADITIONAL ROLE OF A FATHER.

LESBIAN SEPARATIST

▼ *noun*
A lesbian woman who chooses not to associate with males.

SEE ALSO
SEPARATISM, TERF

"There is a lesbian separatist community in Alabama. It is a male-free world!"

 WANT MORE INFO? *THINK*: WOMYN WHO WON'T EVEN BRING THEIR YOUNG SONS TO ALL-FEMALE MUSIC FESTIVALS.

LESBIFLEXIBLE

▼ *adjective*
Describing a woman who identifies as predominantly lesbian but is open to relationships and sexual encounters with men or gender nonconforming partners. This person is not likely to identify as bisexual.

SEE ALSO
HETEROFLEXIBLE, HOMOFLEXIBLE

"Let's play a game to see who is the most flexible! Eeny, meeny, miney, mo, lesbiflexible, homoflexible, heteroflexible? GO!"

 WANT MORE INFO? *THINK*: LESBIAN, BUT OCCASIONALLY ATTRACTED TO SOMEONE OF A DIFFERENT GENDER.

 The use of this term relies on an individual's preference.

LESBIHONEST OR LEZ BE HONEST

▼ *idiom*
A play on "let's be honest," typically used in a lesbian context.

"Lez be honest, who didn't foresee Jodie Foster's coming out?"

 WANT MORE INFO? *THINK:* **LET'S BE REAL. (REAL GAY.)**

LESBO

▼ *noun*
See LESBIAN

LESBOPHOBIA

▼ *noun*
Aversion, fear, or hatred toward female homosexuality and queerness.

RELATED
LESBOPHOBIC *adjective*   **LESBOPHOBE** *noun*

SEE ALSO
ACEPHOBIA, BIPHOBIA, FEMMEPHOBIA, HOMOPHOBIA, QUEERPHOBIA, TRANSPHOBIA

"The student body is launching a campaign against lesbophobia during Women's History Month. Each day, we are going to highlight the accomplishments of queer women on campus to show our support for the lesbian community."

 WANT MORE INFO? *THINK:* **DISLIKE OF OR PREJUDICE AGAINST LESBIANS.**

LET THEM HAVE IT

▼ *idiom*
To reprimand someone strongly.

"I am about to let her have it if she says something else negative out her mouth again. She's killing my vibe!"

 WANT MORE INFO? *THINK:* **TO PUT SOMEONE IN CHECK.**

To overwhelm with fierceness and power.

"J-Hud let them have it in Dreamgirls! 'And I am telling yooooou . . .'"

 WANT MORE INFO? *THINK:* **I WILL OUTDO AND BE MORE SUCCESSFUL THAN YOU!**

 This term is commonly used in the Black gay community and the larger queer and trans people of color (QTPOC) community.

LEZ

▼ *noun*
See LESBIAN

LEZZIE

▼ *noun*
See LESBIAN

LGB

▼ *noun*
An acronym for lesbian, gay, and bisexual.

"In the eighties, the use of LGB replaced the word 'gay' because it wasn't considered inclusive. A decade later, LGBT was introduced as the more inclusive term for the queer community."

 WANT MORE INFO? *THINK:* **THE OLD QUEER CODE (AND NOT THE LONG BEACH AIRPORT CODE).**

LGBTQ(IA+)

▼ *noun*
An acronym for the lesbian, gay, bisexual, transgender, queer and/or questioning community and an umbrella term for all nonhetero–normative identities. The acronym GLBT is also used, where "gay" leads the grouping. LGBTQIA includes the intersex, asexual, agender, and aromantic communities. LGBTQIA+ is an inclusive acronym for all gender identities and sexualities.

Grand Marshal: *LGBTQIA+ roll call! Lesbian, gay, gender nonconforming, bisexual, biromantic, transgender, queer, questioning, intersex, asexual, aromantic, androgynous, flexible, fluid, poly, pan, no label, and every other beautiful human riding on the rainbow we call life?* **Us:** *Heeeeeere!!*

 WANT MORE INFO? *THINK:* **AN INCLUSIVE ACRONYM FOR THE ENTIRE QUEER COMMUNITY.**

DID YOU KNOW Around 1988, activists started a movement for equal rights for lesbian, gay, bisexual, and transgender people. The acronym LGBT was created because simply saying gay or lesbian did not accurately describe the entire community. In 2016, GLAAD created the tenth edition of their media reference guide and included Q—for queer or questioning folks—in the commonly used acronym, forming the initials LGBTQ.

LIBRARY

▼ *noun*
A snarky extension of a read; a form of insult commonly used and referred to within the QTPOC community. Often used in the phrase "the library is open" or "opened up the library."

SEE ALSO
READ

"The library is open, and the kids are reading."

 WANT MORE INFO? *THINK:* **A COLLECTION OF SASSY, DISPARAGING REMARKS.**

 USAGE NOTE This term originated in ballroom culture. It has been appropriated by the larger LGBTQIA+ community and mainstream culture.

L

DID YOU KNOW The library was introduced to mainstream culture in the documentary *Paris Is Burning*. The film provided an intimate look into the ballroom scene of 1980s New York City. Director Jennie Livingston highlighted family values, the support of house culture, exploration of gender expression and sexuality, the creative movement of vogue dance, and the magical language of a marginalized and powerful community of Black and Latinx queens.

LIES AND FAIRYTALES!

▼ *exclamation*
An exclamation used to signal dishonesty and deception.

Morgan: *To say that Forty-five has a casual relationship with the truth would be a gross understatement.*
Wilson: *Everything he says are lies and fairytales!*

 WANT MORE INFO?
***THINK:* DECEIT! DRAMA! FABRICATIONS!**

 This term originated in ballroom culture.

LIGHT IN THE LOAFERS

▼ *idiom*
A dated expression to refer to a homosexual male.

"You know, Mary's son Kirk is light in the loafers. I saw him kissing a man at the docks."

 WANT MORE INFO? *THINK:* **GAAAAAAAAAY AS THE DAY IS LONG.**

LIMP WRIST

▼ *noun*
A behavioral indicator of an effeminate, gay man.

"A limp wrist is a stupid stereotype. Some men with limp wrists are as straight as they come!"

 WANT MORE INFO? *THINK:* **WHEN HE DROPS HIS WRIST AND SAYS, "HEY, GIRL!"**

 This term originated as a derogatory slur for gay men but has been reclaimed by some of the larger LGBTQIA+ community. It may still have negative connotations for some people.

LIPSTICK LESBIAN

▼ *noun*
A super-feminine lesbian. The term "lipstick" can also be used.

SEE ALSO
CHAPSTICK LESBIAN, "The Lesbian Spectrum," *p. 194*

"I can't resist a red lip and a red bottom! Lipsticks are my weakness."

 WANT MORE INFO? *THINK:* **PORTIA DE ROSSI.**

LIPSTICK MAFIA

▼ *noun*
A group of lesbian, bisexual, or queer women who identify as femme or lipstick lesbians.

"Watch out, Tony Soprano. The lipstick mafia is in town."

 WANT MORE INFO? *THINK:* **HIGH-FEMME GAY-GIRL SQUAD.**

 USAGE NOTE This term originated in the lesbian community.

LIVE FOR HER

▼ *idiom*
An expression of appreciation toward someone or something.

Client: *Deepak Chopra meditations just bring light into my world. I live for her!*
Therapist: *Chopra is a man. But that's great you enjoy his meditations.*
Client: *I know he is a man! And I live for her!*

 WANT MORE INFO? *THINK:* **TO ABSOLUTELY ADORE.**

 USAGE NOTE This term originated in the Black gay community. It has been appropriated by the larger LGBTQIA+ community.

LIVING

▼ *verb*
Completely enjoying and embracing one's current experience.

"I am living. The sand, the sun, and this margarita feel marvelous. And there are no kids!"

 WANT MORE INFO? *THINK:* **LIVING, LAUGHING, AND LOVING; THE ULTIMATE STATE OF HAPPINESS.**

 USAGE NOTE This term originated in the Black gay community and is commonly used by the larger queer and trans people of color (QTPOC) community. It has been appropriated by mainstream culture.

LONE STAR

▼ *noun*
See SILVER STAR

LOUNGE LIZARD

▼ *noun*
A person who frequently socializes at bars and lounges. The terms BARFAIRY and BARFLY can also be used.

Gabriel: *You are such a lounge lizard. I can't keep up with you! Abbey on Friday, Micky's and Eagle on Saturday, and . . .*
Preston: *Come on, Gabe, shut up and keep up!*

 WANT MORE INFO? *THINK:* **FREQUENT BAR HOPPER.**

L

LP

▼ *noun*

An acronym for Lesbian Potential: a woman who could possibly be a lesbian based on appearance and demeanor. The term DYKIE FIT can also be used.

"Piper is giving me major LP. I bet she'd be down to hook up."

 WANT MORE INFO? *THINK:* **MAJOR DYKE VIBES.**

 USAGE NOTE This term may be considered a stereotype or derogatory.

LUBE

▼ *noun*

An abbreviated version of *lubricant*. A liquid, gel, or cream used to enhance sexual intercourse or masturbation by reducing friction during sexual acts.

RELATED
LUBE *verb*
LUBRICANT *noun*

"I come in a water base, oil base, silicone base, or even spit. What am I? Your trusty friend lube!"

 WANT MORE INFO? *THINK:* **THE SPLASH OF WETNESS THAT MAKES SEX FEEL EVEN BETTER.**

LUG

▼ *noun*

An acronym for Lesbian Until Graduation, stereotypically used at liberal arts or all-girls schools. Refers to a girl who is lesbian in school but straight after graduation. The terms BUG (bisexual until graduation) and GUG (gay until graduation) can also be used.

"Alison and Lee are total LUGs. I give them each a week after graduation to find a boyfriend."

 WANT MORE INFO? *THINK:* **WHEN MOM SAYS, "YOU KNOW, DEAR, IN COLLEGE I WAS A LESBIAN, TOO."**

 USAGE NOTE Use of this term assumes sexuality cannot be fluid and enforces hetero- and mononormativity.

LURK

▼ *verb*

To hide or move about sneakily.

To cruise. Tends to be used in a negative context.

"Nathan is lurking around the bar for any twink who will bite."

 WANT MORE INFO? *THINK:* **A GAY MAN LOOKING TO GET HIS FREAK ON.**

To be behind in rhythm or a request.

"Dakota, you are a count behind on the choreography! You are lurking! Stay on the beat."

 WANT MORE INFO? *THINK:* **FALLING BEHIND.**

L

The Queens' English

Lyrics and Literature:
The Harlem Renaissance

The Harlem Renaissance birthed some of America's most extraordinary intellects, writers, and entertainers, during an era that was, according to some scholars, just as gay as it was Black.

In 1920s Harlem, New York, a community of queer Black artists, writers, musicians, and performers made their mark on history. Drag balls at the Savoy Ballroom and the Hamilton Lodge were called "spectacles of color," where gays and lesbians would dress in drag, and over three thousand spectators would marvel at the elegant fashion and new styles of song and dance. Queer Black women reigned on stage at venues like Ubangi Club and the Clam House, where lesbian singers Gladys Bentley and Ethel Waters both performed in men's clothing, and famous blues singer Ma Rainey wrote lyrics expressing her love for women.

I went out last night
with a crowd of
my friends,
It must've been
women, 'cause I
don't like no men.
Wear my clothes just
like a fan,
Talk to the girls just
like any old man.

▶ "Prove It on Me," Ma Rainey, 1923

The Harlem Renaissance brought us the Black queer brilliant minds like scholar Alain Locke, performer Josephine Baker, poet Angelina Weld Grimké, and writers Countee Cullen, Alice Dunbar-Nelson, Langston Hughes, Claude McKay, Zora Neale Hurston, Wallace Thurman, and James Weldon Johnson.

Harlem was known for its jazz and blues, speakeasies, and extravagant parties, but it was also known for the vibrant, coded language that emerged to represent the gay Harlem lifestyle. Some of the words we recognize today (including *bull dyke, bull dagger, daddy, hype, in the life, in the closet, nookie, reefer,* and *scram*) came from this dynamic celebration of art, queerness, and Black community.

Marriage Equality

Marriage equality is the recognition of equal marriage rights granted to partners of any and every sexual orientation. Formerly referred to as the right to same-sex marriage (before our understanding of sex and gender had become what it is today—see "The Genderbread Person," p. 56), activists began fighting for the cause as early as the 1970s, when homosexuality was still largely criminalized in the United States.

In May 1996, the Defense of Marriage Act (DOMA) legally defined marriage as the union of a man and a woman and banned federal recognition of same-sex unions. This act denied many LGBTQIA+ couples the benefits granted to heterosexual couples and gave power to the states to refuse the acknowledgment of same-sex marriages.

Massachusetts became the first state to legalize gay marriage, in 2004. Cities in California, Oregon, and New Mexico began issuing marriage licenses to same-sex couples shortly thereafter, and over the course of the next ten years, gay marriage was legalized in thirty-seven states.

The fight for federal recognition of marriage equality would continue until June 26, 2015, when the United States Supreme Court ruled in favor of gay marriage, stating that the fundamental right to marry should extend to same-sex couples. This ruling legalized same-sex marriage in every state in the country. That night, the White House was lit up with the colors of the rainbow, celebrating the victory for marriage equality and love everywhere.

#LOVEWINS

Mm

MAGIC WAND

▼ *noun*
A powerful handheld personal massager commonly used for masturbation and as a sex toy. The term HITACHI may also be used.

"Girl, you have to get yourself a Magic Wand. It's the little black dress of vibrators."

 WANT MORE INFO? *THINK:* **THE OG SEX TOY.**

DID YOU KNOW The original Hitachi Magic Wand was released in 1968— a full year before Neil Armstrong walked on the moon! (That's just to say the Magic Wand can also take you to the moon, and you might see the stars twinkle, too.)

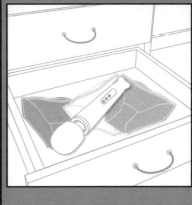

Magic Wand ▲

MAJOR

▼ *adjective*
Describing someone or something impressive.

"Janet Jackson is major! When she performs, I live, I die, then I live again!"

 WANT MORE INFO? *THINK:* **AMAZING.**

 This term is commonly used in the Black gay community and the larger queer and trans people of color (QTPOC) community.

MALE

▼ *adjective*
A biological sex or identity expression often associated with the display of masculine physicality, demeanor, and behavior.

▼ *noun*
A male-identifying person.

> **SEE ALSO**
>
> **"The Genderbread Person,"** *p. 56*

"The term 'male' is inclusive. Just because someone who identifies as a man has a uterus or vagina, doesn't mean they aren't male."

 WANT MORE INFO? *THINK:* **ASSOCIATED WITH BOYS AND MEN.**

MALE PRIVILEGE

▼ *noun*
The inherent rights and immunities granted to men.

> **SEE ALSO**
>
> **PRIVILEGE, CISGENDER PRIVILEGE, STRAIGHT PRIVILEGE, WHITE PRIVILEGE**

Jaxon: *Male privilege? I just can't catch a break! You think I get special treatment because I was born a man? Why?*
Zoe: *Society has conditioned you and everyone else to believe you are superior. It's just our reality. Check yourself, Jaxon.*

 WANT MORE INFO? *THINK:* **THE ENTITLEMENT OF BOYS AND MEN.**

MALE-TO-FEMALE

▼ *noun*
A person who is assigned male at birth but has transitioned or is in the process of transitioning to female. The term is often abbreviated as "MTF" or "M2F."

> **SEE ALSO**
>
> **AMAB, FEMALE-TO-MALE, FEMALE-TO-NONBINARY/ GENDER NEUTRAL/ NEUTROIS, MALE-TO-NONBINARY/GENDER NEUTRAL/NEUTROIS, TRANSFEMININE**

▼ *adjective*
Describing a person who has undergone MTF transition.

"When I first transitioned, I called myself MTF, but as I embraced my trans-ness I started calling myself AMAB. Acknowledging that I was never male has empowered me in a way I cannot put into words."

 WANT MORE INFO? *THINK:* **A TRANS WOMAN.**

 This term may be considered outdated by many members of the LGBTQIA+ community. The use of "AMAB," or "Assigned Male at Birth," is widely accepted because it does not imply an individual's gender identity has changed, instead acknowledging the binding nature of being assigned a specific gender at birth. The use of this term relies on an individual's preference. Please ask for a person's chosen name and pronouns.

MALE-TO-NONBINARY/ GENDER NEUTRAL/ NEUTROIS

▼ *noun*
A person who is assigned male at birth but who identifies as nonbinary, gender neutral, or neutrois. The term is often abbreviated as "MTN."

▼ *adjective*
Describing a person who has undergone an MTN transition.

SEE ALSO

AMAB, FEMALE-TO-MALE, FEMALE-TO-NONBINARY/ GENDER NEUTRAL/ NEUTROIS, MALE-TO-FEMALE

"I took my sister to my MTN Meetup group, and afterwards she told me that she understands who I am now."

 WANT MORE INFO? *THINK:* **KATE BORNSTEIN: AMAB AND IDENTIFIES AS GENDER NONCONFORMING.**

 This term may be considered outdated by many members of the LGBTQIA+ community. The use of "AMAB," or "Assigned Male at Birth," is widely accepted because it does not imply an individual's gender identity has changed, instead acknowledging the binding nature of being assigned a specific gender at birth. The use of this term relies on an individual's preference. Please ask for a person's chosen name and pronouns.

MAMA

▼ *noun*
A term of endearment, especially in the drag community.

"Mama! How was your day off? You know this club misses you when you are gone."

 WANT MORE INFO? *THINK:* **LOVED ONE.**

 This term originated in ballroom culture and is commonly used in the larger queer and trans people of color (QTPOC) community.

M

MAMA AND PAPA RELATIONSHIP

▼ *noun*
A lesbian relationship where one partner identifies as feminine and the other as masculine.

SEE ALSO
BUTCH/FEMME RELATIONSHIP

Eve: *I went to the Schomburg Center yesterday to do some research on Black queer culture. Did you know that mama and papa relationships came from the Black lesbian community in the 1920s, right here in Harlem?*
Imani: *Yeah, I did know that! The Harlem Renaissance was everything.*

 WANT MORE INFO? *THINK:* **A BUTCH/FEMME LESBIAN COUPLE.**

DID YOU KNOW This term is a century old, with historical reference to Black gay slang used in Harlem, New York, during the early 1920s. It is still used in the Black lesbian community and has since been appropriated by the larger LGBTQIA+ community.

MAN PUSSY

▼ *noun*
See BUSSY

MARGINALIZE

▼ *verb*
To treat as insignificant or less than within the social hierarchy and give less access to resources and power than the majority.

RELATED
MARGINALIZATION *noun*

"As a Latinx trans man, I belong to two distinctly different marginalized communities. I'm proud of who I am, but sometimes it's a damn struggle to have all this weight on my shoulders."

 WANT MORE INFO? *THINK:* **TO DEEM PERIPHERAL, UNIMPORTANT, OR POWERLESS.**

MARRIAGE EQUALITY

▼ *noun*

The concept of recognizing same-sex and queer marriage as equal to cisgender heterosexual marriage. The terms GAY MARRIAGE or SAME-SEX MARRIAGE can also be used.

SEE ALSO
"History Lesson: Marriage Equality," *p. 204*

"We fought hard and we fought long for marriage equality!"

 WANT MORE INFO? THINK: THE EQUAL TREATMENT OF LGBTQIA+ PEOPLE WITHIN THE INSTITUTION OF MARRIAGE.

DID YOU KNOW Marriage for same-sex or queer couples was not legal in the United States until 2004, when Massachusetts became the first state to legally recognize same-sex unions. Since then, the movement has taken on a more inclusive term—marriage equality—and on June 26, 2015, the United States Supreme Court ruled that same-sex and queer couples are allowed to marry on the same terms and conditions as opposite-sex couples, with all the accompanying rights and responsibilities.

Marriage equality ▲

MARY

▼ *noun*

A name used to greet and identify other gay people, typically within the gay male community. The terms BETTY, ROSE, and SALLY can also be used.

SEE ALSO
JUDY

"Oh, Mary, Rose, Betty! It's time for popcorn and binge-watching Game of Thrones *again!"*

 WANT MORE INFO? THINK: PAL, BUDDY, CUTIE, FRIEND.

 USAGE NOTE This term originated in the gay male community.

MARY OF THE CLOTH

▼ *noun*
See FLIPCOLLAR FAIRY

MASC

▼ *adjective*
Abbreviation of masculine, referring to the physical and personality characteristics stereotypically associated with men.

"The three of us identify as masc. I'm a boi, Maxwell is a transman of experience, and Tasha is a butch lesbian."

 WANT MORE INFO? THINK: THE OPPOSITE OF FEMME.

 This term is commonly used in the transgender, nonbinary, and gender nonconforming communities.

MASC FOR MASC

▼ *idiom*
Expression referring to a sexual or emotionally intimate relationship between two queer masc-of-center people. This also can be referred to as "masc on masc" or abbreviated as "M4M."

SEE ALSO
BUTCH-ON-BUTCH CRIME, FEMME FOR FEMME

"I got love for M4M couples. Yeah, that's my boo! We both rock a jersey and a fitted."

 WANT MORE INFO? THINK: DESCRIBING A BUTCH COUPLE.

 This term may be considered exclusionary.

MASC-OF-CENTER

▼ *adjective*
Referring to gender identities that lean toward masculinity.

SEE ALSO
FEMME-OF-CENTER

Noshi: *You heard of the Brown Boi Project in Oakland?*
Casey: *No, what's that?*
Noshi: *A group of mad-conscious masc-of-center womxn, trans, queer, and two-spirited folx who work to dismantle the stigma of gender in communities of color. I'm going to take you to their next event!*

 WANT MORE INFO? THINK: MASCULINE-LEANING.

 This term is commonly used in the transgender, nonbinary, and gender nonconforming communities.

DID YOU KNOW B. Cole of the Oakland-based Brown Boi Project coined the term "masc-of-center" to acknowledge the evolution of identity for queer people who lean toward the masculine side of the gender spectrum.

M

MASCULINIZATION

▼ *noun*
See HYPERMASCULINIZATION

MASCULINIZING HORMONE THERAPY

▼ *noun*
A process in which hormones are altered and leveled to produce physiological changes within the body to exhibit secondary sex characteristics. The term HORMONE REPLACEMENT THERAPY can also be used.

> **SEE ALSO**
> **FEMINIZING HORMONE THERAPY**

"The doctor said that once I start MHT and take testosterone, my period may stop."

 WANT MORE INFO? *THINK:* MEDICAL THERAPY USED FOR GENDER AFFIRMATION.

MATILDA

▼ *noun*
See BLUE BOY

MATTRESS QUEEN

▼ *noun*
See PILLOW PRINCESS

MEAT

▼ *noun*
See COCK

MEG

▼ *noun*
See BLUE BOY

MELONS

▼ *noun*
See BOOBS

MESSY

▼ *adjective*
Being inappropriate or intentionally disturbing the peace by creating chaos.

"JD is so messy. He got mad at Ron, threatened him, and threw a drink at him, and then JD was saying they need to talk about their future together? Take that mess home!"

 WANT MORE INFO? *THINK:* ON THE HOT MESS EXPRESS.

 USAGE NOTE This term originated in Black American culture and is commonly used in the Black gay and queer community. The word has also been appropriated by mainstream culture.

M

METOIDIOPLASTY

▼ *noun*
See BOTTOM SURGERY

METROSEXUAL

▼ *noun*
A label for a heterosexual male who has a keen sense of style and takes great pride in his grooming and appearance. A portmanteau of metropolitan and heterosexual.

"Ladies, he's all yours. I know he may look too refined to be straight with his nails done, skin moisturized, and slight gloss of the lips, but he is a rare breed we like to call 'metrosexual.'"

 WANT MORE INFO? *THINK:* **STRAIGHT MAN SO METICULOUS ABOUT HIS LOOKS, YOU MIGHT MISTAKE HIM FOR GAY.**

MINIBALL OR MINI-BALL

▼ *noun*
In ballroom culture, this is a small competition for ball walkers. This type of ball promotes skillful competitors, but the guidelines are less formal, and the competition usually has fewer categories and/ or rules.

"I heard you lost last night. Girl, you better pull up and get her back at the next mini-ball."

 WANT MORE INFO? *THINK:* **PERFORMANCE COMPETITION THAT IS SMALLER THAN A TRADITIONAL BALL.**

MISAPPROPRIATE

▼ *noun*
To appropriate wrongly.

RELATED
MISAPPROPRIATION *noun*

SEE ALSO
APPROPRIATE, REAPPROPRIATE

"Honestly, cultural appropriation should be renamed 'cultural misappropriation' because it's the theft of thousands of years of cultural history."

 WANT MORE INFO? *THINK:* **TO STEAL.**

MISGENDER

▼ *verb*
To incorrectly use a gendered term or pronoun for someone.

SEE ALSO
"Common Pronouns 101," *p. 81*

"It is so important to be aware of misgendering people—it is hurtful and can make a person feel unsafe. When you aren't sure of the person's pronouns, it's best to just use their name."

 WANT MORE INFO? *THINK:* **TO USE THE WRONG GENDER IDENTIFIER.**

M

MISOGYNY

▼ *noun*

An extreme dislike, contempt, and/or ingrained prejudice against women and the overall feminine expression. Not limited to cisgender women, misogyny is often directed at trans and/or intersex women as well as effeminate men and other groups.

SEE ALSO
FEMMEPHOBIA, TRANSMISOGYNY

"I'm sick of the blatant sexism and misogyny in the media today. When will we, as a society, learn that it's not just a man's world anymore?"

 WANT MORE INFO? *THINK:* **CULTURAL, SOCIETAL, SYSTEMIC HATRED TOWARD WOMEN.**

MISS CONGENIALITY

▼ *noun*

A person who tries desperately to be perfect, popular, and liked but is greatly disliked in spite of their efforts.

"You are trying way too hard. Nobody likes your Miss Congeniality ass!"

 WANT MORE INFO? *THINK:* **MISS POPULAR, MISS PERFECT . . . NOT!**

MISS GIRL OR MISS GURL

▼ *idiom*

A term used to command attention or commend a show of sass. The phrase "miss ma'am" can also be used.

"Miss Girl, you are on fiyah lately. I see you had a double shot of espresso this morning."

 WANT MORE INFO? *THINK:* **A LIVELY AND SPIRITED ONE.**

 This term originated in the Black gay community and is commonly used in the larger queer and trans people of color (QTPOC) community. It has been appropriated by mainstream culture.

M

MISS THING OR MISS THANG

▼ *idiom*

A sarcastic way of referring to a self-important person by not calling them by their given name.

"I am going to need you to calm down, Miss Thing. The Uber says it will be here in five minutes."

 WANT MORE INFO? *THINK:* **A DIVA.**

 This term originated in Black American culture and is used in the Black gay and trans community. It has been appropriated by the larger LGBTQIA+ community and mainstream culture.

The Queens' English

MISTRESS

▼ *noun*
See FEMME DOM

MOC

▼ *noun*
An abbreviation for man/men of color, referring to a person who identifies as such.

SEE ALSO
POC, QPOC, QWOC

"Emil Wilbekin founded Native Son to change the way gay Black men are represented in the media. We must dismantle the negative stereotypes put on MOC."

 WANT MORE INFO? *THINK:* **TITUSS BURGESS, NICO SANTOS, WILSON CRUZ— A NONWHITE MALE.**

DID YOU KNOW Men of color, particularly Black and Latinx people, face extreme racial discrimination in accessing equal opportunities in employment, housing, education, and other public benefits. Statistics show that boys and men of color are punished, policed, and incarcerated at disproportionately higher rates than their white male counterparts. Leading organizations like the NAACP and Black Lives Matter, among others, are working tirelessly to change this narrative.

MOMMI

▼ *noun*
An older woman—regardless of sexuality—who oozes with sex appeal, confidence, and feminine dominance; the femme counterpart to DADDY or ZADDY. Not to be confused with the D/s use of MOMMY.

A femme-of-center woman who practices the role of provider and protector in a queer relationship. Typically, this partner exhibits an alluring, confident attitude and is the dominant one in the partnership.

Nic: *Cate Blanchett in* Carol *is such a Mommi.*
Catherine: *Noooo! The ultimate Mommis are the characters from* Big Little Lies.
Erica: *No, no, no, no,* and *no! Sultry blues-singing Margaret Avery in* The Color Purple *is the ultimate Mommi. She was everybody's sweet thang.*

 WANT MORE INFO? *THINK:* **A SEXY OLDER LADY IN OVERSIZED SUNGLASSES WITH A GLASS OF RED WINE.**

MOMMY

▼ *noun*
See FEMME DADDY

M

MONOGAMY

▼ *noun*
The custom of having only one partner at a time in a sexual and/or romantic relationship.

RELATED
MONOGAMOUS *adjective*

SEE ALSO
POLYAMORY

"Twinkle, twinkle, little star, how I wonder where the monogamous people are. Everyone I seem to meet is poly nowadays."

 WANT MORE INFO? *THINK:* **THE PRACTICE OF SEXUAL AND ROMANTIC FIDELITY.**

M

MONONORMATIVITY

▼ *noun*
A belief that sexual and romantic relationships can or should only exist between two monogamous partners.

RELATED
MONONORMATIVE *adjective*

SEE ALSO
HETERONORMATIVITY

"Why is mononormativity considered our culture's 'normal' way to love? Love has huge power that doesn't always have to be confined only between two people."

 WANT MORE INFO? *THINK:* **A VIEW ON RELATIONSHIPS THAT EXCLUDES POLYAMORY.**

MONOSEXISM

▼ *noun*
The belief that monosexuality is superior to bisexuality and other non-monosexual orientations.

SEE ALSO
MONOSEXUAL

Interviewer: *Are you familiar with bisexuality, asexuality, pansexuality, and polysexuality?*
Monosexism: *I'm sorry, I don't understand. Who are they?*

 WANT MORE INFO? *THINK:* **STRICTLY HOMOSEXUAL OR HETEROSEXUAL, NOTHING IN BETWEEN.**

MONOSEXUAL

▼ *adjective*

A person who has a sexual and romantic preference for only one gender.

SEE ALSO
NON-MONOSEXUAL

"A gay person and a straight person are both considered monosexual."

 WANT MORE INFO? THINK: WOULD YOU LIKE AN APPLE AND AN ORANGE? NAH, JUST THE ORANGE, PLEASE.

MOTHER OR MOTHA

▼ *noun*

The symbolic matriarch of a social group and/or a respected mentor. The term may also be spelled "mutha" or "muva."

SEE ALSO
DRAG MOTHER, HOUSE MOTHER, MAMA

"Oh, that's motha right there in the mink coat. He runs this club, and if we stay on his good side he will put us on the VIP list."

 WANT MORE INFO? THINK: THE HEAD HONCHO.

 This term is commonly used in the Black gay and trans community.

MOTHER OF THE HOUSE

▼ *noun*

See HOUSE MOTHER

MOTHER SUPERIOR

▼ *noun*

An older and wiser gay man.

SEE ALSO
AUNT(IE)

"Mother Superior holds the truth! The stories he told me about being openly gay in the 1970s are crazy. I have so much respect for him."

 WANT MORE INFO? THINK: A GAY ROLE MODEL.

 This term is commonly used in the gay male community.

MSM

▼ *noun*

An abbreviation for "men who have sex with men" often used in medical and social research. This abbreviation is not limited to gay men.

SEE ALSO
WSW

"In medical charts, we don't write the word homosexual, we write 'MSM.'"

 WANT MORE INFO? THINK: AN ACRONYM FOR MALE-TO-MALE INTERCOURSE.

MTF

▼ *noun*
See MALE-TO-FEMALE

MTN

▼ *noun*
See MALE-TO-NONBINARY/
GENDER NEUTRAL/NEUTROIS

MUFF DIVER

▼ *noun*
See CARPET MUNCHER

MUSCLE MARY

▼ *noun*
See GYM BUNNY

◀ **MSM**

DID YOU KNOW In 1983, the U.S. Food and Drug Administration (FDA) implemented a lifetime ban of blood donations from men who have sex with men. The FDA changed its lifetime ban in 2015, to a deferral eligibility plan, requiring all MSM to be celibate for one year. Many gay and bisexual men felt that the FDA's deferral plan was discriminatory, and actor Alan Cumming used his creative humor to combat the clause, advising all MSM to accept the "Celibacy Challenge." In 2020, due to the COVID-19 pandemic and low blood supply, the FDA changed the year ban to only a three-month waiting period.

MEMORIZATION IS A FIERCE MENTAL WORKOUT!

CAN YOU MEMORIZE THREE DEFINITIONS TODAY?

M

Nn

NAIL IT

▼ *verb*
To achieve total perfection.

SEE ALSO
DUSTED, TENS

"Lena Waithe nailed it in her rainbow pride cape at the 2018 Met Gala. She will go down in fashion history, right next to Björk's 2001 swan dress and anybody who's ever worn Alexander McQueen."

 WANT MORE INFO? *THINK:* **TO ACCOMPLISH FLAWLESS GREATNESS.**

NANCY BOY

▼ *noun*
An outdated term used to refer to an effeminate gay man. Often shortened to "Nancy" or "Nance."

Damon: *Either he is a virgin or a Nancy boy because I ain't never seen him with a woman.*
Maeve: *Oh, lay off, Damon.*

 WANT MORE INFO? *THINK:* **AN OLD-FASHIONED, SEXIST WAY TO DISPARAGE A MAN'S MASCULINITY,**

 This may be considered a stereotype or derogatory.

NASTY

▼ *adjective*
See FIRE

NAVY CAKE

▼ *idiom*
A gay man who serves in the United States Navy. Often used in the phrase "a piece of navy cake."

"Did you know that Harvey Milk has a ship named after him? He was a gay rights leader, and he served in the U.S Navy. Talk about a piece of navy cake with a tall glass of milk!"

SEE ALSO
ANGEL FOOD

 WANT MORE INFO? *THINK:* **AN AMERICAN NAVY GAY.**

USAGE NOTE This term originated in the gay male community.

N

DID YOU KNOW Harvey Milk was known as one of America's most influential LGBT political officials and was the state of California's first openly gay politician. He was assassinated in 1978, just eleven months after he took office. In 2009, Milk was honored with a posthumous Presidential Medal of Freedom for his gay rights activism.

Navy cake ▲

NEG

▼ *adjective*
An abbreviation for the word "negative," usually referring to negative HIV test results but may also refer to other STDs.

SEE ALSO
POZ

"My test results came back neg, praise be! Unprotected sex is not an option for me anymore."

 WANT MORE INFO? *THINK:* **STD-FREE.**

NEGOTIATION

▼ noun
In BDSM, this is a discussion around the limits, wishes, and demands for a particular power-dynamic scene. After discussion, all partners must come to a consensus before engaging in scene play.

SEE ALSO
BDSM, CONSENT

Paul: *What are your limits?*
Elliot: *I've got no limits!*
Paul: *Damn straight you do! What if I said you have to suck me off while we have some blood-and-knife play and then I'm going to put you in a closet for a whole day?*
Elliot: *Whoa, okay, wait! Negotiation, please!*

 WANT MORE INFO? *THINK:* **THE PRACTICE OF SETTING RULES BEFORE BDSM PLAY.**

 USAGE NOTE This term is commonly used in the BDSM, leather, and kink communities. For all BDSM-related terms, the power exchange is a part of sadomasochistic play and should be consensual between all partners involved.

NELLY

▼ adjective
Extremely effeminate, usually referring to a gay man. The terms NANCY BOY and PERCY can also be used.

SEE ALSO
PANSY

"Charles is too nelly for my taste. I prefer a manlier meat."

 WANT MORE INFO? *THINK:* **ULTRA-GAY.**

USAGE NOTE This term may be considered a stereotype and derogatory.

NEUTROIS

▼ noun
A gender identity that does not conform to the gender binary and is typically thought of as gender neutral. There is no one definition for neutrois; people who identify as neutrois may also identify with the terms AGENDER, GENDERLESS, and/or NONGENDER, among others. The term NULL GENDER can also be used.

SEE ALSO
GENDERQUEER, NONBINARY, GENDER NONCONFORMING

"Identifying as neutrois has allowed me to be part of the nonbinary and trans community. No boundaries, no rules. Gender is what you make of it."

 WANT MORE INFO? *THINK:* **GENDERLESS.**

 USAGE NOTE This term is commonly used in the nonbinary and gender nonconforming community.

N

NEW WAY (VOGUING)

▼ *noun*

The modern technique of vogue house dance established after 1990. This technique is known for its sharpness, flexibility, limb contortions, hand and wrist illusions, and stylized, geometric movement.

SEE ALSO
OLD WAY (VOGUING), VOGUE FEMME

"These up-and-coming children are slaying the new way. Walk for me!"

 WANT MORE INFO? *THINK:* **TUTTING AND LOCKING TO "THE HA DANCE" BY MASTERS AT WORK.**

 This term originated in ballroom culture.

NO BLACKS, NO ASIANS

▼ *idiom*

An exclusionary, racist phrase used in dating apps to indicate a person's prejudice against people of color. The phrase "no Asians, no Blacks, no Hispanics" is also used.

"Damn, his profile says, 'no Blacks, no Asians!' Just because it's online doesn't make your blatant racism invisible."

SEE ALSO
NO FATS, NO FEMMES

 WANT MORE INFO? *THINK:* **PREJUDICE AGAINST DATING QTPOC.**

NO FATS, NO FEMMES

▼ *idiom*

An exclusionary, body-shaming phrase used in dating apps to indicate a distaste for specific types of people who are considered full-bodied and/or femme.

SEE ALSO
NO BLACKS, NO ASIANS

"Identity shaming is an absolute no-no. The No Fats, No Femmes *documentary is an absolute yes-yes! Truly a must-see."*

 WANT MORE INFO? *THINK:* **A BIGOTED PHRASE USED ON GAY DATING APPS.**

 The terms "no Blacks, no Asians" and "no fats, no femmes" originated in gay dating apps. They are exclusionary phrases that much of the gay community is trying to eliminate from its vocabulary.

NO HOST

▼ *idiom*

A phrase typically used in dating profiles indicating the user is unable to provide a physical space to engage in sexual activities.

"I'm tired of these blank profiles on Grindr filled with no hosts. My roommate has been home so much lately, and I can't do shit at my apartment."

 WANT MORE INFO? *THINK:* **"I'M TIRED OF YOU ALWAYS COMING TO MY PLACE. WHY CAN'T WE GO TO YOURS?"**

NO LABEL

▼ *adjective*
Describing a person who does
not identify with any gender or
sexuality labels.

*"I don't have a label. I would like no
label. I feel that one of the joys of
being a gay man is that I can have
all the masculine and macho stuff
and also be a queen. Freedom to
be . . . no apologies."* ▶ James Beaman

 WANT MORE INFO? *THINK:*
**A LABEL AGAINST USING
SEXUALITY STEREOTYPES.**

NONBINARY
OR NON-BINARY

▼ *adjective*
A gender identity that is open to a
full spectrum of gender expressions,
not limited by masculinity and
femininity. Nonbinary people may
express masculinity, femininity, both,
or neither.

*"We don't need to look or act or
be a certain way to be nonbinary.
For me, being nonbinary means
breaking down what it means to
be a gendered person in the world."*
▶ Meredith Talusan

 WANT MORE INFO? *THINK:*
**AN INCLUSIVE TERM FOR
GENDER EXPRESSIONS THAT
ARE NOT CISGENDER.**

SEE ALSO
**ENBY, GENDER
NONCONFORMING,
GENDERQUEER**

N

NONGENDER

▼ *adjective*
See AGENDER

NON-MONO OR
NON-MONOSEXUAL

▼ *adjective*
Having sexual and romantic
attraction to more than one gender.

SEE ALSO
MONOSEXUAL

*"A bisexual person is also
considered non-monosexual
because they are attracted to more
than one expression of gender."*

WANT MORE INFO? *THINK:*
**IDENTIFYING AS ANYTHING
OTHER THAN HETERO- OR
HOMOSEXUAL.**

NON-MONOGAMY

▼ *noun*
The practice of having multiple relationships that are not sexually or romantically exclusive. People may be open or private about this choice and have multiple sexual partners and/or relationships.

RELATED
NON-MONOGAMOUS *adjective*

SEE ALSO
POLYAMORY

"I really don't believe humans are supposed to be with just one person sexually. Non-monogamy is natural to us. It's primal."

 WANT MORE INFO? *THINK:* **ENTERTAINING MORE THAN ONE INTIMATE RELATIONSHIP.**

NO SHADE

▼ *idiom*
Saying something directly without the intent of being offensive. However, people often use "no shade" with a snide tone, intending to criticize. The phrase NO T, NO SHADE is also often used.

SEE ALSO
SHADE

"No shade, but we will never forget when the Oscars messed up the Best Picture award for Moonlight. I know it wasn't 'on purpose,' but that was the first time a film won with an all-Black cast! And it was gay!"

 WANT MORE INFO? *THINK:* **"NO OFFENSE, BUT . . ."**

USAGE NOTE This term originated in ballroom culture. It has been appropriated by the larger LGBTQIA+ community and mainstream culture.

NO T, NO SHADE

▼ *idiom*
A phrase meaning "No disrespect, but . . ."—an evolution of the phrase "all T, no shade," meaning "here's the entire truth, but I meant no shade." Can also be seen as "no tea, no shade."

"No T, no shade, I just want to get paid. You said the coins would be here by the end of April, and here we are, fifteen days into May."

 WANT MORE INFO? *THINK:* **NO OFFENSE.**

USAGE NOTE The term originated in ballroom culture. It has been appropriated by the larger LGBTQIA+ community and mainstream culture.

NOT ABOUT THIS LIFE

▼ *idiom*
Completely uninterested in a particular situation, thing, or person.

"Nope, no way, never. I will not be going to the circus. Clowns freak me out. I am not about that life."

 WANT MORE INFO? *THINK:* **DON'T WANT TO BE INVOLVED.**

N

This term originated in Black American culture and is used in the Black gay and queer community. It has been appropriated by mainstream culture.

NOT FEATURING

▼ *idiom*
Not amused by; uninterested in.

SEE ALSO
FEATURE

"Sage and Tami cannot sit with us. You know I am not featuring those hoes today."

 WANT MORE INFO? *THINK:* **NOT FOND OF.**

 This term originated in ballroom culture and is commonly used in the larger queer and trans people of color (QTPOC) community.

NOT YOUR MINISTRY

▼ *idiom*
A phrase highlighting a person's notable lack of skill or talent in a particular area.

"Please stop singing. Not your ministry, baby girl."

 WANT MORE INFO? *THINK:* **"THAT IS NOT IN YOUR WHEELHOUSE . . ."**

 This term originated in Black American culture and is commonly used in the Black gay and queer community.

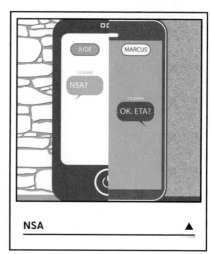

NSA ▲

NSA

▼ *idiom*
An acronym for "No Strings Attached," usually found in online dating profiles to indicate that an individual is open to having sex without attachment or commitment.

Jude: (online chatting, types) *NSA.*
Marcus: *OK. ETA?*

 WANT MORE INFO? *THINK:* **ISO A FUCK BUDDY.**

NULL GENDER

▼ *adjective*
See NEUTROIS

N

GENDER NEUTRAL

Omnigender ▲

Oo

OH, NO YOU DIDN'T

▼ *idiom*
A phrase used to express irritation, distaste, or disbelief at someone's actions.

"Oh, no she didn't! She just ate off my plate without asking. Do I look like a buffet station?"

 WANT MORE INFO? *THINK:* "CAN YOU BELIEVE?"

USAGE NOTE This term originated in Black American culture and is used in the Black gay and queer community. It has been appropriated by mainstream culture.

DID YOU KNOW Black American women coined the phrase "Oh, no you didn't!" to respond to an unfavorable action. The idiom gained mainstream exposure when comedian Martin Lawrence, dressed in drag as the character Sheneneh Jenkins, would say her signature line, "Oh, no you didn't!"

OLD WAY (VOGUING)

▼ *noun*
The technique of vogue house dance established prior to 1990. It is known for its symmetry, precision, and stylized movements based on Egyptian hieroglyphs and high fashion poses. In a ball competition, the movement is often used in a dance duel; the winner must trap the other competitor, rendering them unable to execute another move.

SEE ALSO

NEW WAY (VOGUING), VOGUE, VOGUE FEMME

Sugar: *I know he didn't just play this song! He is about to make me go off! "Love Is the Message" is the anthem for old way!*
Venus: *Baby, no, the anthem is "Din Daa Daa"! He has to play that next!*

 WANT MORE INFO? *THINK:* WILLI NINJA: THE GOD OF VOGUING.

USAGE NOTE This term originated in ballroom culture.

OMNIGENDER

▼ *adjective*
Treating all genders as one, without distinguishing from or discriminating against one or the others.

"It's time to implement omnigender bathrooms in all public places. Why the gender divide?"

 WANT MORE INFO? *THINK:* **ALL FOR ONE AND ONE FOR ALL.**

OMNISEXUAL

▼ *adjective*
A sexual orientation where a person is attracted to all types of humans and has no distinct preferences based on sexuality or gender.

RELATED
OMNISEXUALITY *noun*

SEE ALSO
BISEXUAL, PANSEXUAL

"Omnisexuals desire people for who they are and don't let sexuality or gender get in the way of their attraction."

 WANT MORE INFO? *THINK:* **ATTRACTION NOT LIMITED TO A SPECIFIC GROUP OF PEOPLE.**

ON THE MAKE

▼ *idiom*
Looking for a romantic relationship or casual sex.

SEE ALSO
CRUISE, NSA, ON THE PROWL

"I'm changing my dating profile status from 'looking for friends' to 'on the make.' Mama needs to get laid."

 WANT MORE INFO? *THINK:* **READY TO MAKE SEXUAL ADVANCES.**

ON THE PROWL

▼ *idiom*
Actively looking for sex.

SEE ALSO
CRUISE, NSA, ON THE MAKE

"I just saw him pull out a condom from his wallet. He is on the prowl tonight."

 WANT MORE INFO? *THINK:* **ON A HUNT FOR A SEXUAL FLING.**

O

OOP

▼ *exclamation*

A sound made when you are shocked. It is usually accompanied with a retraction of the neck. The length, tone, and pitch of the sound determines the severity.

"Oop! Did she just fart and not say excuse me? Rude."

 WANT MORE INFO? *THINK:* **WHOA.**

 USAGE NOTE This term originated in Black American culture and is commonly used in the Black gay and queer community.

ORAL TOP

▼ *noun*

A gay, bisexual, or queer man who prefers to receive oral sex over giving it and is also a top when it comes to anal penetration.

SEE ALSO
TOP

"I love being an oral top. My boyfriend sucks the life out of me."

 WANT MORE INFO? *THINK:* **A GAY MAN WHO PREFERS BEING IN CONTROL: HE PENETRATES ON TOP AND RECEIVES FELLATIO.**

USAGE NOTE This term originated in the gay male community and has since been appropriated by the larger LGBTQIA+ community.

O

ORPHAN

▼ *noun*

A person who hangs around couples looking for attention and intimacy. An orphan is often newly single and in need of company.

"Please, I am just asking you and Justin to come over and watch American Horror Story and maybe cuddle a little? I can't help that I'm an orphan right now."

 WANT MORE INFO? *THINK:* **A PERSON IN NEED OF EXTRA TLC.**

OTTER

▼ *noun*
A body label for a gay, bisexual, or queer man who has a lot of body hair and a lean or slim body type.

> **SEE ALSO**
>
> **"Help! What's My Gay Type?,"** *p. 152*

"Ah, my favorite view! An otter in his Speedo, splashing in my swimming pool."

 WANT MORE INFO? *THINK:* **GAY MAN WHO IS ATHLETIC AND HAIRY WHO PROBABLY GOES TO THE GYM FOUR TIMES A WEEK.**

USAGE NOTE This term originated in the white gay male community.

Otter ▲

OUT

▼ *adjective*
Openly LGBTQIA+.

London: *Are you out to your family and coworkers?*
Tessa: *Baby, I am out and PROUD!*

 WANT MORE INFO? *THINK:* **OPEN ABOUT BEING ON THE LGBTQIA+ SPECTRUM.**

▼ *verb*
To make someone's sexual identity public knowledge—either with or without the person's consent. Often used in the phrase "come out," referring to the metaphor of coming out of the closet.

> **SEE ALSO**
>
> **COME OUT, CLOSET**

"You outed that boy on Snapchat and now he is being bullied at school! I am so disappointed in you."

 WANT MORE INFO? *THINK:* **TO REVEAL AN INDIVIDUAL'S QUEERNESS.**

OVAH

▼ *adjective*
Exquisite.

"I finally saw Hamilton, and I am at a loss for words. It was so ovah."

 WANT MORE INFO? *THINK:* **INCREDIBLE.**

USAGE NOTE This term originated in ballroom culture.

◀ OWL

OVER IT OR OVER THIS

▼ *idiom*
Annoyed, fatigued, "done" with
something or someone.

*"I am so over this snow! My delicate,
sensitive skin needs Fire Island
rainbow-loving and sunshine!"*

 WANT MORE INFO? *THINK:*
"I HAVE MOVED ON."

OVERLIVING

▼ *adjective*
Totally happy; overjoyed. The
superlative form of LIVING.

*"I was overliving in Amsterdam this
weekend. I am still on a literal and
figurative high!"*

 WANT MORE INFO? *THINK:*
EUPHORIC.

 This term originated in the
Black gay community.

OWL

▼ *noun*
An acronym for Older Wiser
Lesbian.

"Have you seen the Into *video
series called 'The Old Lesbians'?
Belita, Phyllis, and Sabel are the
cutest dykes I've ever seen. OWLs
are the best!"*

 WANT MORE INFO? *THINK:*
**EDIE WINDSOR AND THEA
SPYER.**

 This term originated in the
lesbian community.

HISTORY LESSON

The Ballroom Scene

Decades after the cultural revolution known as the Harlem Renaissance, an even more fluid, more diverse group of artists took to the very same streets to create a safe space for LGBTQIA+ self-expression in the midst of intense political, racial, and homophobic strife.

By the late 1970s, the extravagant gay drag balls of 1920s Harlem had evolved into a full-fledged underground queer community. The ballroom scene—as captured in the highly acclaimed 1990 documentary *Paris Is Burning*—became home for Black and Latinx gay and trans people in Harlem and other New York City neighborhoods.

During this time, drag emerged as more than just an idea—it was a way of life. A powerful new lexicon exploded from the ballroom scene. Highly energetic balls featured a variety of categories in which queer and trans people of color (QTPOC) of all gender expressions—butch queens, femme queens, trans men, drag queens, butches, and women—could walk for trophies and cash prizes. A commentator with a legendary reputation would act as emcee, freestyling, chanting, and pumping up the crowd while reading and throwing shade at the kids. Walkers competed in categories like Face, Sex Siren, Runway, Vogue, Realness, and Realness with a Twist, hoping for "TENS ACROSS THE BOARD!" or else they'd be chopped.

Along with the feisty language that would eventually trickle into mainstream culture, the ballroom scene embraced the values of family, self-expression through movement and identity, and the art of reading and throwing shade. For queer people who experienced trauma, abuse, or neglect from their biological families, the social houses in ballroom culture became family. These families were built to provide support networks for QTPOC to live freely and embrace their true identity.

In our modern world, LGBTQIA+ culture is finally being celebrated after years of being forced underground. The ballroom scene has seen support in mainstream pop culture. *RuPaul's Drag Race* is a pillar of reality television. FX's groundbreaking *Pose* has the largest cast of trans actors in TV history. Ballroom choreography has influenced pop and R&B greats like Madonna, Beyoncé, Teyana Taylor, and Lady Gaga, and the music has inspired new forms of house and queer hip-hop. Ballroom culture and houses have expanded into major cities across the nation, and balls are held in international cities like London, Paris, Hong Kong, Auckland, and St. Petersburg, providing people all over the world with the opportunity to express themselves, strike a pose, and vogue.

PENDAVIS

A house typically consists of a house mother and/or house father, and the family members are called "the children." Among the first houses created were the Houses of LaBeija, Corey, Wong, Dupree, Christian, Princess, and Pendavis.

COREY

DUPREE

"This culture has existed under our noses for over 40 years."

▶ Ronald Murray

WONG

Polyamorous ▲

Pp

PACKAGE

▼ *noun*
The penis and testicles.

"I wore my mailman costume for Halloween and all I heard the whole evening was, 'Please handle my package with care.' And I did."

 WANT MORE INFO? *THINK:* **THE BANANA AND CLEMENTINES ON** *DAVID* **BY MICHELANGELO.**

PACKING

▼ *verb*
Wearing padding or a phallic object, called a packer, to create a nonflesh penis.

"I like to use an adhesive when I am packing. That way I can wear boxers."

 WANT MORE INFO? *THINK:* **PROSTHETIC PHALLUS TO SUPPORT MASC GENDER EXPRESSION.**

 USAGE NOTE This term is commonly used in the transgender, nonbinary, gender nonconforming, and drag communities.

PADDING

▼ *verb*
Using special undergarments that enhance the figure of the body to look more feminine. Garments such as padded panties, bras, and breast and buttocks forms are often used.

"Padding is safer than silicone injections and cheaper than surgery."

 WANT MORE INFO? *THINK:* **SHAPING THE BODY TO HAVE LARGE BREASTS, BUTT, AND HIPS.**

USAGE NOTE This term is commonly used in the transgender, nonbinary, gender nonconforming, and drag communities.

PAID IT

▼ *verb*
Purposely ignored.

"She paid it. She just walked past and didn't even say hello."

 WANT MORE INFO? *THINK:* **PAY IT NO MIND.**

USAGE NOTE This term originated in ballroom culture.

PAINTED

▼ *adjective*
Beautifully adorned with makeup.

"Okay, your face is painted! You are giving supple, chic, gentle airbrush glory like mother Octavia St. Laurent."

 WANT MORE INFO? *THINK:* **EXQUISITELY MADE UP.**

USAGE NOTE This term originated in ballroom culture and is commonly used in the drag community.

PANDA

▼ *noun*
A gay, bisexual, or queer man of Asian descent who has a large or stocky frame with body hair.

SEE ALSO

BEAR, BEAR COMMUNITY

"In the book, the character is described as 'Japanese, queer, and larger-bodied.' I don't understand why they didn't cast a panda in the role. The actor is so skinny! And straight!"

 WANT MORE INFO? *THINK:* **AN ASIAN IN THE BEAR COMMUNITY.**

USAGE NOTE The term originated in the gay male community. It may be considered a stereotype or derogatory.

PANGENDER

▼ *adjective*
A person who identifies with all—"pan" is a prefix meaning "all"—genders, without distinguishing one from another.

SEE ALSO

BIGENDER, POLYGENDER, GENDERFLUID, GENDERFLUX, NONBINARY

Subin: *Whoa! There's a study that found more than thirty separate gender definitions!*
Angel: *Really? I should take that report to the DMV, so I can get a new license that actually says I'm pangender.*

 WANT MORE INFO? *THINK:* **A PROUD MEMBER OF ALL GENDERS.**

PANSEXUAL

▼ *adjective*
A sexual orientation where a person is attracted to people of all—"pan" is a prefix meaning "all"—genders and sexualities.

▼ *noun*
A pansexual person.

RELATED

PANSEXUALITY *noun*

SEE ALSO

BISEXUAL, OMNISEXUAL

"Some people view 'pansexual' as a more expansive and inclusive label than 'bisexual.' Pansexuals are attracted to all gender identities."

 WANT MORE INFO? *THINK:* **LOVE KNOWS NO GENDER.**

PANSY

▼ *adjective*
Effeminate or girly.

▼ *noun*
A sissy.

SEE ALSO

NELLY

"Don't be such a pansy, Mo. Go talk to him!"

WANT MORE INFO? *THINK:* **DELICATE.**

USAGE NOTE This term originated as a derogatory slur for gay men but has been reclaimed by some of the LGBTQIA+ community. It may still have negative connotations for some people.

DID YOU KNOW In the early 1930s, during the era of Prohibition and a thriving underground bohemian life, drag culture experienced a surge in popularity in big American cities like New York, San Francisco, and Los Angeles. At the time, drag queens were called "pansy performers" and this celebration of queer culture was called the Pansy Craze.

P

PASSING

▼ *adjective*
Describing a transgender person
who is perceived as cisgender.

RELATED
PASS *verb*

SEE ALSO
CLOCK, STEALTH

*"'Passing' is looking cis. Like, I
walked into a straight bar after my
FFS and no one blinked an eye."*

 WANT MORE INFO? *THINK:*
**WHEN A TRANS PERSON
"PASSES" THE TEST OF
ADHERING TO A TRADITIONAL
GENDER EXPRESSION.**

USAGE NOTE This term is controversial
within the transgender
community. Not all trans
and gender nonconforming people feel
the need to "pass" as cisgender, and
many are comfortable shaking up
gender norms.

In the broader queer community,
passing can be linked to other
societal privileges—like being
cisgender, straight, white, able-
bodied, etc.

*"Being straight-passing comes
with its privileges for sure. I
don't ever feel unsafe, but I also
sometimes feel unseen by other
members of the queer community.
It's complicated."*

 WANT MORE INFO? *THINK:*
**APPEARING "NORMAL"
WITHIN A MAJORITY
COMMUNITY.**

PASSION FRUIT

▼ *noun*
A dated term used to refer to a
homosexual man who was not
easily identified as gay due to an
outwardly masculine, straight-
passing appearance.

*"Actor Rock Hudson gave serious
passion fruit back in the 1950s.
That's why fans were so shocked
when they found out he had a
boyfriend."*

 WANT MORE INFO? *THINK:*
**A MASCULINE GUY WHO
DOESN'T "LOOK" GAY.**

PASSIVE

▼ *adjective*
See SUBMISSIVE

PEGGING

▼ *verb*
A form of intercourse where a
person with a vagina penetrates a
partner's anus using a strap-on or
sex device like a dildo.

*"My man says it feels good when
we are pegging. I'm happy he is
open to getting his G-spot rocked!"*

 WANT MORE INFO? *THINK:*
**PENETRATION FROM AN
AFAB.**

PEP

▼ *noun*
An antiretroviral medication used to prevent HIV infection after potential exposure. PEP stands for Post-Exposure Prophylaxis.

SEE ALSO
PrEP

"PEP is an emergency medication that must be taken within three days of potentially being exposed to HIV. A doctor or the nearest hospital can give you a prescription."

 WANT MORE INFO? *THINK:* **EMERGENCY PILLS TO HELP STOP HIV FROM SPREADING.**

PERCHED

▼ *adjective*
Sitting or posing in a confident and/or elegant manner.

"The divine Eartha Kitt was always so pulled and perched on that throne, like the queen she is."

 WANT MORE INFO? *THINK:* **REGAL ... AND MAYBE A LITTLE BIT CUNTY.**

 USAGE NOTE This term originated in ballroom culture and is commonly used in the larger queer and trans people of color (QTPOC) community.

P

PERCY

▼ *adjective*
See NELLY

PGP OR PREFERRED GENDER PRONOUN

▼ *noun*
See PRONOUN

PHALLIC

▼ *adjective*
Relating to or resembling a penis.

"Mario advises us to buy quality phallic packers and underwear."

 WANT MORE INFO? *THINK:* **DICK-LIKE.**

PHALLOPLASTY

▼ *noun*
See BOTTOM SURGERY

PIG PLAY

▼ *noun*
Sexual play and/or intercourse that embraces extreme fetishes and kink.

SEE ALSO
BDSM, KINK

"I love pig play. The dirtier the better."

 WANT MORE INFO? *THINK:* **KINKY SEX.**

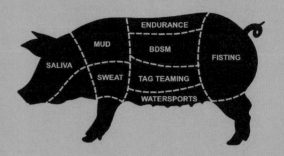

USAGE NOTE This term originated in the BDSM, leather, and kink communities. For all BDSM-related terms, the power exchange is a part of sadomasochistic play and should be consensual between all partners involved.

PILLOW PRINCESS

▼ *noun*
A lesbian, bisexual, or queer woman who prefers being passive in bed, often acting as the receiver of sexual acts, not the giver.

SEE ALSO
BOTTOM

"You're just going to lie there and be a pillow princess? Okay, queen. But tomorrow, you go down on me!"

 WANT MORE INFO? *THINK:* **SHE WHO GETS TAKEN CARE OF IN BED.**

USAGE NOTE This term originated in the lesbian community. It has been appropriated by the larger LGBTQIA+ community and mainstream culture.

DID YOU KNOW The term "pillow princess" was used in the lesbian community as early as the 1990s. In a 1992 issue of *Curve* magazine (called *Deneuve* at the time), an article highlighted a sexual dynamic between butch and femme women, where the butch would initiate sexual play, while the femme played "pillow princess."

PINK PANTHER

▼ *noun*
See CHICKEN QUEEN

PINK TRIANGLE

▼ *noun*

A symbol adopted by the gay community to show pride in being homosexual and resistance against discrimination.

SEE ALSO
BLACK TRIANGLE

"The pink triangle is not just a symbol of gay resistance—it's a symbol of the power we have as a community to reappropriate symbols and words that were historically used to hurt us."

 WANT MORE INFO? *THINK:* A SYMBOL OF GAY LIBERATION.

DID YOU KNOW The pink triangle was first used in Nazi concentration camps to mark male prisoners who were homosexual. During the AIDS crisis in the late 1980s, there was public discussion of putting gay men diagnosed with HIV/AIDS in concentration camps to keep the AIDS epidemic from spreading. One of the first organizations to bring public awareness to the AIDS epidemic was ACT UP, created by Larry Kramer. Their slogan, Silence=Death, was one of the many ways the pink triangle has been reclaimed by the gay community as a symbol for pride, equality, and justice.

PITCHER

▼ *noun*

See TOP

PIV

▼ *adjective*

An acronym for penis-in-vagina.

"Listen, I'm gay. I dig men, but I like PIV sex, too."

 WANT MORE INFO? *THINK:* DESCRIBING HETERO-SEXUAL SEX.

PLATINUM STAR

▼ *noun*

A gay man who has not experienced sexual intercourse with a woman and was born via C-section. This "status" one-ups a GOLD STAR because not only has he not had sex with a woman, but he has never even touched a vagina. The term DOUBLE GOLD STAR can also be used.

SEE ALSO
GOLD STAR, SILVER STAR

"And the award for gayest man goes to . . . ME! Thank you, thank you. I would like to truly thank the Academy and my platinum star status."

 WANT MORE INFO? *THINK:* THE GAYEST OF GAYS.

 USAGE NOTE This term may be considered derogatory.

P

PLEASE AND THANK YOU

▼ *idiom*
A sassy request for someone to do something immediately.

"Can you stop being so loud? Please and thank you!"

 WANT MORE INFO? *THINK:* **"DO AS I SAY."**

PLEASE OR PUH-LEASE

▼ *exclamation*
An expression of disagreement or disbelief.

"Oh child, puh-lease. That woman did not lose fifteen pounds in a week! I hate infomercials."

 WANT MORE INFO? *THINK:* **"COME ON!"**

 This term originated in Black American culture and is commonly used in the Black gay and queer community.

PNP

▼ *noun*
An acronym for party 'n' play. Typically used within the gay male community, party 'n' play refers to a particular type of sexual experience enhanced by drugs (often crystal methamphetamine, cocaine, or ecstasy). The term CHEMSEX can also be used.

"You into PnP? I know somewhere we can get fucked up."

 WANT MORE INFO? *THINK:* **HIGH-RISK SEXUAL PLAY UNDER THE INFLUENCE OF HARD DRUGS.**

 This type of recreational drug activity can be harmful to one's health.

POC OR BIPOC

▼ *noun*
An acronym for "people of color" or "person of color"—an inclusive term for supporting people within a community who face marginalization and erasure because of race or ethnicity. BIPOC, "Black, Indigenous, and people of color" may also be used.

> **SEE ALSO**
> ## MOC, QPOC OR QTPOC, QWOC OR QTWOC, WOC

Juniper: *Hey, I'm looking for any organizations for gay POC. Are there any represented here?*
Fallon: *Yes! Through these double doors, you'll see tables for the Trikone, Shades of Yellow, the Trans Masculine Advocacy Network, and a ton of other social and political groups for LGBTQ POC.*

 WANT MORE INFO? *THINK:* **NOT CAUCASIAN.**

POLAR BEAR

▼ *noun*
An older gay, bisexual, or queer man who has a large or stocky frame with gray body hair.

"Ooh, BEAR Magazine *featured a polar bear daddy on its cover this month. Hubba hubba!"*

 WANT MORE INFO? *THINK:* **A SENIOR MEMBER IN THE BEAR COMMUNITY.**

POLY

▼ *adjective*
A Greek prefix used to identify something that has "many" or "several" parts.

"I celebrate all the ways I am poly! I'm polysexual and polyamorous!"

 WANT MORE INFO? *THINK:* **MORE THAN ONE AND MORE THAN TWO.**

POLYAMOROUS

▼ *adjective*
Having or desiring multiple intimate relationships at one time. The term is often abbreviated as "poly" and "polyam."

"People think being poly is complicated, and sure, it can be, but it's all about setting ground rules and communicating effectively with your partners."

 WANT MORE INFO? *THINK:* **MAINTAINING DIFFERENT TYPES OF INTIMATE RELATIONSHIPS WITH DIFFERENT PEOPLE.**

USAGE NOTE Please note that the abbreviation "poly" is also a shortened version for Polynesian and many polyamorous people prefer using "polyam" out of respect.

P

POLYAMORY

▼ *noun*
The practice of having multiple intimate relationships at once, with consent of all individuals involved.

RELATED
POLYAMORIST *noun*

SEE ALSO
MONOGAMY

"My husband and I practice polyamory. We have opened ourselves up to sexual and emotional intimacy with other partners, and it's done wonders for our relationship."

 WANT MORE INFO? *THINK:* **A MUTUAL AGREEMENT TO HAVE PARTNERS OUTSIDE OF A PRIMARY RELATIONSHIP.**

POLYGENDER

▼ *adjective*
A person who identifies with many genders, without distinguishing one from another.

SEE ALSO
BIGENDER, PANGENDER, GENDER-FLUID, GENDERFLUX, NONBINARY

"My gender expression is vast and always changing. I identify as polygender and genderflux."

 WANT MORE INFO? *THINK:* **IDENTIFYING AS THREE OR MORE GENDERS.**

POLYSEXUAL

▼ *adjective*
Sexually attracted to people of several genders and sexualities. A polysexual person's sexual attraction is not limited to a specific gender identity. However, polysexuality does not indicate an attraction to *all* genders, but a specific set of gender expressions that are particular to each individual.

▼ *noun*
A polysexual person.

RELATED
POLYSEXUALITY *noun*

"Joey is attracted to masc-of-center folks who may identify as male, nonbinary, genderqueer, or gender nonconforming. He's polysexual."

 WANT MORE INFO? *THINK:* **ATTRACTION IS BOUNTIFUL, BUT SPECIFIC.**

POPPA

▼ *noun*
A lesbian who is a minor.

"Check everyone's ID. I know the poppas will want to buy alcohol for Sacred Heart's prom this weekend."

 WANT MORE INFO? *THINK:* **A BABY DYKE.**

POPPERS

▼ *noun*
An inhalant commonly used within the gay male community to induce an instant high and sexual arousal. It also relaxes the muscles, including the anus, making for enhanced sexual experiences.

"I really love Julio. But his dick is so big, I think I might need poppers before he turns me from power bottom to pillow princess."

 WANT MORE INFO? *THINK:* **A RECREATIONAL DRUG USED FOR LONGER AND STRONGER GAY SEX.**

 Using this drug may cause the blood pressure to drop and heart rate to increase.

POST-OP

▼ *noun*
See GENDER AFFIRMATION SURGERY

P

POWER BOTTOM

▼ *noun*
A person who is dominant in bed, controlling the sexual activities, but still receives penetration.

A gay, bisexual, or queer man who acts dominant in bed but prefers receiving penetration.

SEE ALSO
BOTTOM, TOP, SWITCH, VERS

▼ *verb*
To perform sex as a power bottom.

"Honey, I am a power bottom. I throw that ass back and get fucked the way I wanna be."

 WANT MORE INFO? *THINK:* **A BOTTOM IN CHARGE.**

 This term originated in the gay male community but has been appropriated by the larger LGBTQIA+ community.

POWER LESBIAN

▼ *noun*
An influential lesbian with a commanding presence.

"I'm always here for Rachel Maddow showing all those men in suits who's boss. She is such a power lesbian."

 WANT MORE INFO? *THINK:* **A LESBIAN BADASS.**

POWER TOP

▼ *noun*
A person who is dominant in bed, navigating and controlling the sexual activities. A power top may be aggressive and forceful.

A person who acts in dominant ways in bed. A power top does not typically receive penetration—they strictly give it.

SEE ALSO
BOTTOM, TOP, SWITCH, VERS

▼ *verb*
To perform sex as a power top.

"He is a power top—he will be stronger, faster, and harder than anything you've ever had before."

 WANT MORE INFO? *THINK:* **A GAY JACKHAMMER.**

 This term originated in the gay male community. It has been appropriated by the larger LGBTQIA+ community.

POZ

▼ *adjective*
HIV-positive. Also spelled "Pos."

SEE ALSO
NEG

"These young kids better listen and learn. Testing poz is no joke. Safe sex is hot sex."

 WANT MORE INFO? *THINK:* **FIGHTING HIV/AIDS.**

P

DID YOU KNOW HIV was originally called GRID, meaning Gay-Related Immune Deficiency. It was also colloquially known as "gay cancer" before the disease was understood. The *New York Times* was the first to mention GRID, in an article written on May 11, 1982, along with A.I.D., which meant Acquired Immunodeficiency Disease.

PRE-OP

▼ *noun*
See GENDER AFFIRMATION SURGERY

PREP

▼ *noun*
A medication used to reduce the risk of contracting the Human Immuno-deficiency Virus in people who have not been previously exposed and/or at risk. PrEP stands for Pre-Exposure Prophylaxis; it is a highly effective way to prevent HIV infection, if taken as prescribed.

SEE ALSO
PEP

Kailey: *What are all these ads about Truvada?*
Terrance: *Oh, that's PrEP. I'm on it. Andre is, too. It's major. You only take it once a day and there aren't any crazy side effects.*

 WANT MORE INFO? *THINK:* **GROUNDBREAKING MEDICATION USED TO PREVENT HIV INFECTION.**

PRESSED

▼ *adjective*
Overly eager.

"I was so pressed to get Frank Ocean's autograph that when I finally saw him I almost peed my pants!"

 WANT MORE INFO? *THINK:* **IMPATIENT, CRAZY-EXCITED.**

USAGE NOTE This term originated in Black American culture and is commonly used in the Black gay and queer community.

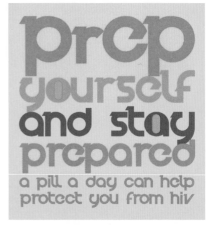

prep yourself and stay prepared
a pill a day can help protect you from hiv

◀ PrEP

DID YOU KNOW Gilead Sciences established a medication-assistance program to help individuals at risk of HIV gain proper medical access to treatments. Truvada for PrEP Medication Assistance Program (MAP) assists eligible HIV-negative adults who are uninsured or need financial assistance.

PRIDE

▼ *noun*
Confidence in one's identity as a lesbian, gay, bisexual, transgender, queer, intersex, asexual, nonbinary, or otherwise nonheteronormative person.

A movement that promotes equal rights and social justice for all members of the LGBTQIA+ community.

SEE ALSO
RAINBOW

"Gay Pride is such a big part of my identity. I'm obsessed with gay culture, gay neighborhoods, gay clubs and institutions, gay TV, films, artists, musicians—I am so proud to be a part of a community that remains strong and united in the face of hate."

 WANT MORE INFO? *THINK:* **QUEER AND PROUD OF IT, BABE.**

DID YOU KNOW In the United States, Gay Pride—or simply, Pride—is celebrated during the month of June in honor of a series of violent demonstrations that occurred at Stonewall Inn, a New York City gay bar, on June 28, 1969. The Stonewall riots are largely credited for starting the cultural conversation around gay rights and continue to be celebrated as a symbol of gay liberation.

P

Gilbert Baker's 1978 Pride flag helped define the modern LGBTQIA+ movement.

A modified version of Baker's flag is commonly seen at Pride parades and in gayborhoods all over the world.

The More Color, More Pride flag was introduced in 2017 by Philadelphia's Office of LGBT Affairs, under Amber Hikes's leadership.

The Progress Pride flag by Daniel Quasar debuted in 2018, incorporating the colors of the Transgender Pride flag.

PRINT

▼ *noun*
See BULGE

PRISSY

▼ *adjective*
See PANSY, SISSY

PRIVILEGE

▼ *noun*
A special right or immunity granted to a particular group of people.

SEE ALSO

CISGENDER PRIVILEGE, MALE PRIVILEGE, STRAIGHT PRIVILEGE, WHITE PRIVILEGE

▼ *verb*
To grant a privilege to.

"A lot of straight people don't understand the privilege they have to simply love the person they love. Love is love—it is our right! We need society to respect all of us!"

 WANT MORE INFO? *THINK:* **THE INVISIBLE WAYS IN WHICH CERTAIN GROUPS OF PEOPLE HAVE FREEDOM BASED ON THEIR IDENTITY.**

PROCESSING

▼ *verb*
In ballroom culture, this refers to a skilled competitor eliminating all others from the competition.

"That queen was processing the girls in Vogue Femme, taking them out one by one, hand by hand."

 WANT MORE INFO? *THINK:* **LEAVING THE OTHER COMPETITORS IN THE DUST.**

 This term originated in ballroom culture.

PRONOUN

▼ *noun*
A grammatical way to refer to someone without naming them, according to gender identity. As our cultural understanding of gender has expanded, pronouns, too, have expanded from the traditional use of she/her/hers and he/him/his to include nonbinary and gender nonconforming identities, such as they/them/theirs.

SEE ALSO

"The Genderbread Person," *p. 56;* **"Common Pronouns 101,"** *p. 81*

Jameelah: *Let's introduce ourselves by sharing our name and pronouns. I'll start! I'm Jameelah and I use she/her/hers or they/them/theirs.*
Jurgen: *I'm Jurgen and I use ze/hir/hirs.*
Izzy: *I'm Izzy and I prefer they/them but also respond to he/him.*
Kiyoko: *I'm Kiyoko and I use she/her pronouns.*

 WANT MORE INFO? *THINK:* **PERSONAL IDENTIFIER THAT REFLECTS ONE'S GENDER EXPRESSION.**

 Pronouns are important identifiers in the transgender, nonbinary, and gender nonconforming communities, as they validate and support a person's gender identity. It is important to respect and properly use a person's pronouns and/or chosen name.

DID YOU KNOW International Pronouns Day was first celebrated on October 17, 2018 in twenty-five countries to acknowledge the many ways gender expression is represented in our queer community. It is annually observed on the third Wednesday of October.

PRO-SEX(UALITY)

▼ *adjective*
See SEX POSITIVE

PUFF

▼ *noun*
See FAGGOT

PULLED

▼ *adjective*
Sophisticated and proper.

"Here I stand, looking perched and pulled, with the third bottle of Moët in my hand. I am grace herself, never forget it."

 WANT MORE INFO? *THINK:* **COSMOPOLITAN.**

 This term originated in ballroom culture.

PULL UP

▼ *verb*
To look and act one's best.

"Everyone must pull up and bring their A game. There are five prospective investors here tonight and we need their support."

 WANT MORE INFO? *THINK:* **PUT ON YOUR SUNDAY CLOTHES AND ACT YOUR SUNDAY BEST.**

 This term is commonly used in ballroom culture.

PUMP

▼ *verb*
To walk with a display of confidence, often mimicking a woman's walk on a high fashion runway.

"You betta pump down that street, diva!"

 WANT MORE INFO? THINK: TO STRUT AND MAKE SURE YOU WERK THOSE HIPS, GURL!

▼ *noun*
A long distance.

"It's a pump to get to the top of the mountain. When you see your dreams come true, it's priceless."

 WANT MORE INFO? THINK: A TREK.

 This term originated in Black American culture. It has been appropriated by the larger LGBTQIA+ community and mainstream culture.

PUNK

▼ *noun*
See PUP

PUNTER

▼ *noun*
See TOP

PUP

▼ *noun*
A young gay or queer male.

> **SEE ALSO**
> **CHICKEN, TWINK, TWUNK**

"He is just a pup with a lot to learn about being gay."

 WANT MORE INFO? THINK: A BABY GAY BOY IN HIS LATE TEENS (AND EARLY TWENTIES).

In kink and fetish play, this is a partner who acts out the role of a puppy, listening to the commands of the Dominant partner.

"I'm a good pup! I waited by the door, wagging my tail when my Handler came home."

 WANT MORE INFO? THINK: PUT ON YOUR LEATHER PUPPY HOOD, KNEE PADS, AND TAIL: IT'S SEXY TIME.

The term is commonly used in the BDSM, leather, and kink communities. For all BDSM-related terms, the power exchange is a part of sadomasochistic play and should be consensual between all partners involved. The first *p* in the word "pup" should always be lowercase and the *H* in "Handler" capitalized when referring to D/s, or power dynamic, relationships.

PUP(PY) PLAY

▼ *idiom*
Part of the kink and fetish scene when a couple role plays a puppy dog and its Handler.

"If you're having trouble understanding the appeal of puppy play, just imagine how amazing it would be if there were a form of group relaxation where you could empty your mind of all your cares . . . lower all of your defenses, and bypass small talk forever. Now imagine that vigorous cuddling and praise are key components of this relaxation technique. And did I mention snacks? You get snacks."
▶ Matt Baume

 WANT MORE INFO? *THINK:* **A FORM OF FETISHIZED PLAY.**

 This term originated in the BDSM, leather, and kink communities. For all BDSM-related terms, the power exchange is a part of sadomasochistic play and should be consensual between all partners involved.

PURE

▼ *adjective*
See GOLD STAR, PLATINUM STAR

PURPLE

▼ *adjective*
See LAVENDER

PUSH THROUGH

▼ *idiom*
To command and take charge of a space or task.

"Push through, choir! Y'all betta sing. The spirit of the Lord is here this morning!"

 WANT MORE INFO? *THINK:* **GET THE JOB DONE.**

USAGE NOTE This term is commonly used in the Black gay community.

PUSSY

▼ *noun*
A vagina.

"Why did I buy us an all-expenses-paid trip to Dinah Shore Weekend? The power of the pussy, of course."

 WANT MORE INFO? *THINK:* **PINK.**

▼ *adjective*
In ballroom culture, this refers to being overtly feminine.

"These queens are iconic because they are pussy. Mother Ashley, Meeka, and Alloura; learn from these legends, children."

 WANT MORE INFO? *THINK:* **FEMME BEAUTY AND GRACE.**

P

"It's time to celebrate! Oh yeah!
#LGBTQFAMILIESDAY !"

Many LGBTQIA+ couples who want to grow their love for each other into a family have children. Some queer people may choose to raise a child in a loving single-parent household. LGBTQIA+ adults have several options on how to build their love nest. When starting a family, it is important to acknowledge that there are unique needs for LGBTQIA+ parents and their kids.

In some cases, a couple or single parent may choose to use donor insemination (often done with lesbians) or have a surrogate (often done with gay males). A child may come from a previous relationship. Many people adopt or foster children. All of these choices are celebrated in our LGBTQIA+ community. Establishing good values, proper communication, and unconditional love and finding a community that offers long-lasting support allow queer parents to build a strong and thriving family dynamic.

The opportunity for a child to have two moms, two dads, or a combination of queer parents is a unique experience. LGBTQIA+ parents and their children often face certain challenges, such as long adoption wait time because of bias or prejudice, complications with legal guardianship, possible emotional instability from an adopted or foster child, children not being socially accepted by their peers, judgment from other parents, and lack of support from immediate family, friends, and/or the children's school.

Laws vary from state to state and are constantly evolving when it comes to recognizing queer parents and their families; if you are able, consult a local family attorney with any questions you may have. On June 26, 2017, the Supreme Court reversed an Arkansas Supreme Court ruling, ordering all states to treat same-sex couples equally to opposite-sex couples in the issuance of birth certificates. This was a big win for our LGBTQIA+ families and a foundation for more wins to come.

PFLAG, Family Equality, COLAGE, *Gay Parent* magazine, Family Acceptance Project, and Family Week in Provincetown are examples of supportive groups, publications, and events that provide support and resources to queer parents and their families.

Qq

QPOC OR QTPOC

▼ *noun*
An inclusive acronym for queer people/person of color or queer trans people/person of color, diverse people who have been marginalized because of race, sex, and gender. This community centers the experiences of its members and provides spaces and language for empowerment.

SEE ALSO
MOC, POC, QWOC, WOC

"Being a queer Person of Color (QPOC) often feels like being on the front lines on the fight for equality in two groups, with both treating you as an 'other.' For me, the challenge has been dealing with racism and colorism in the gay community and homophobia and transphobia in the Black community. . . . The majority of my friends are QPOC because they understand what it's like to be the rainbow sheep in your Black family, and the Black sheep in a white world." ▶ Kayla Inman

 WANT MORE INFO? *THINK:* **AN ACRONYM THAT CREATES SPACE AND EMPOWERMENT FOR MARGINALIZED GENDERS, SEXUALITIES, AND RACES WITHIN THE LGBTQIA+ COMMUNITY.**

USAGE NOTE Other iterations of this acronym exist, one of the most popular being QTBIPOC: queer, trans, Black, Indigenous, and people/person of color.

DID YOU KNOW Due to the adversity queer and trans people of color face—because of racism, queerphobia, and transphobia— many QTPOC, youth especially, find themselves at high risk for homelessness, poverty, and violence. As a result, activist groups have formed to serve and protect QTPOC youth and the community at large, such as the National Black Justice Coalition, Audre Lorde Project, QLatinx, and Fabulous Independent Educated Radicals for Community Empowerment (FIERCE).

QUEEN

▼ *noun*

A gay, bisexual, or queer man, usually flamboyant in nature. Femininity is often celebrated and glorified in the gay male community, so there are many labels using the word "queen." Alternate spellings include QWEEN, KWEEN, and KWANE.

RELATED
QUEENY *adjective*

A term of endearment for a friend (of any gender and/or sexuality).

In ballroom and drag culture, "queen" is a term used to unite all LGBTQIA+ people, blurring the line between genders and celebrating queerness.

SEE ALSO
BUTCH QUEEN, FAUX QUEEN, FEMME QUEEN, DRAG QUEEN

"['Queen' is] the line between us. The unity. Because we are family. We are queens—*but he's a guy queen, and I'm a girl queen."*
▶ Nicole Bowles

 WANT MORE INFO? *THINK:* **A GAY, A BFF, AND/OR A MEMBER OF THE BALLROOM COMMUNITY.**

QUEENAGER

▼ *noun*

A teenage queen. The term QUEER TEEN can also be used.

Arrow: *Let me give you the cafeteria tour. The lacrosse and dance teams sit over by the east doors. The speech club sits here . . .*
Luna: *That's fine, but where do the queenagers sit?*
Arrow: *I thought you would never ask! We all sit over there, by the big windows.*

 WANT MORE INFO? *THINK:* **ADOLESCENT QUEER.**

Queening out ▼

Queer teen / Queenager ▲

Q

DID YOU KNOW

In 2010, gay activists Dan Savage and Terry Miller created the It Gets Better Project in direct response to the increasing rates of suicide among LGBTQIA+ youth. In an effort to build a supportive community around those struggling with bullying and mental health issues related to gender, identity, and sexuality, Savage and Miller created a video-sharing platform to empower and uplift the youth and connect them with adults who could affirm that life does indeed get better. Since its inception, the It Gets Better Project has collected over sixty thousand video entries from people all around the world, reminding LGBTQIA+ youth that hope is out there, and it does get better.

QUEENING OUT

▼ *idiom*
Heightened emotional behavior or fits.

"He was queening out just because he saw a rat! It's New York! Get over it."

 WANT MORE INFO? *THINK:* **ACTING MELODRAMATIC.**

The act of a queer male exaggerating femininity.

"I am ready to queen out for Troy's birthday! The theme is glitter and gold!"

 WANT MORE INFO? *THINK:* **FEMME-ING IT UP.**

QUEER

▼ adjective
An umbrella term describing anyone who identifies as something other than heterosexual and/or cisgender.

▼ noun
A queer person.

"I just wish more of my fellow queers would come out sometimes. It's nice out here, you know?"
▶ Elton John

 WANT MORE INFO? *THINK:* ANYONE ON THE LGBTQIA+ SPECTRUM.

▼ verb
To make something queer; to analyze, deconstruct, and challenge thoughts or ideas rooted in heteronormativity.

"The queering of literary classics brings diversity to young readers. I can't wait to share 'Ash,' the queer version of 'Cinderella,' with my future children."

 WANT MORE INFO? *THINK:* THE ACTS OF GENDER-BENDING, CHALLENGING SEXUAL NORMS, AND QUESTIONING MASCULINE AND FEMININE IDEALS.

USAGE NOTE Once derogatory, the term has been reappropriated by much of the LGBTQIA+ community to be an inclusive identifier for anyone within it. However, not all members of the LGBTQIA+ community are comfortable with this term and refrain from using it.

DID YOU KNOW The word "queer" came into popular use in the gay community in the early 1900s after being used for hundreds of years to mean strange or peculiar. For many years, the term was used in a derogatory way to describe homosexuals, until the 1980s, when activists reclaimed the word as a politically provocative way to take ownership of their identities.

Q

QUEER GEEK

▼ *noun*
A queer enthusiast of technology, comics, video games, podcasts, and other topics that empower LGBTQIA+ nerds.

Ivy: *I'm rallying up the queer geek squad to volunteer for Flame Con next month. Sai and Astrid are in!*
Emile: *Amazing! Lacie and Shanita are too! #flamies #GeeksOUT #geeksjustwannahavefun*

 WANT MORE INFO? *THINK:* **FLAME CON.**

QUEER PARENT(S)

▼ *noun*
A queer person or couple raising a child or children. For couples who identify as "same-sex," the term SAME-SEX PARENT(S) can also be used.

RELATED
QUEER PARENTING *verb*

SEE ALSO
"Queer Parents and the Family Dynamic," *p. 252*

"In the 1960s, a gay man adopts in California, in the '70s, a lesbian couple starts a family through pregnancy, and in the '90s, a transman gives birth—this is queer history for queer parents!"

 WANT MORE INFO? *THINK:* **LGBTQIA+ PARENTS WHO DO BEDTIME STORIES, PARENT/ TEACHER CONFERENCES, AND TIKTOK DANCES FOR THEIR KIDS.**

QUEERPHOBIA

▼ *noun*
Aversion, fear, or hatred toward queerness.

RELATED
QUEERPHOBIC *adjective*   **QUEERPHOBE** *noun*

SEE ALSO
ACEPHOBIA, BIPHOBIA, FEMMEPHOBIA, HOMO- PHOBIA, LESBOPHOBIA, TRANSPHOBIA

"Our state representative's queerphobic rhetoric is problematic not only for political reasons, but for the safety of the LGBTQIA+ community."

 WANT MORE INFO? *THINK:* **DISCRIMINATION TOWARD QUEER PEOPLE.**

QUEERPLATONIC PARTNER

▼ *noun*
A partner in a queerplatonic relationship. The terms SQUISH or ZUCCHINI can also be used. The term may be abbreviated as "QP" or "QPP."

SEE ALSO
QUEERPLATONIC RELATIONSHIP

"Victoria and I work together, cry together, braid each other's hair, communicate intimately, and support and love each other as queerplatonic partners."

WANT MORE INFO? *THINK:* **A LOVING, NONROMANTIC, NONSEXUAL BESTIE AND PARTNER.**

 USAGE NOTE This term originated in the asexual and aromantic communities. It has been appropriated by some of the larger LGBTQIA+ community.

QUEERPLATONIC RELATIONSHIP

▼ *noun*
An extremely close, passionate attachment between two friends that has a strong emotional connection that may extend beyond the boundary of a "normal" friendship. These relationships do not develop into sexual or romantic partnerships. A person in a queerplatonic relationship can be called a QUEERPLATONIC PARTNER, SQUISH, or ZUCCHINI.

"Your aura is beautiful, and you affirm me with such goodness. We've developed the most extraordinary queerplatonic relationship, and I've never felt safer."

 WANT MORE INFO? *THINK:* **A LOVING BOND BETWEEN TWO PEOPLE THAT DOES NOT FIT THE MODEL OF A TRADITIONAL FRIENDSHIP OR SEXUAL RELATIONSHIP.**

 USAGE NOTE This term originated in the asexual and aromantic communities. It has been appropriated by some of the larger LGBTQIA+ community.

QUEER TEEN

▼ *noun*
Youth, usually between the ages of twelve and nineteen, who identify as queer or LGBTQIA+.

SEE ALSO
QUEENAGER

"To all the queer teens who continue to stand up for yourselves, for others, and what you believe in, the LGBTQIA+ community thanks you!"

 WANT MORE INFO? *THINK:* **LGBTQIA+ YOUTH.**

DID YOU KNOW Media representation of queer teens has encouraged and supported LGBTQIA+ youth in a dynamic way. Films, YouTube channels, music, and social media have provided important outlets for queer teens to connect on social issues, organize grass-roots projects, create peer groups, and inspire each other. Some noted influencers who use their social media platforms to empower the young queer community are Troye Sivan, Hayley Kiyoko, Tyler Oakley, Amandla Stenberg, Connor Franta, Lil Nas X, and Miles Jai.

QUEER THEORY

▼ *noun*
A field of critical theory that grew out of women's and gender studies; a form of critical thinking that dismantles traditional assumptions about sex, sexuality, and gender as they relate to our social environment.

"The work of so many philosophers, writers, and great thinkers paved the way for queer theory."

 WANT MORE INFO?
THINK: **LOOKING AT ALL EXPRESSIONS OF HUMANITY THROUGH A CRITICAL, QUEER LENS.**

QUESTIONING

▼ *adjective*
An identifier for an individual who is curious about or exploring their gender identity or sexual orientation.

"To tell you the truth, I'm still questioning my sexuality. When I find new labels I connect with, I get curious. There is such liberation in self-discovery and I'm going to take my time exploring."

 WANT MORE INFO? *THINK:*
EXPLORING ONE'S IDENTITY.

QWEEN

▼ *noun*
See QUEEN

QWOC OR QTWOC

▼ *noun*
An inclusive acronym for queer women/woman of color or queer and transgender women/woman of color, members of a group of diverse women who have traditionally been marginalized because of race, sex, and gender. This community centers the experiences of its members and provides spaces and language for empowerment.

SEE ALSO
MOC, POC, QPOC OR QTPOC, WOC

"QTWOC will not be overlooked anymore! Femininity, queerness, and melanin are our superpowers and we are a force to be reckoned with."

 WANT MORE INFO? *THINK:*
AN ACRONYM THAT AMPLIFIES THE VOICES OF MARGINALIZED WOMEN/ FEMMES, SEXUALITIES, AND RACES WITHIN THE LGBTQIA+ COMMUNITY.

Q

Rainbow _____ ▲

Rr

RACK

▼ *noun*
A pair of breasts.

SEE ALSO
BOOBS, JUGS, TITTIES

"Sis, your rack looks sick in that bikini. You have to get it!"

 WANT MORE INFO? *THINK:* **A SET OF NICE TITTIES.**

RAINBOW

▼ *noun*
A symbol of colors associated with the diversity and empowerment of the LGBTQIA+ community.

SEE ALSO
FULL SPECTRUM, PRIDE

▼ *adjective*
Bearing the colors of the rainbow.

"The rainbow flag and the rainbow itself are symbols that remind us love is love, no matter what size, shape, or color it comes in."

 WANT MORE INFO? *THINK:* **PRIDE.**

DID YOU KNOW The rainbow flag was created in 1978. Politician Harvey Milk challenged an artist named Gilbert Baker to create an image that promoted hope for the gay community amid the progressive movement toward gay liberation in the late seventies. The original flag consisted of eight colors: hot pink for sexuality, red for life, orange for healing, yellow for the sun, green for nature, turquoise for art, indigo for harmony, and violet for spirit. In 2017, the Philadelphia Office of LGBT Affairs debuted a flag that includes black and brown stripes to celebrate people of color within the community. In 2018, Daniel Quasar designed the Progress Pride Flag, incorporating the colors of the transgender pride flag into the rainbow flag. (See p. 247.)

REACHING

▼ *verb*
An attempt to make something work but not quite achieving the desired result.

"Baby, you are reaching with that bright blue! Who dyed your hair? Papa Smurf?"

 WANT MORE INFO? *THINK:* **TRYING, BUT . . . D+.**

 USAGE NOTE This term is commonly used in the Black gay community.

READ

▼ *noun*
A skillful insult, piece of criticism, or mocking observation, usually rooted in some truth.

SEE ALSO
LIBRARY, READ FOR FILTH

▼ *verb*
To insult or disrespect.

"Shade comes from reading. Reading came first. Reading is the real art form of insult. You get in a smart crack and everyone laughs and kikis because you found a flaw and exaggerated it . . . then you got a good read going." ► Dorian Corey

 WANT MORE INFO? *THINK:* **READING IS FUNDAMENTAL!**

 USAGE NOTE This term originated in ballroom culture. It has been appropriated by the larger LGBTQIA+ community and mainstream culture.

READ FOR FILTH

▼ *idiom*
A harsh, merciless attack on someone's character.

SEE ALSO
LIBRARY, READ

"Javier got read for filth by his mama because of all those porn charges on her DirecTV bill."

 WANT MORE INFO? *THINK:* **REPRIMANDED.**

 USAGE NOTE This term originated in ballroom culture.

READ SOMEONE THEIR RIGHTS

▼ *idiom*
To publicly point out someone's flaws. The attack can be mild, earnest, and honest, or it can be spiteful with major intent to hurt.

"Miss Thing thought she was going to read someone their rights with her finger all in Kiara's face. But I gave that hussy the nastiest stare-down and she knew not to try us!"

 WANT MORE INFO? *THINK:* **TO OPENLY CRITICIZE OR HUMILIATE.**

 USAGE NOTE This term originated in ballroom culture. It has been appropriated by the larger LGBTQIA+ community and mainstream culture.

REALLY GIRL

▼ *idiom*
Questioning a statement or action.

"Really girl? You just gonna jump the line? We have all been patiently standing here. You can kindly find your way to the back!"

 WANT MORE INFO? *THINK:*
"ARE YOU SERIOUS?"

 This term originated in Black American culture and is used in the Black gay and queer community. It has been appropriated by the larger LGBTQIA+ community and mainstream culture.

REALNESS

▼ *noun*
A quality someone possesses when they have the ability to copy and bring to life a specific look or behavior. The term is often used in succession with another adjective or noun.

"You are giving major Olivia Pope realness in this white coat today."

 WANT MORE INFO? *THINK:*
"IF YOU DON'T RECOGNIZE THE REALNESS, SHADE ON YOU!"
▶ Sugur Shane, "Buddah Vs Sugur"

In ballroom culture, this is a category in a competition where a participant is judged on their ability to embody a particular look or persona in an authentic, realistic way. Popular subcategories include Femme Queen Realness, Schoolboy Realness, Executive Realness, and Thug Realness.

"The Prodigy boys are in Armani from head to toe. We are snatching the realness category tonight!"

 WANT MORE INFO? *THINK:*
A COMPETITION CATEGORY JUDGING HOW REAL YOU LOOK.

 This term originated in ballroom culture. It has been appropriated by mainstream culture.

REAPPROPRIATE

▼ *verb*
To reclaim a word or expression that was once derogatory and give it positive meaning.

RELATED
REAPPROPRIATION *noun*

SEE ALSO
APPROPRIATE, MISAPPROPRIATE

"The LGBTQIA+ community has reappropriated so many terms, like sissy, fag, and dyke, and we're prouder than ever to use these former slurs to radically celebrate our queerness! Yes, we are dykes, we are faggots, we are nellies and sissies and pansies, and we are proud!"

 WANT MORE INFO? *THINK:*
TO TAKE BACK WHAT WAS TAKEN AND MAKE IT WERK.

R

REPULSED

▼ *adjective*
A term used by some asexuals describing their view of sex—whether it is engaging in sex or the idea of sex in general—as repulsive. The term may be used in the phrases "repulsed asexual" or "sex-repulsed."

SEE ALSO
SEXUALLY AVERSE

"I experience an attraction to masculine people, but I am sex-repulsed. I don't do the nasty business. Hearts, not parts!"

 WANT MORE INFO? *THINK:* **STRONGLY DISLIKES SEX.**

 This term is commonly used in the asexual community.

RING OF KEYS

▼ *idiom*
A symbol representing lesbian identity and visibility. This phrase comes from a song in the Broadway musical *Fun Home*, when a young girl sees a butch woman and, for the first time, a living embodiment of her own identity. Often used in the phrase "ring of keys moment."

SEE ALSO
THE BECHDEL TEST

"I listened to the Nancy podcast episode about 'ring of keys' moments yesterday, and it made my inner baby dyke just melt into a puddle of lesbian love."

 WANT MORE INFO? *THINK:* **THAT MOMENT WHEN REPRESENTATION MATTERS MOST.**

R

RING SNATCHER

▼ *noun*
See TOP

ROLE PLAY

▼ *verb*

To act out a particular scene, where each person involved takes on a specific role. Role-playing can be sexual or nonsexual. When used in the context of D/s play or BDSM, this is usually a power dynamic between Dominants and their submissives.

RELATED
ROLE-PLAY or ROLE-PLAYING *noun*

SEE ALSO
DOM/SUB RELATIONSHIP, BDSM

Rory: *Do you want to role play tonight?*
Eli: *Ooh, yummy! Be my railroad conductor, and I'll be your damsel in distress.*

 WANT MORE INFO? *THINK:* **TO ACT OUT FANTASY SCENARIOS.**

 This term is commonly used in the BDSM, leather, and kink communities. For all BDSM-related terms, the power exchange is a part of sadomasochistic play and should be consensual between all partners involved.

ROMANTIC ORIENTATION

▼ *noun*

Similar to sexual orientation, this term allows people to identify who they are romantically attracted to. The term "affectional orientation" is also used.

"The desire to intimately connect with someone does not have to include sex. A woman who is sexually averse, for example, may have the tendency to fall in love with women, identifying as asexual and homoromantic. Sexual intimacy is only part of a relationship's dynamic."

 WANT MORE INFO? *THINK:* **SEXUAL ORIENTATION: WHO YOU SLEEP WITH. ROMANTIC ORIENTATION: WHO YOU FALL IN LOVE WITH.**

 This term is commonly used in the asexual community.

ROOT

▼ *noun*

A person, piece of media, or situation that may have been an early sign of being LGBTQIA+.

Joon: *My root was definitely either playing with my sisters' Barbies or—weirdly—Captain Hook in the cartoon version of* Peter Pan? *I love a fancy queen.*
Claire: *That's not weird at all. My root was She-Ra. Followed swiftly by Jennifer Connelly in the film* Labyrinth. *HOT!*

 WANT MORE INFO? *THINK:* **THE "REASON" YOU'RE QUEER.**

R

The Queens' English

ROSE

▼ *noun*
See MARY

ROUGH TRADE

▼ *noun*
See TRADE

RUGGED

▼ *adjective*
See BUTCH

RUG MUNCHER

▼ *noun*
See CARPET MUNCHER

RUMPY TO RUMPY

▼ *idiom*
Male-to-male sexual intercourse. The phrase "rumper to rumper" can also be used.

Chaz: *Pull up to my rumpy, baby! Rumper to rumper—let's get it onnnnnnn.*
Dylan: *Oh my God, Chaz! Please stop. Please stop now.*

 WANT MORE INFO? *THINK:* BUTT TO BUTT. DUDE TO DUDE. MALE-ON-MALE SEX.

Religion and LGBTQIA+ Believers

There are many LGBTQIA+ people who identify as religious. We center our lives around our faith and the teachings of a higher power. However, many gay and queer people who choose to live in faith often face harsh discrimination from religious institutions, spiritual leaders, and even family members because our sexual orientation or gender expression is deemed incongruous with the practices of a particular faith.

Faith-based spaces for the queer community are important, and several religious and spiritual institutions have welcomed diversity, promoting compassion and love for all people in their spiritual teachings. Noted religious communities include the Metropolitan Community Church founded by Troy Perry, the Buddhist Fellowship, the Institute for Judaism and Sexual Orientation, The Naming Project, Many Voices, and Muslims for Progressive Values.

HISTORY
LESSON

coexist

LGBTQIA+
AND RELIGION
CAN SHARE
THE SAME
WORLD.

HISTORY LESSON

Stonewall

ON JUNE 28, 1969, a series of intense demonstrations by gay and transgender protesters began at the Stonewall Inn, a gay club in New York City. That night, police raided the club and arrested several patrons and employees. This was not the first time a bar or club in Greenwich Village—a well-known gayborhood—was raided. For years, the police and the New York State Liquor Authority would target and antagonize gay establishments in the city.

> "It was a rebellion, it was an uprising, it was a civil rights disobedience– it wasn't no damn riot."
>
> ▶ Stormé DeLarverie

Rioting followed for days after the first punch was thrown (allegedly by Black lesbian and drag performer Stormé DeLarverie), continuing up and down Christopher Street and throughout the neighborhood. These demonstrations eventually propelled the organization of the gay rights movement, which regarded Stonewall as the catalyst for social and political change.

Prominent drag queens and trans activists like Sylvia Rivera and Marsha P. Johnson were instrumental in spearheading the fight for equality and advocating for gay and transgender rights after the Stonewall events. Together they founded Street Transvestite Action Revolutionaries (STAR) and the Gay Liberation Front.

These organizations paved the way for others to follow, and Rivera and Johnson, both trans women of color, are now considered two of the most revered icons in LGBTQIA+ history.

> "IF YOU WANT GAY POWER, THEN YOU'RE GOING TO HAVE TO FIGHT FOR IT. AND YOU'RE GOING TO HAVE TO FIGHT UNTIL YOU WIN."
>
> ▶ Sylvia Rivera

Ss

S&M

▼ *noun*
See BDSM

SAFE WORD

▼ *noun*
A code word or set of words used during sexual activity, and especially in BDSM scene power play, to signal one partner's discomfort, fear, or desire to stop an activity. A common set of safe words are "green" meaning safe, "yellow" meaning slow down, and "red" meaning stop.

SEE ALSO

CONSENT, NEGOTIATION

"What do you think of pineapple or blackberry? No wait, how about banana for our safe word?"

 WANT MORE INFO? *THINK:* **A RED LIGHT IN THE BEDROOM THAT IS ALWAYS TAKEN SERIOUSLY.**

USAGE NOTE This term originated in the BDSM community and is commonly used in the leather and kink communities. For all BDSM-related terms, the power exchange is a part of sadomasochistic play and should be consensual between all partners involved.

SAGA

▼ *noun*
An acronym standing for "Sexuality and Gender Acceptance."

"Should the community use SAGA instead of LGBT, I mean LGBTQ, I mean, LGBTQIA+. I mean . . . never mind."

 WANT MORE INFO? *THINK:* **AN INCLUSIVE CATCHALL TERM FOR QUEER EQUALITY.**

SALLY

▼ *noun*
See MARY

SAME-GENDER LOVING

▼ *noun*
Having an attraction to people of the same gender. Can be abbreviated as "SGL."

"Same-gender loving ain't different from any other type of loving. Love is love, man."

 WANT MORE INFO? *THINK:* **AN INCLUSIVE TERM FOR SAME-SEX INTIMACY.**

USAGE NOTE This term originated in the Black gay and queer community. It has been appropriated by the larger LGBTQIA+ community.

DID YOU KNOW The expression "same-gender loving" was popularized in the Black American community in the early 1990s when activist Cleo Manago used it to refer to homosexuality and bisexuality as a means of empowering Black queers.

SAME-SEX MARRIAGE

▼ *noun*
See MARRIAGE EQUALITY

SAME-SEX PARENTS

▼ *noun*
See QUEER PARENT(S)

SAPPHIC

▼ *adjective*
Of or relating to lesbianism; derived from the lesbian Greek poet Sappho, of the island Lesbos.

RELATED
SAPPHISTRY *noun*

Kennedy: *Baby, I wrote you a love poem. May I read it to you?*
Fana: *You know I love your Sapphic poetry! Read it to me, my sweet Mary Oliver, my Nikki Giovanni.*

 WANT MORE INFO? *THINK:* **LADY-LOVIN'.**

SAPPHO DADDY-O

▼ *noun*
A straight man who enjoys the company of lesbians.

"Grayson is our crew's Sappho daddy-o. He always kills it in our fantasy soccer league and comes to everyone's annual anniversary parties."

 WANT MORE INFO? *THINK:* **ONE OF THE DUDES.**

SASHAY

▼ *verb*
To walk with swagger; to show off with exaggerated movements of the hips and shoulders.

SEE ALSO
SHANTAY

"I love you darling, and keep your head up high, but it is time for you to sashay away. You have been eliminated from the competition!"

 WANT MORE INFO? *THINK:*
A CONFIDENT, FEMININE GAIT.

 This term was popularized by American drag queen and entertainer RuPaul and is commonly used in the drag community. It has been appropriated by mainstream culture.

SATURDAY NIGHT LESBIAN

▼ *noun*
A dated term for a woman who discreetly displays affection for other women, limiting her homosexuality to weekend social engagements—at a club, bar, or special outing.

"She is only gay on the weekend. A true Saturday night lesbian."

 WANT MORE INFO? *THINK:*
A COVERT LEZ.

S

SCENE

▼ *noun*
In BDSM, "scene" refers to an exchange of power between two or more people through role-play. Each scene should always be negotiated and consensual for all parties involved.

SEE ALSO
BDSM, DOM/SUB RELATIONSHIP, ROLE PLAY

"If you aren't ready to be paddled or flogged, try a little cops-and-robbers scene to warm up."

 WANT MORE INFO? *THINK:*
A ROLE-PLAYING SCENARIO.

 This term originated in the BDSM, leather, and kink communities. For all BDSM-related terms, the power exchange is a part of sadomasochistic play and should be consensual between all partners involved.

SCENE, THE

▼ *noun*
The atmosphere or current social location.

Devin: *I'll be there soon—five minutes away. What's the scene giving?*
Lloyd: *Everything you can dream and more. Girl, hurry up!*

 WANT MORE INFO? *THINK:* **A PLACE TO MEET UP AND SOCIALIZE.**

 This term is commonly used in the Black gay community and the larger queer and trans people of color (QTPOC) community.

SCHNAUZER

▼ *noun*
A small penis.

RELATED
SCHNAUZER TAIL *noun*

"I go for schnauzers. Smaller fits better."

 WANT MORE INFO? *THINK:* **A TEENY WEENIE.**

 This term originated in the gay male community.

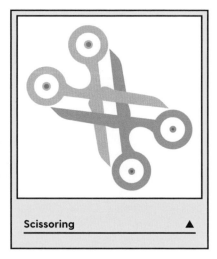

Scissoring ▲

SCISSORING

▼ *verb*
A sexual act, where clitoral stimulation is achieved by two people rubbing their vulvae together. The term comes from a common position used to achieve this, where lesbians open their legs like two pairs of scissors in order to connect vaginas.

SEE ALSO
BUMPER-TO-BUMPER, TRIB

"We were scissoring all night. My legs hurt, but I came three times."

 WANT MORE INFO? *THINK:* **BUMPING DONUTS, PUSSY LOCKING, CLIT-CLATTING, PRAWN WRESTLING. YOU GET THE IDEA.**

 This term originated in the lesbian community.

SCREAM

▼ *verb*
See GAG

SELLING

▼ *verb*
Displaying high levels of self-confidence, a fierce attitude, behavior, or style. Often used in the phrase "selling it." The term SERVING can also be used.

"She was serving, she was selling, she was slaying all night!"

 WANT MORE INFO? *THINK:* **SELLING AND SERVING CONFIDENCE IS HOW YOU MAKE YOUR ENEMIES EAT THEIR WORDS.**

 USAGE NOTE This term originated in ballroom culture and is commonly used in the larger queer and trans people of color (QTPOC) community. It has been appropriated by mainstream culture.

SEMI-CLOSETED

▼ *adjective*
Open about one's sexuality with members of the queer community, but not publicly with the hetero-sexual community.

"Don't frown on someone who is semi-closeted. Everyone protects their sexuality in different ways. Being semi-closeted is no different."

 WANT MORE INFO? *THINK:* **ONE FOOT IN THE CLOSET, ONE FOOT OUT.**

SEPARATISM

▼ *noun*
A practice of separation of a certain group of people from the larger whole. Separatism is often advocated for on the basis of culture, gender, government, religion, or sexuality.

RELATED
SEPARATIST *adjective, noun*

SEE ALSO
IDENTITY POLITICS, LESBIAN SEPARATIST, TERF

Scott: *What if all gay men lived on one island? That's my idea of utopia.*
Titus: *Well, sorry to burst your utopian bubble, but separatism isn't my idea of fun.*

 WANT MORE INFO? *THINK:* **MAKING CLIQUES AND LEAVING PEOPLE OUT.**

SERVE FISH

▼ *idiom*
To deliver feminine realness. This idiom was first used in drag culture, referring to queens who looked convincingly female.

SEE ALSO
FISH

"Serve fish, honey! Give me mahi-mahi and tuna in that slinky little dress and thigh-highs!"

 WANT MORE INFO? *THINK:* **TO DISH OUT ULTRA-FISHY FEMININITY.**

SERVING

▼ *verb*
See SELLING

SEVERE

▼ *adjective*
Of epic proportion; larger than life.

"Baby, our new temperature-controlled organic mattress just arrived! Our sleep is about to be so severe!"

 WANT MORE INFO? *THINK:* **FIERCE.**

 USAGE NOTE This term is commonly used in the Black gay community and the larger queer and trans people of color (QTPOC) community.

SEX

▼ *noun*
A category of humans based on reproductive organs and functions.

SEE ALSO
"The Genderbread Person," *p. 56*

"My sex is female, but my gender expression is more expansive. I identify as queer in every sense of the word: genderqueer, sexually queer . . . I'm a queerdo!"

 WANT MORE INFO? *THINK:* **MALE, FEMALE, OR INTERSEX.**

Sexual intercourse or play.

Gene: *Are we having sex tonight, pookie bear?*
Alan: *Come on. You know it's not Thursday.*

 WANT MORE INFO? *THINK:* **HANKY PANKY.**

SEX ASSIGNED AT BIRTH

▼ *noun*
See CISGENDER

SEX NEGATIVE

▼ *adjective*
Having an unfavorable attitude toward sex, sexuality, and sexual diversity. A sex negative person views sexual exploration as undisciplined, problematic, and risky.

"Because of moral and cultural beliefs, many cultures around the world are sex negative. Mastur- bation is looked down on, only missionary heterosexual sex is considered 'acceptable,' and some laws even restrict public display of affection."

 WANT MORE INFO? *THINK:* **SEX-SHAMING.**

SEX POSITIVE

▼ *adjective*
Having a progressive, open attitude toward sex, sexuality, and sexual diversity. A sex positive person views safe and consensual sexual activity as healthy and liberating. The term PRO-SEX can also be used.

"Come one, come all! Join us— gay, queer, poly, straight, and BDSM enthusiasts—in the sex positive movement."

 WANT MORE INFO? *THINK:* **POSITIVELY EMBRACING SEXUALITY AND SEXUAL EXPRESSION.**

S

SEX REASSIGNMENT SURGERY

▼ *noun*
See GENDER AFFIRMATION SURGERY

SEX WORKER

▼ *noun*
A person who offers sexual services for money. Common jobs include exotic dancer, phone sex operator, webcam sex performer, escort, pornographic actor, and Dominatrix.

RELATED
SEX WORK *noun*

"You cannot erase sex workers. Sex work is part of our history and we must erase the stigma."

 WANT MORE INFO? *THINK:* **SOMEONE EMPLOYED IN THE SEX INDUSTRY.**

DID YOU KNOW The discrimination transgender people face often leads to homelessness, unemployment, and violence. Reports have shown that more than 60 percent of transgender women are unable to find or maintain jobs because of their identity. Many trans women participate in sex work to pay for their basic needs. On June 15, 2020, the Supreme Court declared the Civil Rights Act of 1964, which outlaws employment discrimination, also protects LGBTQ people, providing the necessary civil rights protection for trans people in the workplace.

SEXUALITY

▼ *noun*
A complex identity based on a person's sexual orientation, feelings, preferences, and practices.

SEE ALSO
"The Genderbread Person," *p. 56*

Lucas: *My sexuality is this basket of chili cheese fries!*
Zadie: *Come on, it's more complicated than that.*
Lucas: *All right, all right. I identify as a pansexual, homoromantic, femme-of-center queer man. Happy?*

 WANT MORE INFO? *THINK:* **THE COMBINATION OF PREFERENCES THAT CONSTRUCTS YOUR SEXUAL IDENTITY.**

DID YOU KNOW In 1948, Alfred Kinsey created the Kinsey Scale to research the depths of a person's sexual orientation. He believed that sexuality is fluid and could range along the spectrum between homosexuality and heterosexuality. Kinsey published two reports on his research, *Sexual Behavior in the Human Male* (1948) and *Sexual Behavior in the Human Female* (1953) and is recognized as "the father of the sexual revolution." Dr. Kinsey's research and the Kinsey Institute have been a critical source for sexuality, gender, love, and reproduction study and discussion.

SEXUALLY AVERSE

▼ *adjective*
Feeling uneasy or disgusted by the act of sexual intercourse.

SEE ALSO
ASEXUAL, REPULSED, SEX NEGATIVE

"Hannah really doesn't want to fool around, because she is sexually averse. Just communicate with her, okay?"

 WANT MORE INFO? *THINK:* **DISLIKES SEX.**

 This term is commonly used in the asexual community.

SEXUAL ORIENTATION

▼ *noun*
The sexual, emotional, and romantic attraction a person has toward others.

SEE ALSO
"The Genderbread Person," *p. 56*

"No person should be discriminated against because of sex, age, race, creed, or sexual orientation."

 WANT MORE INFO? *THINK:* **INNER SEXUAL COMPASS POINTS TOWARD MEN, WOMEN, BOTH, NEITHER, ALL, OTHER.**

S

SHADE

▼ *noun*
A statement or look filled with subtle criticism or a blunt insult.

RELATED
SHADY *adjective*

SEE ALSO
NO SHADE, THROW SHADE

▼ *verb*
To subtly insult or blatantly show contempt for.

"Shade is, 'I don't tell you you're ugly, but I don't have to tell you because you know you're ugly.' And that's shade." ▸ Dorian Corey

 WANT MORE INFO? *THINK:* **SLANDER.**

 This term originated in ballroom culture. It has been appropriated by the larger LGBTQIA+ community and mainstream culture.

SHANTAY

▼ *verb*
Similar to sashay, this term was coined by famous drag queen and entertainer RuPaul, in the 1993 hit song "Supermodel (You Better Work)." RuPaul has said the term means "to weave a bewitching spell." The alternate spelling "shanté" can also be used.

SEE ALSO
SASHAY

"Shantay, you stay!"

 WANT MORE INFO? *THINK:* **ENCHANTÉ, YOU CAPTIVATE THE CROWD!**

DID YOU KNOW Internationally known drag queen, actor, singer, and producer RuPaul Andre Charles is considered one of the most influential queer people in entertainment today. In 1993, his debut single, "Supermodel (You Better Work)," skyrocketed him to mainstream fame. In 2009, RuPaul's popular reality television show, *RuPaul's Drag Race*, became the first of its kind, bringing viewers into the once intimate world of drag culture.

SHE/HER/HERS

▼ *pronouns*
A set of pronouns used for femme or female-identifying people.

SEE ALSO
"The Genderbread Person," *p. 56,* **"Common Pronouns 101,"** *p. 81*

"I identify as a soft butch lesbian. I use she/her/hers pronouns."

A set of pronouns that can reference anything that is animate or inanimate.

"Ugh, she has been sold out for a month, when am I going to get my new iPhone?"

 WANT MORE INFO? *THINK:* **FEMME IDENTIFIER.**

DID YOU KNOW Feminine names and pronouns are commonly used as terms of endearment in the gay male community and also served as a form of protection in a time when being openly gay was dangerous. Queer men spoke about same-sex relationships in public or in letters by using women's names (see MARY or JUDY, for example) or by switching pronouns of their lovers from "he" to "she." Many cisgender gay men continue to use feminine pronouns to refer to one another. While some consider it subversive, some consider it problematic, too.

SHE'S BEEN DANCED

▼ *idiom*
A phrase used after a person has finished a drink or a smoke and is thoroughly satisfied.

"Ahhhh, well she's been danced! Darling, can you order me another martini?"

 WANT MORE INFO? *THINK:* **A HAPPY RESPONSE AFTER A GOOD SOCIAL HAPPY HOUR.**

SHOW QUEEN

▼ *noun*
A person who is a musical theater or drag show enthusiast.

"Todrick Hall is the ultimate show queen. He was in Broadway's Kinky Boots, *on* RuPaul's Drag Race, *and his album* Straight Outta Oz *slays!"*

 WANT MORE INFO? *THINK:* **SOMEONE WHO LISTENS TO BROADWAY SHOW TUNES ALL DAY, EVERY DAY.**

SICKENING

▼ *idiom*
Astonishingly impressive.

"Oh my Gawd, that Chanel bag is sickening!"

 WANT MORE INFO? *THINK:* **BREATHTAKING.**

 This term originated in ballroom culture. It has been appropriated by mainstream culture.

SIDE

▼ *noun*
A gay man who enjoys all aspects of sexual intercourse with the exception of anal penetration.

"Jin and Leon both identify as tops. In order to make it work, since Jin refuses to take dick, he's a side and Leon is an oral top. You still with me?"

 WANT MORE INFO? *THINK:* **NO BUTT STUFF.**

 This term is commonly used in the gay male community.

SIE/SIE/HIRS

▼ *pronouns*
See "Common Pronouns 101," p. 81

SILVER STAR

▼ *noun*
A gay or lesbian person who has only had one sexual experience with the opposite sex. Typically, this "hetero" sexual encounter confirms the person's homosexuality. When used in the lesbian community, the term LONE STAR can also be used.

Carla: *I hooked up with Greg and it felt weird as hell. I really am a lesbian.*
Danielle: *You're a silver star lesbian, babe. Embrace it.*

 WANT MORE INFO? *THINK:* **ONE AND DONE.**

S

SIR

▼ *noun*

A person who facilitates power dynamic and scene play as the Dominant figure. This term can be used in both nonsexual and sexual capacities.

SEE ALSO
DADDY DOM, DOMINANT, LEATHER COMMUNITY

"In leather relationships, a Sir guides and teaches his submissive. It's important as a Sir to reflect the attitudes and disciplines you want to teach your leather boy. He will be watching you."

 WANT MORE INFO? *THINK:* **SOMEONE WHO DEMANDS RESPECT IN A D/S RELATIONSHIP.**

 USAGE NOTE This term originated in the BDSM, leather, and kink communities. For all BDSM-related terms, the power exchange is a part of sadomasochistic play and should be consensual between all partners involved. The *S* in "Sir" should always be capitalized when referring to D/s, or power dynamic, relationships.

SIS

▼ *noun*

See SISTER OR SISTA

SISSY

▼ *noun*

An effeminate boy or man. This term typically implies weakness.

Mr. Russell: *Your son looks like a sissy with that pink hat on.*
Mrs. Russell: *Don't be a dick, Ron.*

 WANT MORE INFO? *THINK:* **PANSY.**

 USAGE NOTE This term originated as a slur for gay men, but it has been reclaimed by some members of the LGBTQIA+ community. It may still have negative connotations for some people.

SISSY THAT WALK

▼ *idiom*

A command used in drag and ballroom culture—to strut in the most feminine way possible.

"When she strutted down the runway, shouts of 'Sissy that walk!' proved that she had the audience in the palm of her hand."

 WANT MORE INFO? *THINK:* **MAKE IT FEMME, MAKE IT FAB.**

USAGE NOTE This term is used in the drag community and ballroom culture.

SISTER OR SISTA

▼ *noun*
A term of endearment used to acknowledge social kinship and/or friendship within a community of people. In the Black gay and QTPOC communities, the term SIS can also be used.

A friend.

"Sis, I'm always gonna have your back. I got you no matter what."

 WANT MORE INFO? *THINK:* **A CLOSE FRIEND.**

 This term originated in Black American culture and is commonly used in the larger queer and trans people of color (QTPOC) community. It has been appropriated by the larger LGBTQIA+ community and mainstream culture.

SITTING

▼ *adjective*
Looking polished and divine.

"Diego is the queen of glam! He will have your face sitting after a makeover with him."

 WANT MORE INFO? *THINK:* **LIKE A MASTERPIECE.**

 This term originated in ballroom culture. It has been appropriated by the larger LGBTQIA+ community.

SIZE QUEEN

▼ *noun*
A person who is only attracted to large penises.

"Size Queen Anthem: 'I like big dicks and I cannot lie. Magnum XL or goodbye.'"

 WANT MORE INFO? *THINK:* **A QUEEN WHO LIKES A BIG DICK.**

 This term originated in the gay male community.

SKIN ROOM

▼ *noun*
See BATH HOUSE

SLAY

▼ *verb*
To impress or amuse; to nail it.

"I did not come to play with you hoes, I came to slay, bitch!"
▶ Big Freedia

 WANT MORE INFO? *THINK:* **TO DOMINATE THE COMPETITION; TO KILL IT.**

 This term originated in ballroom culture. It has been appropriated by the larger LGBTQIA+ community and mainstream culture.

SLICE

▼ *verb*
To cut out.

"If he tries to text me one more time, I am going to slice him. We are done!"

 WANT MORE INFO? *THINK:* **TO REMOVE AND DELETE.**

 USAGE NOTE This term is commonly used in ballroom culture.

SNATCHED

▼ *adjective*
Extremely lean and toned, as it relates to physique.

"Snatched means the body is together! You are lovely, lean, and shapely. And to be in this dance company, we have to be snatched for the gawds! So that means you have to eat air, drink hope, and take a wheatgrass shot for dessert."

 WANT MORE INFO? *THINK:* **EXTREMELY FIT.**

Small or inadequate.

"I am about to die from thirst and you bring me this snatched cup of water?"

 WANT MORE INFO? *THINK:* **A LESS THAN AMPLE AMOUNT.**

 USAGE NOTE This term originated in ballroom culture. It has been appropriated by the larger LGBTQIA+ community and mainstream culture.

SNATCHING WIGS

▼ *idiom*
Humiliating or exposing someone.

"She needs to keep it cute before I snatch her wig and embarrass her in front of our whole dressing room!"

 WANT MORE INFO? *THINK:* **BLOWING UP SOMEONE'S SPOT.**

Stealing or earning a desired title or claim to fame, even (or especially) when someone already holds the position.

"She is snatching wigs, snatching crowns, and snatching trophies. She stole the whole competition."

 WANT MORE INFO? *THINK:* **SWEEPING THE COMPETITION.**

Someone doing something so incredible, shocking, or downright *good* that you metaphorically lose your hair.

"Beyoncé is always out there snatching wigs with her secret album drops and insane live performances. She is the reason I live!"

 WANT MORE INFO? *THINK:* **BEING FIERCE AS HELL.**

 USAGE NOTE This term originated in the drag community. It has been appropriated by the larger LGBTQIA+ community and mainstream culture.

S

SOFT BUTCH

▼ *noun*

A lesbian who presents in a masculine or androgynous way, with some feminine touches and/or behaviors.

> SEE ALSO
>
> **CHAPSTICK LESBIAN, FUTCH, STEMME, "The Lesbian Spectrum,"** *p. 194*

"I'm looking for a lady who wears the pants most of the time but will put on some lipstick and dazzle me in a suit. A soft butch is hard to find."

 WANT MORE INFO? *THINK:* **ELLEN PAGE.**

 USAGE NOTE This term originated in the lesbian community.

SOFT STUD

▼ *noun*

A lesbian, bisexual, or queer woman who leans toward a masculine or androgynous gender presentation with a sharp eye for style. This woman tends to be softer-presenting or more feminine than a stud.

> SEE ALSO
>
> **FUTCH, STEMME, STUD**

Remy: *Now, where do you think soft stud falls on the lesbian spectrum? Between femme and boi?*
Diamond: *Hmm, maybe? It's definitely close to futch and stemme.*

 WANT MORE INFO? *THINK:* **LENA WAITHE.**

 USAGE NOTE This term originated in the Black lesbian community. It has been appropriated by the larger lesbian community.

SOLO POLYAMORY

▼ *noun*

A polyamorous practice in which an individual does not have a primary partner (or belong to a triad) with whom they might live or share finances. Instead, solo poly people maintain their relationships with themselves as the "primary partner."

"I have a few partners, but I live by myself and don't really see myself settling down with anyone anytime soon. Solo polyamory is my thing because I still get to experience the best parts of love and sex."

 WANT MORE INFO? *THINK:* **PRIMARY RELATIONSHIP: WITH ONESELF.**

 USAGE NOTE This term is commonly used in the non-monogamous community.

S

The Queens' English

SOLO SEX

▼ *noun*
Masturbation.

"Don't be embarrassed by solo sex. I have explored my whole body and my orgasms are insaaaaane."

 WANT MORE INFO? *THINK:* **SELF-STIMULATION.**

SPAGHETTI

▼ *idiom*
Someone who identifies as straight until they get intimate with a queer person or person of the same gender.

Margot: *I'm sorry if I led you on, but I don't like girls. I'm straight.*
Willow: *Yeah, so is spaghetti—until it's wet.*

 WANT MORE INFO? *THINK:* **STRAIGHT WHEN DRY, GAY WHEN WET.**

 S

SPILL THE T

▼ *idiom*
To deliver news or gossip. The *T* stands for "Truth."

"Sis, spill the T! Tell me what's happening over there."

 WANT MORE INFO? *THINK:* **"LET'S HAVE SOME TEA AND A KIKI."**

USAGE NOTE This term originated in ballroom culture. It has been appropriated by the larger LGBTQIA+ community and mainstream culture.

GURL! You betta SPILL THE T!

Ooooh! You KNOW I gots the T! Meet me at the spot at 3PM!

SPOOKED

▼ *verb*
See CLOCK

SQUIRT

▼ *verb*
To ejaculate, as a female.

Daphne: *Omigod! Did I just squirt? I'm so embarrassed!*
Penelope: *Baby, that was so hot.*

 WANT MORE INFO? *THINK:* SHE SHOOTS, SHE SCORES.

SQUISH

▼ *noun*
See QUEERPLATONIC PARTNER
or ZUCCHINI

SRS

▼ *noun*
See SEX REASSIGNMENT SURGERY

STEALTH

▼ *adjective*
Describes a transgender person moving through daily life passing as cisgender. This individual makes a deliberate choice to not disclose to the public their trans identity.

SEE ALSO
PASSING

"I am a man of trans experience, but I am stealth in most areas of my life. Only my family, girlfriend, and my therapist know that I am not cis."

 WANT MORE INFO? *THINK:* **PASSING AS A CIS MAN OR WOMAN WITHOUT BEING DISCOVERED AS TRANS.**

 USAGE NOTE One should be sensitive or refrain from using this term to identify a transgender person.

STEMME

▼ *noun*
A lesbian, bisexual, or queer woman who either switches effortlessly between masculine and feminine looks or captures a fashionable combination of both. The word is a combination of STUD and FEMME. Alternate spellings include "stem."

"A stemme can wear a dress and look bomb, and then all of a sudden go and sag her pants and look bomb. That's why it's so rare to be a stemme because you got to do both and do it right." ▶ Amber Whittington

 WANT MORE INFO? *THINK:* **SOMETIMES SHE SERVES A LITTLE JUSTIN BIEBER, SOMETIMES SHE SERVES CHANEL IMAN.**

 USAGE NOTE This term originated in the Black lesbian community. It has been appropriated by the larger lesbian community.

S

STONE

▼ *adjective*
Describing a person who strictly chooses to perform sexual acts, usually refusing to have one's genitals touched.

"A stone butch is the most common form of someone who's stone, but femmes can be stone, too. I dated a stone femme—a lipstick lesbian—who just wanted to make me cum for days on end."

 WANT MORE INFO? *THINK:* **PREFERS TO TOUCH AND NOT BE TOUCHED.**

 USAGE NOTE This term originated in the lesbian community. It has been appropriated by the larger LGBTQIA+ community.

STONE BUTCH

▼ *noun*
A masculine lesbian or otherwise masculine person who strictly chooses to perform sexual acts, usually refusing to have one's genitals touched.

SEE ALSO
BUTCH, STUD

"Stone butch code: I touch you there, you don't touch me anywhere."

 WANT MORE INFO? *THINK:* **SEXUALLY DOMINANT.**

 USAGE NOTE This term originated in the lesbian community. It has been appropriated by the larger LGBTQIA+ community.

STORM

▼ *verb*
Acting out of confidence about one's appearance or attitude.

"It's my birthday, and I am storming up in this bitch like I own it."

 WANT MORE INFO? *THINK:* **"I GOT YOU (I FEEL GOOD)" BY JAMES BROWN.**

USAGE NOTE This term originated in the Black gay community.

STP

▼ *noun*
An abbreviation for stand-to-pee, referring to a device that enables transgender men or nonbinary people to urinate in public facilities in a standing position.

"I used to sit down to pee in public bathrooms and felt like I was being clocked. It made me feel paranoid. So, now I use my STP."

 WANT MORE INFO? THINK: **PACK 'N' PEE PROSTHETICS.**

STRAIGHT

▼ *adjective*
Heterosexual.

"These straight guys and their horrible pickup lines. I really feel for my hetero sisters."

 WANT MORE INFO? *THINK:* **BOY MEETS GIRL.**

STRAIGHT BOYFRIEND

▼ *noun*
A straight man who is a platonic companion to a gay man. This friendship places respect and value on each person's sexual orientation.

Daniel: *Awww! What did my straight boyfriend buy me today?*
Muhammad: *These are flowers for Kate. It's our anniversary.*
Daniel: *You are so sweet! Can you please give Jasper pointers on how to be more romantic?*

 WANT MORE INFO? *THINK:* **STRAIGHT BESTIE TO A GAY MAN.**

STRAIGHT PRIVILEGE

▼ *noun*
The inherent rights and immunities granted to straight people.

SEE ALSO
PRIVILEGE, CISGENDER PRIVILEGE, MALE PRIVILEGE, WHITE PRIVILEGE

"It must be nice to have straight privilege. I can imagine it would be nice to not have to come out as straight. Or to be able to kiss your partner in public without getting glared at. Oh, right, and not to have to worry about getting 'let go' from your job because of your sexual orientation."

 WANT MORE INFO? *THINK:* **THE ENTITLEMENT OF STRAIGHT PEOPLE.**

STRAP-ON

▼ *noun*
A sexual device that consists of a belt or harness and a model penis. Mostly used by individuals with vaginas to simulate sexual penetration. Often shortened to "strap."

"I bought this new strap-on, so I'll catch up with y'all another day. My girl and I got business tonight."

 WANT MORE INFO? *THINK:* **A HARNESS WITH A DILDO ATTACHMENT.**

STUD

▼ *noun*
A lesbian with a masculine demeanor and appearance. Other characteristics include having a great sense of style and confident swagger.

SEE ALSO
SOFT STUD, "The Lesbian Spectrum," *p. 194*

"Some say there is nothing that a man can do that a stud can't do better."

 WANT MORE INFO? *THINK:* **A MASC LADY STUNNER.**

 This term originated in the Black lesbian community. It has been appropriated by the larger lesbian community.

STUD FOR STUD

▼ *adjective*
An intimate relationship between two masculine lesbians. The phrase "stud on stud" can also be used.

SEE ALSO
BUTCH-ON-BUTCH CRIME

"Personally, I am into stud for stud relationships. My girlfriend and I are both butch and consider ourselves studs. Screw the butch/ femme binary bullshit."

 WANT MORE INFO? *THINK:* **BUTCH FOR BUTCH, MASC FOR MASC.**

 This term originated in the Black lesbian community. It has been appropriated by the larger lesbian community.

STUNT

▼ *idiom*
See DOING SHOWS

SUBMISSIVE

▼ *adjective*
Passive.

▼ *noun*
The partner in a relationship, power-play exchange, or sexual encounter that services a Dominant partner. The term is often abbreviated as "sub," and referred to within the context of Dom/sub relationships in BDSM.

SEE ALSO
DOM/SUB RELATIONSHIP, DOMINANT

"Yes, Mistress, I am your submissive. I exist to serve only you. Please spank me if I don't do as I am told."

 WANT MORE INFO? *THINK:* **ONE WHO TAKES ORDERS.**

 This term is commonly used in the BDSM, leather, and kink communities. For all BDSM-related terms, the power exchange is a part of sadomasochistic play and should be consensual between all partners involved. The s in the word "submissive" should always be lowercase when referring to D/s, or power dynamic, relationships.

SWEET

▼ *adjective*
Describing an effeminate gay man.

SEE ALSO
NELLY

"Child, you know he is sweet as a Georgia peach!"

 WANT MORE INFO? *THINK:* **SWEET TEA: BLACK GAY MEN OF THE SOUTH BY E. PATRICK JOHNSON.**

 This term originated in the Black gay community. It has been appropriated by the larger LGBTQIA+ community and mainstream culture.

SWEET'N LOW

▼ *adjective*

A man who may engage in same-sex or queer romantic or sexual relationships but is discreet about it.

SEE ALSO
DOWN LOW, FRAME, DISCREET, CLOSETED

"DeMarcus is living that sweet'n low life. I wish he'd just embrace his sexual lifestyle—whatever it is—and come outta that closet!"

 WANT MORE INFO? *THINK:* **A MAN WHO KEEPS GAY ENCOUNTERS PRIVATE.**

 USAGE NOTE This term originated in the Black gay community.

SWITCH

▼ *noun*

A person who, when engaging in sexual activities, switches from top to bottom or Dominant to submissive with ease.

SEE ALSO
VERS

"Jill and I are switches, so our sex life is always keeping us guessing. It's never the same twice!"

 WANT MORE INFO? *THINK:* **ABLE TO EXPERIENCE BOTH SIDES OF A POWER DYNAMIC IN BED.**

▼ *verb*

To walk with an exaggerated sway of the hips.

SEE ALSO
PUMP

"I see you switching them hips from left to right, right to left. Yo, 'bout to come dance with you, sexy."

 WANT MORE INFO? *THINK:* **SASHAY, SHANTAY, AND SWISH AWAY.**

 USAGE NOTE This term originated in Black American culture and is commonly used in the Black gay and queer community.

SWITCH HITTER

▼ *noun*

A bisexual.

Kenneth: *Do you write with your left or right hand?*
Grant: *I use my right more, but I'm ambidextrous.*
Kenneth: *That makes sense. I mean, you are a switch hitter!*

 WANT MORE INFO? *THINK:* **LIKE IN BASEBALL, WHERE THE BATTER SWITCHES FROM THE LEFT TO THE RIGHT SIDE OF THE PLATE DEPENDING ON THE PITCHER'S DOMINANT HAND.**

USAGE NOTE This term may have negative connotations as it limits bisexuality to the gender binary. It is inappropriate to use this label if a person has not self-identified as such.

S

Whether you identify as transgender, demigender, gender nonconforming, cisgender, or beyond, every aspect that encompasses your identity is yours and always will be. You deserve to be **LOVED, RESPECTED,** and **ACCEPTED** for who you are. Do not change or bend to please anyone. Society must be educated and your queer queens will push to educate them!

YOU ARE UNIQUE. The transgender community challenges society's narrow molds and teaches the world an important lesson: One's assigned sex at birth does not determine one's gender identity. Surgeries, hormones, binding, and tucking can help affirm your gender but do not make you who you are. And while it may be for some, passing is not always the goal for transgender people.

"I ♥ BEING TRANS!"
Let's say it again, **"I ♥ BEING TRANS!"**

As varied transgender identities become more well-known with the public faces of Laverne Cox, Janet Mock, Alex Blue Davis, Ian Alexander, Danica Roem, Brian Michael Smith, Peppermint, Mj Rodriguez, Dominique Jackson, and Caitlyn Jenner, the trans community's visibility is rapidly increasing. Be authentic to you and project the happiest version of yourself. We all see you and you are never alone. Every day you teach us what true courage and resilience looks like. Your LGBTQIA+ community supports you!

Gender spectrum is a and there are many identities to explore. It may take a few steps to live in your most genuine self. It is healthy to think about who you are and whether your current identity is the right one for you.

— GENDER —
is the journey of seeking the fullest expression of yourself, because living in your truth is the ultimate
— SELF LOVE.—

Tt

T

▼ *noun*
Testosterone.

"A lot of body changes happen when you start taking T. I had no idea how much hair I'd grow and what insane acne I'd get. It was like going through puberty all over again."

 WANT MORE INFO? *THINK:* **HORMONES.**

USAGE NOTE This term is commonly used in the transgender, nonbinary, and gender nonconforming communities.

T, THE

▼ *noun*
The truth.

SEE ALSO
NO T, NO SHADE; SPILL THE T

"Girl, turn on MSNBC. The T is Russia had something to do with that election!"

 WANT MORE INFO? *THINK:* **THE HOT GOSSIP.**

USAGE NOTE This term originated in ballroom culture. It has been appropriated by the larger LGBTQIA+ community and mainstream culture.

TACO BLOCK

▼ *verb*
See COCK BLOCK

TAINT

▼ *noun*
The perineum; the soft tissue between the scrotum and anus, or vulva and anus.

"Bottom Etiquette 101: Clean your taint thoroughly."

 WANT MORE INFO? *THINK:* **THE FUN ZONE UP TO THE BUTTHOLE.**

TEA ROOM

▼ *noun*
A public restroom sometimes appropriated by gay, bisexual, or queer men for sex.

"In the olden days, gay men had limited places to hook up, and a tea room was a common place to go. You can now thank me for today's Gay History 101 lesson."

 WANT MORE INFO? *THINK:* **A PUBLIC LOCATION WHERE MEN CRUISE FOR HOOKUPS**

TENDER

▼ *adjective*
Used to describe a queer person who embraces vulnerability, in spite of society's gendered emotional expectations.

"I'm just your average city-dwelling tender queer, trying to make a living selling 'zines, teaching breath work, accepting my flaws, and organizing monthly volunteer trips to the local women's shelter."

 WANT MORE INFO? *THINK:* **EMBRACING SOFTNESS AND EMOTIONS WHILE LISTENING TO TRACY CHAPMAN AND SAM SMITH.**

TENS

▼ *noun*
In ballroom culture, this refers to the preliminary round of competition, where walkers perform to receive a perfect score—a ten from each judge—moving them on to the main competition.

"Judges score? Tens, tens, tens! Tens across the board!

 WANT MORE INFO? *THINK:* **SCORES NEEDED TO ELIMINATE THE COMPETITION AND TAKE THE GRAND PRIZE!**

 This term originated in ballroom culture. It has been appropriated by mainstream culture.

TERF

▼ *noun*

An acronym for Trans-Exclusionary Radical Feminist: a feminist who excludes trans women from their brand of feminism.

SEE ALSO
LESBIAN SEPARATIST, SEPARATISM, TRANSMISOGNY, TRANSPHOBIA

"Get these TERFs spewing hateful, transphobic speech outta my timeline!"

 WANT MORE INFO? *THINK:* **A PERSON WHO BELIEVES THAT IF ONE IS NOT BORN A CIS WOMAN, THEY DON'T MATTER.**

DID YOU KNOW Viv Smythe, a trans-inclusive feminist writer and blogger, is credited with coining the term TERF as a shorthand phrase to identify feminists who consider themselves radical and refuse to recognize transgender females as women.

TGNC

▼ *adjective*

A commonly used acronym for the transgender, nonbinary, and gender nonconforming communities.

SEE ALSO
GENDER NONCONFORMING, TRANSGENDER, GENDER-QUEER, NONBINARY

"The TGNC community empowers gender complexity. There are over seven billion people on this planet and many of us don't fit into the socially structured cishet model."

 WANT MORE INFO? *THINK:* **UMBRELLA TERM FOR TRANS AND NONBINARY FOLKS.**

DID YOU KNOW The transgender, nonbinary, and gender nonconforming communities have always challenged society's narrow molds, acknowledging that a person's assigned sex at birth does not have to determine a person's gender. In recent years, the emergence of public figures like Lana and Lilly Wachowski, Alok Vaid-Menon, Asia Kate Dillon, Jacob Tobia, Jill Soloway, and Indya Moore have provided unprecedented visibility of the TGNC community, encouraging people to think of gender as a personal journey of self-expression and fulfillment.

T

THE GAG IS

▼ *idiom*
A phrase meaning "the truth is" or "the funny thing is . . ."

"Verizon said they were going to cut my phone off, but the gag is I already switched to Metro."

 WANT MORE INFO? *THINK:* **THE SHOCKING TRUTH.**

 USAGE NOTE This term originated in ballroom culture and is commonly used in the larger queer and trans people of color (QTPOC) community. It has been appropriated by mainstream culture.

THEY/THEM/THEIRS

▼ *pronouns*
A set of pronouns frequently used by nonbinary and gender nonconforming people.

SEE ALSO

"The Genderbread Person," *p. 56,* **"Common Pronouns 101,"** *p. 81*

DID YOU KNOW The word "they" has been used as a singular pronoun since the 14th century. *The AP Stylebook* allows the usage of singular "they" in cases where a subject doesn't identify as male or female.

"When I tell people that my pronouns are they/them/theirs, I usually get either a completely awkward and confused look or the supportive 'I don't know what that means, but good for you' look. I use the singular they because it works for me."

 WANT MORE INFO? *THINK:* **IDENTIFIERS FOR GENDER- QUEER AND NONBINARY PEOPLE.**

 USAGE NOTE This set of pronouns is commonly used in the transgender, nonbinary, and gender nonconforming communities.

THEYBIE

▼ *noun*
A child raised without gender whose parents use "they/them" pronouns to refer to their child.

A self-identified gender nonconforming child or youth.

"We're raising little North here as genderqueer. We don't want to put the unnecessary pressure of conforming to gender roles on our precious little theybie."

 WANT MORE INFO? *THINK:* **PINK, BLUE, AND EVERY COLOR IN BETWEEN.**

T

THOT

▼ *noun*
Acronym for "that ho over there," referring to a person with a voracious sexual appetite.

RELATED
THOTTY *adjective*

"I wouldn't try to holla at him. He's a true thot, with a master's in Thot-ism."

 WANT MORE INFO? *THINK:* **THE PODCAST** *FOOD 4 THOT.*

 This term originated in the Black American culture. It has been appropriated by the LGBTQIA+ community and mainstream culture.

THREE-BEER QUEER

▼ *idiom*
See GAY AFTER THREE

THROW SHADE

▼ *idiom*
To subtly insult or blatantly show contempt for.

"They are always throwing shade on The Real Housewives. Thank you, Andy Cohen, for good reality TV!"

 WANT MORE INFO? *THINK:* **TO SPREAD NEGATIVITY LIKE WILDFIRE.**

 This term originated in ballroom culture. It has been appropriated by the larger LGBTQIA+ community and mainstream culture.

TILAPIA

▼ *noun*
See TUNA

TITTIES

▼ *noun*
Breasts. The term "tits" can also be used.

SEE ALSO
BOOBS, RACK

"A cups, C cups, D cups, F cups! Titties, titties, titties, titties, rocking everywhere!"

 WANT MORE INFO? *THINK:* **SQUEEZING AND HUGGING ON THE TWINS.**

TOMBOY

▼ *noun*
A girl—regardless of sexuality—who is slightly masculine in behavior and appearance.

"I love a tomboy who wears high-top sneakers and snapbacks."

 WANT MORE INFO? *THINK:* **SIMILAR TO SOFT BUTCH, CAN REFER TO YOUNGER LESBIANS.**

 This term is commonly used in the lesbian community.

T

TONGUE POP

▼ *noun*
A sound or click made with the tongue, used for emphasis in a variety of situations.

"Don't come for me! You're just jealous because your tongue pop sucks. Go on YouTube and watch Alyssa Edwards's 101 class!"

 WANT MORE INFO? *THINK:* **ONOMATOPOEIA USED PRIOR TO MAKING A POINT.**

 USAGE NOTE The term originated in Black culture. It has been appropriated by the larger LGBTQIA+ community and mainstream culture.

DID YOU KNOW The tongue pop is very common to many traditional African languages and dialects. Black Americans, especially women, continue to use the tongue pop to indicate disapproval. The sound has since been adopted by gay and drag communities.

SAY CLOCK WITH YOUR TONGUE

TOO MUCH

▼ *idiom*
When a look or behavior becomes overdone.

SEE ALSO
EXTRA

"He just does too much. Sequins, glitter, beads, and bells?"

 WANT MORE INFO? *THINK:* **OVER-THE-TOP AND TACKY.**

TOP

▼ *noun*
The dominant person in a sex act; when referring to same-sex male encounters, it often refers to the partner giving anal penetration. The term PITCHER can also be used.

▼ *verb*
To dominate sexually; to engage in sexual activity as a top.

SEE ALSO
BLOUSE, CLOWN TOP, POWER TOP, SWITCH, BOTTOM, VERS

Rodney: *What happened? You fainted while you were talking to that guy over there.*
Dwayne: *He told me he was a top. Thank Gawd, gurr!*

 WANT MORE INFO? *THINK:* **THE POSITION OR ACT OF BEING DOMINANT DURING SEX.**

 USAGE NOTE This term originated in the gay male community. It has been appropriated by the larger LGBTQIA+ community.

TOP SURGERY

▼ *noun*
Medical procedure for a person to change the physical appearance of breasts or chest, often performed to better suit one's gender identity. Often shortened to "top."

"Top surgery will differ depending on the individual. Some trans or gender nonconforming people may want tissue removed for a flatter chest, while others may want implants for a curvier shape."

 WANT MORE INFO? *THINK:* **SURGERY FOR GENDER AFFIRMATION.**

 This term is commonly used in the transgender, nonbinary, and gender nonconforming communities.

TOXIC MASCULINITY

▼ *noun*
Expressions of masculinity that encourage men to suppress emotions and maintain an aggressive and often prideful persona, hindering them from experiencing a healthy emotional balance.

"Toxic masculinity is a cultural disease that views femmes— women, gay men, and femme queers—as inferior."

 WANT MORE INFO? *THINK:* **MASCULINITY AND MACHISMO THAT NEGATIVELY AFFECT MEN'S JUDGMENT AND EMOTIONAL HEALTH.**

TRADE

▼ *noun*
A casual sexual partner for a gay, bisexual, or queer man. The term ROUGH TRADE or phrase "piece of trade" can also be used.

"I am about to call up my trade. I need some company."

 WANT MORE INFO? *THINK:* **A HOOKUP, A PIECE OF ASS.**

A male who identifies as heterosexual, but occasionally has same-gender or queer sexual encounters.

> **SEE ALSO**
> ### DOWN LOW, SWEET'N LOW

"No more chasing trade who will spew homophobic slurs in the day and then privately text you late at night." ▶ Ernest Owens

 WANT MORE INFO? *THINK:* **A QUEER MAN WHO PRESENTS AS STRAIGHT.**

In the Black gay community, this term refers to a masculine man not easily identified as gay due to a lack of stereotypical traits.

Nico: *Damn! Who is that huggin' on Hakim?*
Reggie: *Gurl, that fine-ass trade is Khalil. Trade is poppin' outside!*

 WANT MORE INFO? *THINK:* **A MASCULINE GAY GUY WHO DOES NOT "LOOK" GAY.**

 This term is commonly used in the gay male and transgender communities.

TRANNY

▼ *noun*
An abbreviation for the word "transsexual"; a person assigned one sex at birth who has used surgery and/or medication to transition to another sex.

SEE ALSO
TRANSSEXUAL

"I don't like the word 'tranny.' Try trans or transgender instead."

 WANT MORE INFO? *THINK:* **DATED TERM FOR A TRANS PERSON.**

 The use of this term relies on an individual's preference. Do not assume that an individual wants to be identified by the term. It is considered a slur and highly derogatory.

TRANSAMOROUS

▼ *adjective*
Experiencing attraction to a transgender person. Usually a person is exploring dating and relationships with transgender people, although the connection may be discreet.

SEE ALSO
CHASER

"Clifton's wife is cisgender, but Clifton is also transamorous."

 WANT MORE INFO? *THINK:* **ATTRACTED TO TRANS PEOPLE.**

TRANS ATTRACTED

▼ *adjective*
To be romantically and sexually attracted to transgender people. Not to be confused with CHASER, which may imply a fetish toward transgender people.

"I'm trans attracted. I like cis women as well as trans women, but there's a lot of stigma associated with being openly attracted to trans women . . . unfortunately."

 WANT MORE INFO? *THINK:* **ROMANTICALLY ATTRACTED TO TRANSGENDER PEOPLE FOR WHO THEY ARE.**

TRANSFEMININE

▼ *adjective*
A term used to describe a transgender, nonbinary, or gender nonconforming person who identifies as feminine. The term "transfemme" can also be used.

"There are some people in power who value the leadership of transfeminine women. Our collective trans experience needs to be heard in order to make inclusive, powerful change."

 WANT MORE INFO? *THINK:* **IDENTIFYING AS BOTH TRANS AND FEMME.**

 This term is commonly used in the transgender, nonbinary, and gender nonconforming communities.

T

TRANSFEMINISM

▼ *noun*
A brand of feminism that actively supports and amplifies the needs and equality of transgender women and other queer-identifying people.

"This Women's March we will be heard loud and clear, that we believe in transfeminism. One day soon, all women—ALL WOMEN—will be treated fairly."

 WANT MORE INFO? *THINK:* **A BELIEF THAT TRANS LIBERATION IS A FUNDAMENTAL PART OF FEMINISM.**

TRANSGENDER

▼ *adjective*
Of, relating to, or being a person who identifies with a gender identity and/ or expression that differs from their assigned sex at birth. The term is often shortened to "trans."

"Being trans has nothing to do with my sexuality. I am a transgender male and I am attracted to women, so I identify as straight."

 WANT MORE INFO? *THINK:* **IDENTIFYING AS A GENDER THAT DOES NOT NECESSARILY MATCH UP WITH YOUR BIRTH CERTIFICATE.**

USAGE NOTE A common misuse of the word "transgender" is to say a person is "transgendered." Transgender is explicitly not a noun. A person should not be called "a transgender."

 DID YOU KNOW The term "transgender" acts as an umbrella term that includes trans men, trans women, and other people who do not identify with the gender they were assigned at birth; this may include people who are gender nonconforming, nonbinary, pangender, bigender, agender, genderqueer, and/or genderfluid. Some trans people use the help of medicine and/or surgery to transition, some do not.

T

TRANSGENDER HORMONE THERAPY

▼ *noun*
See HORMONE REPLACEMENT THERAPY

TRANSITION

▼ *noun*
The process of someone affirming their gender identity when it differs from the gender they were assigned at birth. This is not a process that "changes" someone from a man to a woman or vice versa; it is the journey toward living a more authentic life—one that reflects a person's true gender identity and/or expression. Medical procedures may be pursued, or they may not.

▼ *verb*
To pursue affirming one's internal gender identity and external gender expression.

"Making the decision to transition was the best thing I ever did for myself. I'm more me than I have ever been." ▶ Persephone Valentine

 WANT MORE INFO? *THINK:* **COMING OUT AS TRANS.**

USAGE NOTE Due to the sensitive and intimate nature of transitions, it is important to respect the way each individual speaks about their own transition. A transition should not be viewed as the ultimate achievement for a trans person. Each person's journey is unique and should be respected as such.

 DID YOU KNOW Medical procedures such as Hormone Replacement Therapy (HRT), Gender Confirmation Surgery (GCS), and Facial Feminization Surgery (FFS) may be pursued but are not necessary for a person to transition.

TRANS KID OR TRANSGENDER KID

▼ *noun*
A young transgender person. The terms "trans youth" and "transgender children" can also be used.

"Each summer, my family and I go to a camp for trans kids. It's the best week of the summer. Everybody is nice to me, and I don't feel different there. I feel cool!"

 WANT MORE INFO? *THINK:* **A CHILD WHO ASSERTS AND EXPRESSES THEIR TRANS IDENTITY.**

T

TRANS MAN OR TRANSMAN

▼ *noun*
A transgender person who was assigned female at birth (AFAB) but whose gender identity is male.

SEE ALSO
TRANSMASCULINE

"Becoming a transman was a long but incredible journey. I started taking hormone blockers when I was eleven. By eighteen, I had started taking testosterone and had top surgery on my twenty-first birthday."

 WANT MORE INFO? *THINK:* **CHAZ BONO, BRIAN MICHAEL SMITH, TOM PHELAN.**

TRANSMASCULINE

▼ *adjective*
Describing a transgender, nonbinary, or gender nonconforming person who identifies as masculine. The term "transmasc" can also be used.

"Now that I identify as transmasculine, I'm experiencing the effects of male-favored sexism firsthand. It's nuts!"

 WANT MORE INFO? *THINK:* **IDENTIFYING AS TRANS AND MASCULINE.**

USAGE NOTE This term is commonly used in the transgender, nonbinary, and gender nonconforming communities.

TRANSMISOGYNY

▼ *noun*
A brand of misogyny that fosters dislike, contempt, and/or ingrained prejudice against trans women.

SEE ALSO
MISOGYNY

"If our generation wants to eradicate misogyny, we must also demand that trans women are included in the fight for equality. Transmisogyny is a blatantly hateful version of misogyny."

 WANT MORE INFO? *THINK:* **AN OPPRESSIVE DOUBLE WHAMMY.**

TRANSPHOBIA

▼ *noun*
Aversion, fear, or hatred toward trans people.

RELATED
TRANSPHOBIC *adjective* **TRANSPHOBE** *noun*

SEE ALSO
ACEPHOBIA, BIPHOBIA, FEMMEPHOBIA, HOMO-PHOBIA, LESBOPHOBIA, QUEERPHOBIA

"When laws are made prohibiting trans people from serving in the military, that's TRANSPHOBIA!"

 WANT MORE INFO? *THINK:* **DISLIKE OF OR PREJUDICE AGAINST TRANSGENDER PEOPLE.**

TRANSSEXUAL

▼ *adjective*
Of, relating to, or being a person who identifies with a different sex than their assigned sex at birth.

"My aunt Linda still identifies as a transsexual—she is proud of being a trans trailblazer, going through some shit in the sixties and seventies, and coming out as the most kickass version of herself."

 WANT MORE INFO? *THINK:* **A DATED, POTENTIALLY INSENSITIVE VERSION OF "TRANSGENDER."**

 USAGE NOTE The use of this term relies on an individual's preference. Do not assume that an individual wants to be identified as such, as it is considered derogatory by many.

DID YOU KNOW While some transgender individuals still use "transsexual" as an identifier, it is largely considered a dated term. In 1965, psychiatrist John F. Oliven of Columbia University coined the term "transgenderism" to replace the then-popular "transsexualism." He posited that "transsexual" was misleading, because a person's decision to alter their gender expression was, in most cases, very much separate from their sexuality.

TRANSVESTITE

▼ *noun*
A dated term for a cross-dresser who is typically (but not always) a man.

SEE ALSO

CROSS-DRESSER

"I was so embarrassed when my grandmother asked my neighbor if he was a transvestite. But he was so nice and told her with a smile, 'Honey, I do love these clothes and I have a beautiful scarf that would look great on you!'"

 WANT MORE INFO? *THINK:* **SOMEONE WHOSE DRESSING AS ANOTHER GENDER FULFILLS THEM.**

 USAGE NOTE This term is often misused to refer to transgender people and/or cross-dressers, which is considered derogatory and offensive, thus the term is not commonly used.

TRANS WOMAN OR TRANSWOMAN

▼ *noun*
A transgender person who was assigned male at birth (AMAB) but whose gender identity is female.

SEE ALSO

TRANSFEMININE

"I am a transwoman and I am living my life authentically, beautifully and expecting all great things to come my way!"

WANT MORE INFO? *THINK:* **LAVERNE COX, AMANDA LEPORE, KIM COCO IWAMOTO.**

TRIB

▼ *verb*
To rub one's vulva on a partner's body for sexual stimulation.

RELATED
TRIBADISM *noun*   **TRIBADE** *noun*

SEE ALSO
SCISSORING

"I love tribbing with my girl. It makes my kitty feel good, too."

 WANT MORE INFO? *THINK:* **LESBIAN SEX ACT OF RUBBING IT OUT ON ONE'S PARTNER.**

USAGE NOTE This term originated in the lesbian community.

◄ **Trans woman**

TRIED IT

▼ *idiom*
Overstepped boundaries.

"Ooh, you tried it by eating my last chocolate chip cookie!"

 WANT MORE INFO? *THINK:* **STAY IN YOUR LANE.**

USAGE NOTE This term originated in ballroom culture and is used in the larger queer and trans people of color (QTPOC) community.

TUCK

▼ *verb*
To conceal penis and testicles by tucking them between the legs and taping the area in a particular way. This is a practice utilized by transgender women or cisgender men who perform in drag.

SEE ALSO
GAFF, "Tucking & Binding 101," *p. 130*

Lee Ann: *Where in the world is it?*
Anthony: *First time at a drag show, huh? She always does a fierce tuck.*

 WANT MORE INFO? *THINK:* **DICK PLAYING HIDE-AND-SEEK.**

USAGE NOTE This term is commonly used in the transgender, nonbinary, gender nonconforming, and drag communities.

TUH

▼ *exclamation*
See CH

TUNA

▼ *noun*
A derogatory word for a cisgender woman.

A feminine-presenting person.

"Why is there so much tuna in here? Is this not a gay club?"

 WANT MORE INFO? *THINK:* **FEMALE.**

 USAGE NOTE This term is used in the drag community and larger gay male community.

TURNED OR TURNT

▼ *adjective*
Exciting or extremely high-energy. The term "lit" is also used.

"Last night was turnt! We had ten bottles in the VIP lounge."

 WANT MORE INFO? *THINK:* **HYPED.**

▼ *verb*
Surpassed.

"Black Panther turnt every other Marvel superhero movie. #wakandaforever!"

 WANT MORE INFO? *THINK:* **SHATTERED, WAS SUPERIOR TO.**

 USAGE NOTE This term originated in Black American culture and is used in the Black gay and queer community. It has been appropriated by mainstream culture.

TWINK

▼ *noun*
A body label for a gay, bisexual, or queer man who has a youthful appearance and a small body frame. He also has very little to no facial and body hair.

> **SEE ALSO**
> **CHICKEN, PUP, "Help! What's My Gay Type?,"** *p. 152*

"Super-tight jeans, plaid shirt, and the face of a cherub? Yep, that's a twink."

 WANT MORE INFO? *THINK:* **TWINKIE—A LITTLE, SOFT, AND DELICIOUS SNACK.**

 USAGE NOTE This term originated in the white gay male community.

TWIRL

▼ *verb*
To dance or move with great skill or urgency.

"Everyone twirled for their life in this season's finale of So You Think You Can Dance!*"*

 WANT MORE INFO? *THINK:* **WORK THE DANCE FLOOR.**

 USAGE NOTE This term is commonly used in ballroom culture and the drag community.

TWO-SPIRIT OR TWO SPIRIT

▼ *noun*
For Western-world understanding, this umbrella term is used to identify the history of gender and sexuality diversity celebrated in Indigenous Native American culture, and that a third gender role is identified and commonly expressed within that culture. Each Indigenous tribe refers to third gender people by different names; for example, Lakota people use the word winkte, the Zuni tribe lhamana, and the Navajo tribe nádleehí. The inclusion of two-spirited people is often seen in the queer community's acronym, LGBTQ2.

RELATED
TWO-SPIRITED *adjective*

"Tobey and I spoke more about two-spirit identity. 'Life is sacred.' That keeps ringing in my head."

 WANT MORE INFO? *THINK:* **THE DIVERSITY OF IDENTITY WITHIN NATIVE AMERICAN CULTURE.**

Two-spirit ▲

DID YOU KNOW The term "two-spirit" was coined at the Native American Gay and Lesbian Gathering in 1990 in an effort to solve what Native scholars called "the problem of naming." The term gives Native people a unifying term to use for a variety of gender and sexuality-based roles. Two-spirit people are often revered for fulfilling a unique role in their society—from healing and guiding others to spiritual protection.

T

TWUNK

▼ *noun*
A body label for a gay, bisexual, or queer man with a small but muscular body frame. A portmanteau of twink and hunk.

SEE ALSO
"Help! What's My Gay Type?," *p. 152*

"Samuel's been to the gym! He's graduated from twink to twunk!"

 WANT MORE INFO? *THINK:* **A TWINK WITH MUSCLE.**

 USAGE NOTE This term originated in the white gay male community.

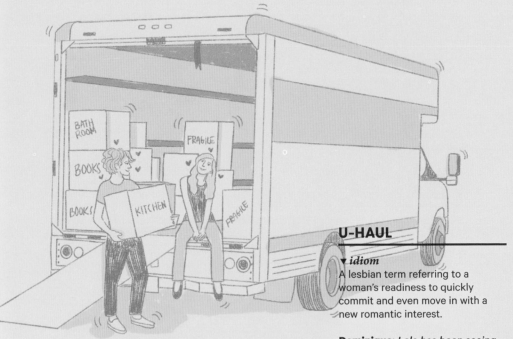

U-HAUL

▼ *idiom*
A lesbian term referring to a woman's readiness to quickly commit and even move in with a new romantic interest.

Dominique: *Lela has been seeing Hope for a week. I call U-Haul in about five more days.*
Iris: *No way. They'll be U-Hauling tomorrow!*

 WANT MORE INFO? *THINK:* **THE ULTIMATE LEZZIE STEREOTYPE.**

 USAGE NOTE This term originated in the lesbian community.

Uu

UNICORN

▼ *noun*

A queer person, often a bisexual woman, who is open to having a threesome and/or relationship with a heterosexual couple. This term is typically used on dating apps for straight couples looking for a third.

Olivia: *Omigod, look! I just matched with the hottest girl I've ever seen.*
Miko: *Oh, honey, no. Look, she and her hubby want you for a threesome. She thinks you're a unicorn. Swipe left.*

 WANT MORE INFO? *THINK:* **SOMEONE INTERESTED IN BEING A HETERO COUPLE'S THIRD.**

URSULA

▼ *noun*

A butch lesbian who enjoys celebrating bear culture.

> SEE ALSO
>
> **BEAR, GOLDILOCKS**

"There goes Ursula and her best friend, Mr. Bear."

 WANT MORE INFO? *THINK:* **A LADY LUMBERJACK.**

U.S.A. GAYBORHOODS

Gayborhoods have become the geographical center for LGBTQIA+ people. Our communities are usually identified by pride rainbow flags and signs hanging from windows and storefronts of bars, nightclubs, restaurants, residences, and shops. Gayborhoods cater to the safety and inclusiveness of all people who identify on the queer spectrum and have transformed cities into rainbow havens for LGBTQIA+ culture.

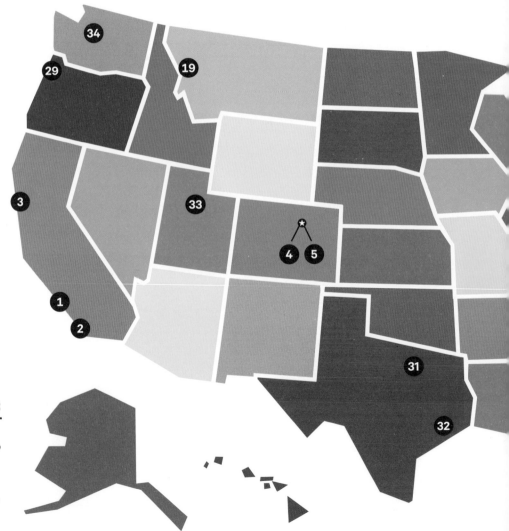

1. WEST HOLLYWOOD, LOS ANGELES, CA
2. HILLCREST, SAN DIEGO, CA
3. THE CASTRO, SAN FRANCISCO, CA
4. CAPITOL HILL, DENVER, CO
5. NORTH RIVER, DENVER, CO
6. DUPONT CIRCLE, WASHINGTON, DC
7. REHOBOTH, DE
8. WILTON MANORS, FL
9. WYNWOOD, MIAMI, FL
10. MIDTOWN, ATLANTA, GA
11. ANDERSONVILLE, CHICAGO, IL
12. BOYSTOWN, CHICAGO, IL
13. FRENCH QUARTER, NEW ORLEANS, LA
14. BYWATER, NEW ORLEANS, LA
15. MARIGNY, NEW ORLEANS, LA
16. THE SOUTH END, BOSTON, MA
17. PROVINCETOWN, MA
18. THE GROVE, ST. LOUIS, MO
19. MISSOULA, MT
20. ASHEVILLE, NC
21. ASBURY PARK, NJ
22. ALLENTOWN, BUFFALO, NY
23. HUDSON, NY
24. FIRE ISLAND, LONG ISLAND, NY
25. CHELSEA, NEW YORK CITY, NY
26. HELL'S KITCHEN, NEW YORK CITY, NY
27. WEST VILLAGE, NEW YORK CITY, NY
28. SHORT NORTH, COLUMBUS, OH
29. PORTLAND, OR
30. THE GAYBORHOOD, PHILADELPHIA, PA
31. OAK LAWN, DALLAS, TX
32. MONTROSE, HOUSTON, TX
33. THE MARMALADE, SALT LAKE CITY, UT
34. CAPITOL HILL, SEATTLE, WA

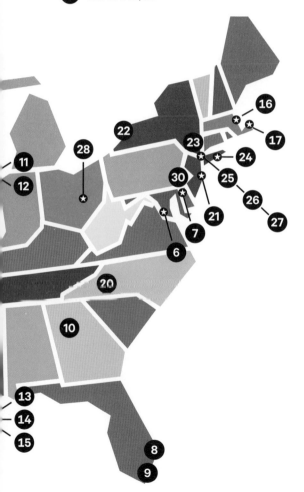

VIOLENCE & HATE CRIME

EPIDEMIC

"When we allow violence against some, we enable violence against all."

▶ **DaShanne Stokes**

Homophobia, biphobia, transphobia, queerphobia, xenophobia, racism, sexism, genderism, misogyny, transmisogyny, and ableism are forms of hate that plague our LGBTQIA+ community. Mainstream culture has often labeled us as outcasts, deplorables, and sinners, subjecting our community to generations of abuse. By definition, a hate crime is an intimidating, aggressive, and/or violent crime, usually motivated by prejudice against a specific race, religion, sexual orientation, gender expression, or bias.

President Barack Obama understood the prevalence of these crimes when he passed the Matthew Shepard and James Byrd Jr. Hate Crimes Prevention Act. This act expanded on the previous United States Federal Hate Crime Law to protect against crimes based on gender, sexual orientation, gender identity, or disability. Even still, the American Medical Association has tracked a disproportionate increase in violence toward members of the trans community, with particularly shocking statistics on the increased murders of Black trans women. In 2020, when yet another unarmed Black man was callously murdered by a police officer, the Black Lives Matter (BLM) movement propelled the world to open their eyes to the hate and injustices experienced by all Black people—including Black LGBTQIA+ people. The mission of BLM is to dismantle the hate that is deeply rooted in our history and current society.

Despite the pain our community has endured, our tenacity was built upon hate. Our power as a community blazes to life in our fight, our persistence, our fire, our resilience, and our courage. Even though much work has been done to protect queer bodies, we still have a long way to go.

HOPE IS BUILT UPON RESISTANCE. WE FIGHT. WE PROTEST. WE WILL NOT BE ERASED.

Vv

VAGETARIAN

▼ *noun*
A person with a sexual preference for vaginas.

"My vagetarian diet consists of her on my face."

 WANT MORE INFO? *THINK:* **A CUNNILINGUS AFICIONADO.**

USAGE NOTE This term may have negative connotations in the transgender, nonbinary, and gender nonconforming communities.

VAGINOPLASTY

▼ *noun*
See BOTTOM SURGERY

VANILLA

▼ *adjective*
Describes banal, traditional sexual behaviors.

Aiden: *Vanilla versus kink, choose one.*
Joel: *Good ol' wholesomeness for me. I'll take vanilla for five hundred please.*

 WANT MORE INFO? *THINK:* **BASIC SEX.**

VEGETARIAN

▼ *noun*
A gay, bisexual, or queer man who does not perform oral sex on other men.

"No, I don't do meat. I am a vegetarian."

 WANT MORE INFO? *THINK:* **A MAN OR GENDER NONCONFORMING PERSON WHO DOESN'T FELLATE.**

VERS(E) OR VERSATILE

▼ *noun*
Sexual position preference where a person enjoys both giving and receiving penetration.

SEE ALSO
SWITCH

Devon: *Do you prefer to top or bottom?*
Quan: *Yes.*
Devon: *Wait, what?*
Quan: *Both—I'm verse.*

 WANT MORE INFO? *THINK:* **EQUAL OPPORTUNITY TO ANY SEXUAL POSITION.**

 This term originated in the gay male community. It has been appropriated by the larger LGBTQIA+ community.

VERS(E) BOTTOM

▼ *noun*
A gay, bisexual, or queer man who prefers receiving penetration but is sometimes open to giving sexual penetration.

"People ask me why I'm a vers bottom. Well, if a twink is cute, but just not that tall, I might have to top him."

 WANT MORE INFO? *THINK:* **A PERSON WHO PREFERS TO TAKE THE DICK, BUT EVERY ONCE IN A BLUE MOON LIKES TO GIVE IT.**

 This term originated in the gay male community. It has been appropriated by the larger LGBTQIA+ community.

VERS(E) TOP

▼ *noun*
A gay, bisexual, or queer man who prefers giving penetration but is sometimes open to receiving sexual penetration.

"Yeah, I like to top, but I'm a verse top. If I meet the right guy at this party, I may have to work the bottom."

 WANT MORE INFO? *THINK:* **A PERSON WHO PREFERS TOPPING, BUT EXPLORES BOTTOMING, TOO.**

 This term originated in the gay male community. It has been appropriated by the larger LGBTQIA+ community.

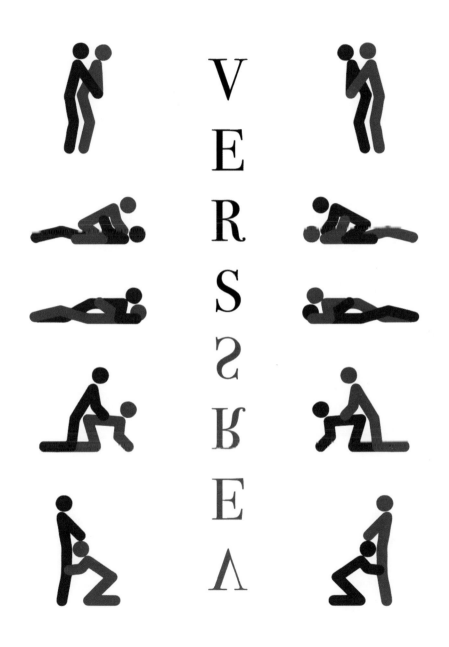

V

VITO RUSSO TEST, THE

▼ *noun*
A test inspired by the Bechdel Test used to examine how queer characters are represented in film. A film that passes the test has an LGBTQIA+ character who is not solely defined by their sexuality and is crucial to the plot of the film.

SEE ALSO
THE BECHDEL TEST

"I just read up on this year's Vito Russo Test results and the TV industry is at an all-time high with LGBTQIA+ representation, projected to rise again in the next year! I agree with theSkimm: 'GLAAD to see more diversity on TV.'"

 WANT MORE INFO? *THINK:* **A BAROMETER FOR POSITIVE QUEER REPRESENTATION IN FILM AND TELEVISION.**

DID YOU KNOW In 1985, LGBTQ activist, author, and film historian Vito Russo cofounded the Gay and Lesbian Alliance Against Defamation (presently known as GLAAD) to change the negative stereotypes and depictions of homosexuality in media. Russo's passion for fair representation for LGBTQIA+ people paved the way for filmmakers and journalists alike to write more inclusively, using guides like his book *The Celluloid Closet* and the Vito Russo Test as tools to analyze their work.

VOGUE

▼ *noun*
A modern house dance that combines stylized movement and model-like poses with intricate angular arm and leg movements. Voguing is an evolving art form that originated in the 1980s as an artistic form of "throwing shade." Styles include NEW WAY, OLD WAY, and VOGUE FEMME.

▼ *verb*
To dance in the style of vogue.

"I saw Amina voguing down at the pier and she is ready to take the title."

 WANT MORE INFO? *THINK:* **"STRIKE A POSE, THERE'S NOTHING TO IT. VOGUE!"**
  ▶ **Madonna**

▲ Vogue

DID YOU KNOW
By the late 1980s, voguing was a fully developed house dance technique that evolved from the work of Black and Latinx dancers in Harlem. Willi Ninja, known as the godfather of voguing, is widely credited for bringing the art form to mainstream culture. The technique was inspired by high fashion models' poses in *Vogue* magazine, Egyptian hieroglyphics, and African art. In the 1990s, Madonna's video of her hit song "Vogue"—which featured dancers like Jose and Luis Xtravaganza and was inspired by New York's underground ballroom culture—became an international chart-topper.

USAGE NOTE
This term originated in ballroom culture. It has been appropriated by mainstream culture.

VOGUE FEMME

▼ *verb*
The modern technique of vogue house dance that was established around 1995. This technique is noted for its rhythm, dramatics, and extreme femininity; it consists of five main elements: catwalk, hands performance, spins and dips, duckwalk, and floor performance.

SEE ALSO

BALL, BALLROOM SCENE, NEW WAY, OLD WAY, VOGUE

"The New York Awards Ball was so lit this year! The butch queens ate it in Vogue Femme."

 WANT MORE INFO? *THINK*: WALK THE RUNWAY OR BE CHOPPED, HI-YAH!

 USAGE NOTE
This term originated in ballroom culture.

V

Will & Grace ▲

Ww

WALKING

▼ *verb*

In ballroom culture, this term means competing in a ball competition before a panel of judges.

RELATED
WALKER, *noun*

"Are you walking Face tonight? It's going for fifteen hundred dollars."

 WANT MORE INFO? *THINK:* **TO COMPETE IN A CATEGORY ON A RUNWAY OR DANCE FLOOR.**

WENDY

▼ *noun*

A Caucasian person (of any gender). The term BECKY can also be used.

Daquan: *When did Wendy and Becky get the memo to start coming to Black churches?*
Tamia: *When they got tired of falling asleep at their churches.*

 WANT MORE INFO? *THINK:* **WHITE PEOPLE.**

WENT IN

▼ *verb*

Went all out.

"Leonardo went in on Mona Lisa! Smile, boo!"

 WANT MORE INFO? *THINK:* **ACHIEVED EXCELLENCE.**

Was extremely engaged.

"Oh girl, last night was everything! We went in watching Pose. *You missed it!"*

 WANT MORE INFO? *THINK:* **WAS COMPLETELY INVESTED.**

USAGE NOTE This term originated in Black American culture and is commonly used in the Black gay and queer community. It has been appropriated by mainstream culture.

WENT TO A PLACE

▼ *idiom*
To have an out-of-body experience or to daydream.

"Baby, I went to a place when I got my Swedish massage! I saw rainbows, waterfalls, and felt all the body tingles."

 WANT MORE INFO? *THINK:* **TRAVELED TO A WORLD OF SUGAR, SPICE, AND EVERYTHING NICE.**

USAGE NOTE This term is commonly used in the Black gay and queer community.

WHAT ARE YOU GIVING?

▼ *idiom*
Questioning someone's appearance or behavior. This can be lighthearted or antagonistic. The term can also be used to inquire about particular situations (e.g., her biology exam, this ugly throw pillow, Rihanna's makeup, etc.). The phrases "what she gave" and "what it gave" can also be used.

"What are you giving? No makeup, hair in a bun, and sweatpants, this isn't like you. Do you need a hug?"

 WANT MORE INFO? *THINK:* **"I DON'T UNDERSTAND WHAT'S GOING ON HERE."**

USAGE NOTE This term is commonly used in the Black gay community and the larger queer and trans people of color (QTPOC) community.

WHAT'S THE GAGA?

▼ *idiom*
A phrase used to ask someone about the latest gossip or news. This phrase is a variation on the idiom "WHAT'S THE T?"

"I know you know, Evan. Are we getting promotions next quarter? What's the gaga?"

 WANT MORE INFO? *THINK:* **"WHAT'S THE LATEST?"**

WHAT'S THE GOODIE?

▼ *idiom*
See WHAT'S THE T?

WHAT'S THE T?

▼ *idiom*
A phrase used to ask someone about current events or the latest goings-on in one's life. "T" refers to the "Truth." The phrase "WHAT'S THE GOODIE?" can also be used.

SEE ALSO
THE T, SPILL THE T

"What's the T? You moving to Atlanta, or nah?"

 WANT MORE INFO? *THINK:* **"WHAT'S THE DEAL? WHAT'S THE GOSSIP?"**

USAGE NOTE This term originated in ballroom culture. It has been appropriated by the larger LGBTQIA+ community and mainstream culture.

W

WHITE FEMINISM

▼ *noun*

Feminist thoughts and theories that are rooted in white privilege, lacking an intersectional look at oppressed women of other races, classes, and abilities.

"The #MeToo movement has been an incredible movement, calling out toxic masculinity in all areas of leadership. But let's not let white feminism take over what Tarana Burke started. This feminist fight is for every woman."

 WANT MORE INFO? *THINK:* **BIASED FEMINISM THAT DOES NOT TAKE EVERYONE'S EXPERIENCE INTO ACCOUNT.**

WHITE PRIVILEGE

▼ *noun*

The inherent rights and immunities granted to white people.

SEE ALSO
PRIVILEGE, CISGENDER PRIVILEGE, MALE PRIVILEGE, STRAIGHT PRIVILEGE

"White privilege begins at birth. Your skin color gives you a sense of protection, access, entitlement, and means to move about your life without being a target."

 WANT MORE INFO? *THINK:* **THE ENTITLEMENT OF WHITE PEOPLE.**

WIG

▼ *noun*

Someone's hair or hairstyle. Often used within the Black, drag, and transgender communities but can be used by anyone.

"I was going to ask you who did your weave because that wig is done!"

 WANT MORE INFO? *THINK:* **HAIR, EXTENSIONS, LOCS, BRAIDS, LACE FRONTS, FADES, UNITS, YOU NAME IT.**

WILL & GRACE

▼ *noun*

A close and playful friendship between a gay man and a woman, derived from the popular sitcom *Will & Grace*.

SEE ALSO
GAY HUSBAND

"They wish they were Jack and Karen, but we are totally Will and Grace."

 WANT MORE INFO? *THINK:* **A TIGHT BOND BETWEEN A GAY MAN AND HIS BEST FEMME.**

W

WITCH

▼ *noun*
A person who practices witchcraft.

"That witch I met at the feminist society's viewing of The Craft *was everything."*

 WANT MORE INFO? *THINK:* **YOUR QUEER FRIEND WHO LOVES TAROT, CRYSTALS, AND ASTROLOGY.**

DID YOU KNOW In the mid to late twentieth century, many feminists explored witchcraft, regarding the practice as an embodiment of the divine feminine and female power. In today's world, witchcraft has created a community for LGBTQIA+ people. Not only is it a form of spirituality rooted in a celebration of femininity and otherness, but it acts as a form of self-care, healing, and protection against the cruel outside world.

WOC

▼ *noun*
An abbreviation for woman/women of color, referring to a person who identifies as such.

SEE ALSO
MOC, POC, QPOC, QWOC

"When [WOC] speak out of the anger that laces so many of our contacts with white women, we are often told that we are 'creating a mood of hopelessness,' 'preventing white women from getting past guilt,' or 'standing in the way of trusting communication and action.'" ▶ Audre Lorde

 WANT MORE INFO? *THINK:* **A NONWHITE FEMALE.**

WOLF

▼ *noun*
A body label for a gay, bisexual, or queer man who is lean and muscular, with an average amount of body hair. These men are typically sexually aggressive.

SEE ALSO
"Help! What's My Gay Type?," *p. 152*

Caleb: *These body labels are confusing. Am I a wolf or an otter? What's the difference? What are the hair requirements again?*
Jack: *I say wolf. You have a good muscular build—not slim—and you are only semi-hairy.*

 WANT MORE INFO? *THINK:* **A MUSCULAR, HAIRY HOTTIE.**

 This term originated in the white gay male community.

W

WOMXN

▼ *noun*
An alternate spelling of the word woman, used to fuel the idea that women can exist without "man" or "men."

"We are womxn. Strong, Black, brown, red, yellow, white, masc, femme, trans, fluid, queer, fat, skinny, shapely, and bold womxn."

 WANT MORE INFO? *THINK:* **A SYMBOL OF WOMAN'S LIBERATION FROM MAN.**

DID YOU KNOW The term "womyn" became popular in the 1970s, with the rise of second-wave feminism. In 1975, the term first showed up in an issue of *Lesbian Connection*, describing a local womyn's festival occurring in July of that year. In 1976, it showed up in print again, advertising the Michigan Womyn's Music Festival. Many womyn's music festivals became notorious for discriminating against and excluding trans women—claiming they weren't "born womyn"—so many feminists and trans allies began to move away from the spelling of womyn, replacing the Y with a more inclusive X.

WORK

▼ *exclamation*
A complimentary exclamation of high praise. Can also be seen as "werk" or "werq."

SEE ALSO
YOU BETTER WORK

"You sewed her wedding dress in a week, Jermaine? WORK! That lace is absolutely stunning."

 WANT MORE INFO? *THINK:* **"GET IT! YOU DID THAT AND DID IT WELL!"**

USAGE NOTE This term originated in the Black gay community. It has been appropriated by the larger LGBTQIA+ community and mainstream culture.

WSW

▼ *noun*
An abbreviation for "women who have sex with women" often used in medical and social research. This abbreviation is not limited to homosexual women.

SEE ALSO
MSM

"Her chart states that she is thirty-six years of age, single marital status, and a WSW."

 WANT MORE INFO? *THINK:* **AN ACRONYM FOR FEMALE-TO-FEMALE SEX.**

W

Xx

XE/XEM/XYRS

▼ *pronouns*
See "Common Pronouns 101," p. 81

X-RATED

▼ *adjective*
Extremely sexually explicit.

"X-rated, hardcore gay porn is my jam."

 WANT MORE INFO? *THINK:*
PORNOGRAPHIC.

XTRA

▼ *adjective*
See EXTRA

(E)XTRAVAGANZA

▼ *noun*
A spectacular and elaborate show.

"Tonight will be the biggest xtravaganza of all time!"

 WANT MORE INFO? *THINK:*
A LAVISH EVENT.

A prominent gay and transgender social house in ballroom culture that is famous for being the first social family structure for the Latinx community.

"We honor our legendary father, Hector, and mother, Angie, for giving us the House of Xtravaganza! We will forever honor your name."

 WANT MORE INFO? *THINK:*
ONE OF THE MOST WELL-KNOWN GAY BALLROOM HOUSES IN NEW YORK CITY.

Yy

YAS

▼ *exclamation*

An affirmative exclamation. The number of *A*s and *S*s can vary depending on the tone and use. The gesture of quickly waving the index finger with approval is sometimes done to emphasize the expression. Often used in the phrases "yas, queen," "yas, girl," and "yas, gawd."

"Yaaassssss! She slayed that question. Miss Georgia is about to win the crown!"

 WANT MORE INFO? *THINK:* **"I SUPPORT AND BELIEVE IN YOU."**

USAGE NOTE This term originated in ballroom culture. It has been appropriated by the larger LGBTQIA+ community and mainstream culture.

YES, GAWD!

▼ *exclamation*

A phrase to proclaim extreme approval and/or support. Variations on the phrase include YES, GIRL! and YES, QUEEN!

Nez: *I got a book deal! I am going to be a published author!*
Lamar: *YES, GIRL! YES, GAWD! Won't He do it!*

 WANT MORE INFO? *THINK:* **"YOU GO, GIRL!"**

USAGE NOTE This term originated in ballroom culture. It has been appropriated by the larger LGBTQIA+ community and mainstream culture.

YES, GIRL!

▼ *idiom*
See YES, GAWD!

YES, QUEEN!

▼ *idiom*
See YES, GAWD!

YESTERGAY

▼ *noun*
A "former" homosexual who currently identifies as heterosexual.

SEE ALSO
EX-GAY

Noah: *Wait, is Mason married to a woman? Did the truth just go hide back in the closet?*
Ross: *Clearly this is another case of a yestergay.*

 WANT MORE INFO? *THINK:* **SOMEONE WHO IS "NO LONGER GAY."**

 USAGE NOTE This term negates any notion that a person could be sexually fluid, bisexual, queer, or any number of fluid identifiers. It forces sexuality to exist within a binary and can therefore be construed as negative or harmful.

YOU BETTER WORK

▼ *idiom*
An exuberant affirmation. The phrase may also be spelled "you betta werk."

SEE ALSO
WORK

Tonya: *I'm nervous about the interview tomorrow. I really need that job.*
Alyson: *Girl, you've got the goods, so you better work!*

WANT MORE INFO? *THINK:* **THE BEST POSITIVE REINFORCEMENT ONE CAN GIVE/RECEIVE.**

USAGE NOTE This term was coined by American drag queen RuPaul. It has been appropriated by the LGBTQIA+ community and mainstream culture.

> You better work
> (Cover Girl)
> Work it, girl
> (Give it a twirl).

▶ **RuPaul,**
"Supermodel (You Better Work)"

YOU COULD NEVER

▼ *idiom*
An expression of superiority.

"Take my man? Ha! You could never!"

 WANT MORE INFO? *THINK:* **"YOU'LL NEVER BE ON MY LEVEL."**

 This term is commonly used in the Black gay and queer community.

YOU DID THAT

▼ *idiom*
A compliment given for something exceptional.

"The Queens' English is here for all you queers! To the LGBTQIA+ community: you did that! We created a language of our own, hell yeah!"

 WANT MORE INFO? *THINK:* **HEAR YE, HEAR YE: THIS IS A JOB WELL DONE!**

 This term originated in the Black gay and queer community.

YOU TRIED IT

▼ *idiom*
See TRIED IT

Y

327

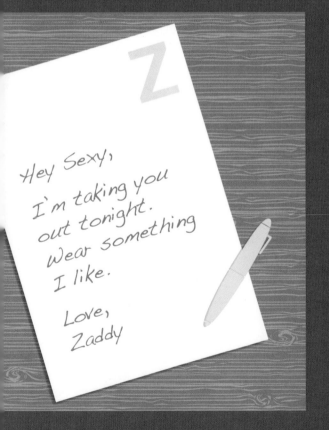

Hey Sexy,
I'm taking you out tonight.
Wear something I like.

Love,
Zaddy

ZADDY

▼ *noun*

A person—typically masc or male-identifying—who is extremely eye-catching and put together. A zaddy exudes a confident demeanor and oozes sexiness.

SEE ALSO
DADDY, MOMMI

Isaac: *Zaddy alert, zaddy alert!*
Dre: *That guy over there? Uh-uh, I don't see it.*
Isaac: *Zaddy is in the eye of the beholder. Now, if you'll excuse me, I need to introduce myself!*

 WANT MORE INFO? *THINK:* **A FIIIIIINE PHYSICAL SPECIMEN WITH SWAGGER TO SPARE.**

USAGE NOTE This term originated in Black American culture and is used in the Black gay and queer community. It has been appropriated by mainstream culture.

Zz

ZAMN

▼ *exclamation*
An overly emphatic "damn!"

"Zamn, zaddy, you look tasty in that Dior suit! I'm ready to walk down the aisle and say "I do!""

 WANT MORE INFO? *THINK:* **OH MY!**

USAGE NOTE This term originated in the Black gay and queer community. It has been appropriated by mainstream culture.

ZE/HIR/HIRS

▼ *pronouns*
See "Common Pronouns 101," p. 81

ZIE/ZIR/ZIRS

▼ *pronouns*
See "Common Pronouns 101," p. 81

ZUCCHINI

▼ *noun*
A partner in a queerplatonic relationship. The terms QUEER-PLATONIC PARTNER or SQUISH can also be used.

SEE ALSO
QUEERPLATONIC RELATIONSHIP

Malcolm: *I have seen you two attached at the hip almost every day. Is that your man now?*
Donnie: *Nah, he's my squish. My zucchini.*

 WANT MORE INFO? *THINK:* **SOUL MATE.**

USAGE NOTE This term originated in the asexual and aromantic community.

RESOURCES

ACT UP / actupny.org

The Ali Forney Center / aliforneycenter.org

The Audre Lorde Project / alp.org

Bisexual Resource Center / biresource.org

bklyn boihood / bklynboihood.com

Black Lives Matter / blacklivesmatter.com

Broadway Cares/Equity Fights AIDS / broadwaycares.org

Brown Boi Project / brownboiproject.org

Camp Aranu'tiq / camparanutiq.org

Center for Black Equity / centerforblackequity.org

CenterLink / lgbtcenters.org

COLAGE / colage.org

Covenant House / covenanthouse.org

Family Equality Council / familyequality.org

FIERCE / fiercenyc.org

Gender Spectrum / genderspectrum.org

GLAAD / glaad.org

GLBTQ Legal Advocates & Defenders / glad.org

GLMA / glma.org

GLSEN / glsen.org

GMHC / gmhc.org

GSA Network / gsanetwork.org

Homeless Youth Alliance / homelessyouthalliance.org

Human Rights Campaign / hrc.org

Immigration Equality / immigrationequality.org

Institute for Judaism & Sexual Orientation / ijso.huc.edu

interACT / interactadvocates.org

Intersex Society of North America / isna.org

It Gets Better Project / itgetsbetter.org

Keshet / keshetonline.org

Kinsey Institute / kinseyinstitute.org

Lambda Legal / lambdalegal.org

Lambda Literary Foundation / lambdaliterary.org

Lesbian, Gay, Bisexual & Transgender Community Center / gaycenter.org

LGBT National Help Center / glnh.org

Los Angeles LGBT Center / lalgbtcenter.org

Many Voices / manyvoices.org

Marsha P. Johnson Institute / marshap.org

Metropolitan Community Churches / mccchurch.org

Muslims for Progressive Values / mpvusa.org

NAACP / naacp.org

The Naming Project / thenamingproject.org

National Black Justice Coalition / nbjc.org

National Center for Lesbian Rights / nclrights.org

National Center for Transgender Equality / transequality.org

National Coalition for the Homeless / nationalhomeless.org

National LGBT Bar Association / lgbtbar.org/annual

National LGBT Chamber of Commerce / nglcc.org

National LGBTQ Task Force / thetaskforce.org

National Queer Asian Pacific Islander Alliance / nqapia.org

New Alternatives / newalternativesnyc.org

NLGJA: The Association of LGBTQ Journalists / nlgja.org

PFLAG / pflag.org

The Pipeline Project / lgbtpipeline.org

QLatinx / qlatinx.org

The Queens' English / thequeensenglishus.com

Resource Center / myresourcecenter.org

Ruth Ellis Center / ruthelliscenter.org

SAGE (Advocacy & Services for LGBT Elders) / sageusa.org

SF LGBT Center / sfcenter.org

Sylvia Rivera Law Project / srlp.org

Thrive Youth Center / thriveyouthcenter.com

Transgender Law Center / transgenderlawcenter.org

Trans Women of Color Collective / twocc.us

The Trevor Project / thetrevorproject.org

Trikone / trikone.org

True Colors United / truecolorsunited.org

Victory Fund / victoryfund.org

ACKNOWLEDGMENTS

Thank you to all of the voices who have contributed to the creation, design, and production of *The Queens' English*. I am awestruck! You not only helped make my dream come true, but also renewed my passion for it daily. I figured I would thank each person with a star, so look up at the sky tonight. There will be a star with your name on it.

Sincere thanks to the Philadelphia Dance Company—*all* my PHILADANCO! guys and dolls—and its fearless leader, Joan Myers Brown. The idea to write the dictionary started here and I am so grateful for how you provided me with a creative space to discover all my talents. Thank you for supporting me for over a decade and teaching me the language of the queens.

Huge round of applause goes to my most supportive parents, John and Rose Davis. I love you! Thank you for believing in me and reminding me to stay creative, persistent, dedicated, and patient. Nothing great can come if you cannot endure the challenges and learn the lessons along the way.

Ebony Barrett—sis, you are my light and number one fan. I love you, Pono, and Sir. Priscilla Jackson, you motivate and believe in me in ways that pull me up to the mountaintop. Teneise Ellis, your love covers me and makes me whole: "I am you, you are me." Thank you, A. Maverick Lemons, for blessing the dictionary with its name, and Hassan Ellis, for creating its beautiful rainbow crown. Maisha Pinkard, you stand by me and for me in ways I never knew I needed. Eleven, thank you for starting me on my journey into the beautiful life of free thinking and free being. Lamar Baylor, you are awesome, selfless, and kind; I thank you for being with me every step of the way. Shout-out and all my love to my complete varsity cheering squad—all my family, all my friends, and all my supporters.

I would like to thank James Harris, Kyle Jones, Daniel Banks, and Persephone Valentine for being instrumental in my writing journey and moving me along with ease, strength, and comfort. To my creative brother, Troy Lambert, I adore you. Your creative input and thoroughness truly brought this dictionary to life. Your illustrations along with the works from Cassandra Fountaine, Mark Uhre, and Shanée Benjamin are extraordinary, and I thank you all.

I am most grateful to the many individuals who participated in interviews and group discussions, including my amazing cast members who helped along the way. Your wisdom, input, words, and stories created this body of work!

Wow, what an incredibly talented production team I have! To my rock-star literary agent, Leila Campoli, the first person to believe that *The Queens' English* would be a resource for all people and who worked effortlessly to find the best home for it: thank you for representing me and my creation. To my editor, Sara Neville, our journey is one for the books, literally! Thank you for advocating for this manuscript. Your passion for this work is endless. Thank you to the production and design team at Clarkson Potter and Penguin Random House, especially Mark McCauslin, Danielle Deschenes, and Kim Tyner, for transforming the vision of *The Queens' English* into a tangible, creative masterpiece. Look at what we have done, the lives we have touched, the understanding we are providing.

So, I say thank you! You did that! You slayed, pushed through, snatched wigs, and showed up! My heart is warm with gratitude.

ABOUT THE AUTHOR

 Chloe O. Davis is a proud Black bisexual woman and debut author who works in the entertainment industry in New York. A graduate of Hampton University and Temple University, she has centered her creative platform on amplifying the narratives of Black culture and heightening the awareness of the LGBTQIA+ community.

Davis's work as a dancer, actor, and creative has allowed her to travel to all fifty states and internationally. In addition to performing at premier theaters across the country, such as New York City Center, the Apollo Theater, the Kennedy Center, the Muny, and the Berkeley Repertory Theatre, she has appeared on PBS *Great Performances* with *Porgy and Bess* at the Metropolitan Opera, *Jesus Christ Superstar Live in Concert* on NBC, and *Southern Landscape* performed by the Philadelphia Dance Company (PHILADANCO!).

Clarkson Potter/Publishers
New York | clarksonpotter.com
POTTER Cover design: Danielle Deschenes